MULTICULTURALISM and EDUCATION

SUNY Series

FRONTIERS IN EDUCATION

Philip G. Altbach, Editor

The Frontiers in Education Series draws upon a range of disciplines and approaches in the analysis of contemporary educational issues and concerns. Books in the series help to reinterpret established fields of scholarship in education by encouraging the latest synthesis and research. A special focus highlights educational policy issues from a multidisciplinary perspective. The series is published in cooperation with the Graduate School of Education, State University of New York at Buffalo.

MULTICULTURALISM and EDUCATION

Diversity and Its Impact on Schools and Society

THOMAS J. LA BELLE
and CHRISTOPHER R. WARD

State University of New York Press

Published by
State University of New York Press, Albany

For information, address State University of New York
Press, State University Plaza, Albany, NY 12246

Production by M. R. Mulholland
Marketing by Theresa A. Swierzowski

Library of Congress Cataloging-in-Publication Data

La Belle, Thomas J.
    Multiculturalism and education : diversity and its impact on
schools and society / Thomas J. La Belle and Christopher R. Ward.
        p. cm. — (SUNY series, frontiers in education)
    Includes bibliographical references (p.   ) and index.
    ISBN 0-7914-1939-8. — ISBN 0-7914-1940-1 (pbk.)
    1. Multicultural education—United States. 2. Education—Social
aspects—United States. 3. Pluralism (Social sciences)—United
States. I. Ward, Christopher R., 1948-   . II. Title.
III. Series.
LC1099.3.L3   1994
370.19'6'0973—dc20   93-5712
                                                            CIP

10 9 8 7 6 5 4 3 2 1

*To friends Marvin and Virginia Lee and
William and Bette Rankin*

Thomas J. La Belle

For Peggy and Calvin

Christopher R. Ward

Contents

Part IV. MULTICULTURALISM, EDUCATION, and CHANGE

Introduction

We have written this book as proponents of pluralism and diversity and in recognition of the contribution that primary and secondary schools, as well as colleges and universities, make to integrating individuals and groups in society. We believe that multiethnic and multiracial societies should make efforts to ensure equity and justice for individuals whose minority background, physical features, economic status, and goals differ from dominant groups. We also believe that such societies need to build on differences in lifestyles, values, and beliefs as a means to enrich all individuals and groups by studying other cultures, learning other languages, establishing fair and equitable methods of treatment, and generally making an effort to understand the behavior and thought of others through their eyes and value systems.

But this book is not about our particular position on multiculturalism; nor is it a book about how to teach multiculturalism in the classroom. Although we review pedagogical and curricular approaches to multiculturalism and address the issues of educating the student from differing social and cultural backgrounds, we do not instruct how and what to teach to enhance diversity. Thus the reader will find few answers to the many "how to" questions, such as how to mediate between groups, how to select books and instructional materials for multicultural classrooms, or how to ensure the scholastic success of the immigrant or the disenfranchised student from a national minority population. Instead, the reader will find an educational foundations text which was written primarily for the individual who already is, or the student who desires to become, a teacher, administrator, or other professional educator in the United States and who seeks to learn more about the issues surrounding multiculturalism there and in selected other countries.

As we approach multiculturalism, we are struck by the simultaneous movement in the world toward more globalization in economics and politics, thereby testing the boundaries of nations, accompanied by the need for ethnic and other culturally based populations to maintain group identities and support networks. In our treatment of multiculturalism, therefore, we have made an effort to unmask the rhetoric of a societal melting pot and to recognize the efforts of each group, old and new, to stake a claim in society and further their

1

respective efforts to achieve what is important to them. Thus we assume that societies which are challenged will be able to reflect both national interests and the interests of specific groups. Our interest is in how formal education is used by groups to meet this challenge. We are especially concerned with racial, ethnic, and social class groups, but at times we reflect the interests of other populations, including gays and lesbians, women, and the disabled.

Thus the book is an introduction to the ways in which multiculturalism—individual and group difference—finds its way into schools through the policies of school boards, the expectations of parents, and the lifestyles of the students, teachers, administrators, and staff who study, recreate, and work in such institutions. It is about how individuals and groups—primarily in the United States, but borrowing liberally from selected international experiences as well—compete, among other things to, influence what gets taught, which books get placed on the library shelf, who gets placed in which ability group, and which language within a mixed classroom of students gets used. It is about how individuals and groups form clubs and cliques, how the community becomes associated with or distances itself from a school, and how those who attend see their values portrayed or ignored. It is also about how individuals and groups protect vested interests through what goes on in schools and how they use schools to gain access to opportunities and resources, especially after they graduate and enter the work force.

Rather than try to provide a road map for educators or other professionals through multiculturalism and education, we attempt to provide an analysis of the ways in which educational institutions have become arenas for playing out the goals and objectives of those affected by them. Conflict and struggles for power and control rather than harmony characterize many of these relationships. And although many acts which lead to the conflicts are in retrospect petty and may appear insignificant in a set of daily activities, their occurrence can often lead to considerable unrest and tension. The classroom teacher who fails to recognize a child's home language or who calls on the minority child less often; the racist epitaph on the corridor wall; the ethnic harassment which characterizes the coach while working with his or her team members; the derogatory editorial column in the school newspaper aimed at members of a particular ethnic group; and the teacher who does not acknowledge the contributions of all members of society to the creation and stability of that society are all potential sources of conflict and struggle. And each may alter the course of integration in a particular locale as individuals move from visible harmony to struggle and conflict and back to at least a veneer of civility.

In most societies multiculturalism has a long history. The first two chapters introduce multiculturalism, chapter 1 from a historical perspective and chapter 2 from a contemporary view. Chapter 1 traces multiculturalism and education in the United States from the nineteenth century, pointing to the role the more powerful economic and political groups had in shaping the nature and goals of the schooling process. Minority groups were excluded from participating in educational policy making, and their values, language, and presence in the curriculum was limited, if existent at all. At the turn of the twentieth century, it was popular to think of schools as a means for homogenizing or eliminating differences within the population, thus ensuring that the large numbers of immigrants coming to the United States from Europe, as well as Native Americans, would assimilate to the customs and behaviors of those already in place. The chapter moves from the melting pot orientation of the early twentieth century to the various efforts since the 1940s to recognize group difference. Attention is drawn to the often bitter and divisive struggles among competing groups to shape educational policy and practice.

Chapter 2 focuses on the new urgency the issues of multiculturalism have taken on in the 1990s and the ways in which the debate over what should be taught in schools builds both on group interest and on national concerns. From religious interests and nationalistic concerns to the advocates of preserving ethnic heritage and the need to portray group contributions to regional and national economic and political development, the debate has sometimes been hot and heavy. The new waves of immigrants in the 1980s and 1990s, combined with the changing demographics of minority populations already in place, assist in explaining why multiculturalism has become a threat to vested interests and a vehicle for societal change. From court cases regarding what the language of instruction in classrooms should be to the resegregation of desegregated schools both in the central city and in suburbs, chapter 2 explores the conceptual and philosophical bases of multiculturalism, the backlash to those who would advocate diversity, and the realities associated with trying to bring together these often conflicting views to shape educational policies and to implement them.

Section II discusses the relationships among social class and cultural groups in society, first at a general level and then at the national, community, and family levels. Chapter 3 proposes that all societies have some form of ethnic and social class segmentation which characterizes their past and present. The chapter then presents a conceptual framework for understanding how such groups are economically, politically, and culturally integrated in society based on socioeconomic power and cultural group interests. As the integration occurs, social class and ethnic groups struggle to simultaneously pull the society toward satisfying particular group concerns while maintaining some national commonality. This struggle, sometimes relying on coercion, and at other times based on consensus or interdependence, is especially visible in schooling as groups seek to influence policy and process while acquiring and using credentials and diplomas to gain access to societal opportunities.

Chapter 4 shifts focus from the integration of groups to the ways formal education interacts with different political and social entities. For example, the presentation of the nation as having an interest in schools is a tool that ensures a common, societywide ideology while simultaneously undermining local allegiances which might challenge the status quo. The national interest is therefore conservative and designed to maintain stability, including the interests of the most powerful political and economic populations.

The family, on the other hand, is portrayed as having more particularized interests in schools, interests which ensure continuity with locally based values yet provide opportunities for success for children in the wider social, economic, and political marketplace. The relationship between family style and school success is addressed by arguing that there are many ways in which families can be organized and can function to successfully prepare children for school achievement and by pointing out guidelines for family interventions which can enhance school functioning. We also discuss the relations between communities and schools, outlining various models of collaboration drawn from a number of international examples. Chapter 4 not only attempts to portray what goes on in schools as a reflection of these national, family, and community influences but also points to the need to disentangle such influences in ways which will increase the likelihood of student success.

Section III takes a look inside educational institutions by focusing first on patterns of behavior which characterize interactions among individuals from different socioeconomic and cultural populations, and second on the value systems which guide that behavior. Chapter 5 addresses how schools have responded to equality of opportunity mandates emanating from the larger society, how social interaction patterns are shaped and occur in the regular curriculum and in student activities outside the classroom, how students from differing backgrounds achieve in school, and what explanations are offered for those levels of achievement. The discussion then turns to the values, cognitive patterns, and languages brought to school by students and how such characteristics interact with those represented by the school, its curricula, and its teachers and administrators. We argue that educational personnel need to avoid the negative effects of labeling by placing into social and cultural context student behavior inside schools. In effect, this means knowing more about how students cope and survive *outside* schools and how they bridge what and how they learn *there* with the expectations and processes of schooling.

Chapter 6 concerns the values of groups and how they shape educational policy and practice. We demonstrate how competing group values influence the overarching policies of what gets taught as well as what is expected from educational institutions. The discussion first centers on whether a society can or should be characterized—by its members or others—through a core set of values, or whether a society should be viewed as exhibiting a variety of value systems which are associated with multiple group interests. We argue that it is important to recognize the competing nature of value systems and to recognize how various groups in society seek to have the schools achieve their particular view of the world. Then we discuss some of the dominant values in the United States and the conflicts surrounding them, such as the need to work hard to be successful; the need to achieve even if it leaves peers behind; the assumption that excellence and equity are compatible; the need to demonstrate independence and creativity yet not threaten the bounds of conformity; the need to preserve individualism in the face of common expectations for all; the separation of church, state, and education, and the pressures from special religious interest groups; and the continuity between family values and those that guide schooling. Finally, we discuss several international examples of how values drive education change on the one hand and are reflected in subsequent educational organizations and policies on the other.

Chapter 7 addresses the social change process and chapter 8 provides a review of pedagogical approaches to multicultural education. Chapter 7 assumes the importance of education as an arena for negotiation among individual and group interests and asks whether narrowing the political and economic resource gap between socioeconomic and cultural groups can be achieved and how education might contribute. Three approaches to social change, plotted along two continua—equilibrium to conflict and prescriptive to process—are offered as a way to think about these issues. The approaches to change are referred to as human capital, revitalization, and new social movements. The human capital approach, involving programs like job training and community development, is aimed primarily at increasing economic opportunity for individuals and works primarily through self-help and individual social mobility. It has had relatively little success in shifting power or resources and is dependent on the existence of a growing, vibrant economy. Revitalization efforts tend to challenge the status quo; they range from the civil rights movement of the 1960s to national revolutions, like Cuba or Nicaragua. Such efforts are dependent on visionary leaders and appear to be most effective as vehicles for political change. The third approach to change—new social movements—is exemplified by environmental activists and advocates of women's rights and has the greatest impact on changing traditions and day-to-day behaviors and on expanding networks of like-minded individuals. Then we point to the need to learn from the economic, political, and social results of these three approaches and the need to identify how each can be strengthened by learning from the others.

Chapter 8 reviews the literature on approaches to multicultural education at the classroom and institutional level and raises the question of how educators can learn more about the communities in which they work and the communities from which their students come. The focus is on primary and secondary schools, higher education, and other settings such as libraries and the extracurriculum. Following an analysis of multicultural approaches from a pedagogical perspective, there is a discussion of bilingual education as a means for bringing the learner's experience into the classroom, followed by a review of ethnic studies and multicultural programs at the higher education level. Then we discuss campus climate and how colleges and universities are dealing with conflict among and between groups on their campuses. Finally, the chapter presents ways the committed educator can draw on the concepts and tools of anthropology to develop an understanding of an educational setting and to become more effective in developing multicultural education programs and working in multicultural settings.

Part 1

Multiculturalism: History and Contemporary Perspectives

CHAPTER 1

Multiculturalism and Education: Historical Developments in the United States

Over the last two centuries the relationship between education and intergroup relations has changed dramatically in the United States, shaped not only by the dynamics of intergroup relationships but also by social, political, and economic forces. Historical accounts of multicultural education generally agree on the stages of its development after World War 1. However, less attention has been given to what might be called multicultural education's "pre-history": Intergroup relations and education preceding the great European immigration early in the twentieth century when there was not yet a formalized concept of multicultural or multiethnic education.

This early period was critical to shaping contemporary multicultural education in the United States. During these years a dominant view formed of how groups should relate and how schools should support these relationships. For example, in the nineteenth century, the conflict between what parents from various subordinate groups (ethnic, racial, religious, and economic) wanted for their children and what the Northern European, Protestant-dominated school systems taught, emerged as an important educational issue. Subordinate groups have continued to raise this issue over the last century. In one highly publicized case in New York City in the late 1960s, African American and Latino parents concerned about the gap between what they wanted for their children and what they saw the schools providing fought for community control of schools.

During the nineteenth century, under the prevailing dominant-subordinate group relations, the dominant group used schools to integrate and socialize children from various ethnic groups; supported boarding schools to break the cultural and tribal bonds of Native Americans; excluded as much as possible African Americans, who sought entrance into the education system with hopes schooling could lead to good jobs and social mobility; and largely ignored three hundred years of Hispanic presence and influence in America.

9

Emerging Dominant Group Values and Schooling

At the beginning of the nineteenth century schools played a limited role in most people's lives. Extended families and communities, not formal education, shaped values and prepared youth for a world of work still largely rural and based on the household. The importance of schools grew, and their relevance to intergroup relations became more critical, with two developments: a growing sense of what it meant to be a United States citizen, and the decline of the family as the center of economic activity. With these two developments, schools increasingly became the institution to enculturate the young to be Americans and to socialize future workers in the habits and attitudes needed in an industrializing economy (Lazerson 1977).

Diversity suffered as a particular model developed of what it meant to be an American citizen. Protestant values unrelated to a person's religion became the new ideals. Ironically, the separation of work and home intensified the family's role in the socialization of children; youngsters no longer moved in with other families to do apprenticeships at an early age, so an individual child's success became his or her family's responsibility (Lazerson 1977). Many immigrants held values which were shaped by rural, peasant cultures and which contrasted sharply to the values of the industrial work place and the increasingly bureaucratized schools which prepared youth for these factories and firms. Even as they struggled for economic survival, immigrants were attacked for possessing inferior cultural or child-rearing traits. Eventually, for the dominant group's educational bureaucracy, "differing cultural values and familial behavior patterns made ethnic groups and families the enemy" (Lazerson 1977, 21).

Religion, Bilingualism, and the Exclusion of African Americans

Tyack's study of urban schooling, *The One Best System* (1974), describes a nineteenth century system that homogenized most groups (including Catholics), gave concessions only to those groups with sufficient political power, and excluded African Americans.

Nineteenth-century American schools, with their mandate to prepare youth for citizenship, not only promoted Protestant values but also displayed anti-Catholic attitudes and disdain for the Irish and other immigrants. However, as the Catholic population grew—by 1907, 17 percent of the total U.S. population was Catholic compared to 1 percent a century earlier—Catholics established their own schools and eventually entered the mainstream culture. Group conflict, both between Protestants and Catholics and among different nationalities within Catholicism, prompted the formation of parochial schools. Various attempts at reconciliation, such as allowing clergy and nuns to teach in public school, failed. Moreover, in cities with large groups of new immigrants, the model of territorial parishes gave way to parishes which were based on language and ethnicity, parishes where parents could enroll their children in schools over which they had some control. In Chicago in 1902, for example, over half of all Catholic parochial school children were in ethnically designated schools (Lazerson 1977).

Group power determined what individuals obtained from the education system. Urban political machines, which depended on the support and goodwill of neighborhood residents—many of them immigrants—supported religious and cultural minorities in their individual and group battles with public education. These politicians smoothed the interaction between immigrant ethnic groups and an increasingly bureaucratic, centralized education system with a pragmatic attitude: "If textbooks contained scurrilous comments about immigrants, then the textbooks should be removed from the schools" (Tyack 1974, 94–95).

For some groups, power meant that their children could be educated in their native tongue. In the mid-nineteenth century cities such as St. Louis and Cincinnati supported bilingual education efforts, principally for German, whose speakers held relatively high status and political power. By the end of the century, however, German groups, recognizing the importance of English for access and acceptance, were asking that their language be taught as an elective, not used as a language of instruction. The conflicts over instruction in languages other than English became a symbolic battle between those who wanted to impose a single standard of belief and those who supported pluralistic education (Tyack 1974, 109). The disappearance of bilingualism marked a decline in cultural pluralism in the schools that would not be reversed until the 1960s, when there emerged a renewed emphasis on multicultural education.

During the mid-nineteenth century the urban areas of the North saw mostly segregated schools for African Americans, even when the law required these institutions open to all children, as in New York after 1873. Moreover, where integration did occur, the dismantling of African-American schools meant that African American teachers lost jobs, because in integrated schools the staff were almost exclusively white. In one of the most segregated cases, the public schools in Pittsburgh, although enrolling nearly 3,000 African American students in 1908, did not have even one African American teacher (Tyack 1974, 117).

Assimilation and Differing Group Values toward Formal Schooling

As immigration increased in the late nineteenth and early twentieth centuries, many educators came to believe that an important purpose of public education was to assimilate the large number of immigrants and their children. Thus the relation between intergroup relations and education came to be one in which public schools were openly an instrument for the dominant group to enculturate and socialize subordinate groups' young.

The schools taught attitudes, behaviors, and language needed for success in an urban, industrial society. However, these attitudes and behaviors, as well as the English language, were often at odds with parents' values. In response to the use of the public schools to mold immigrant children into middle-class, Protestant values and American cultural norms, individual groups organized their own education efforts. For example, Norwegians established colleges in the late nineteenth century and pushed for Norwegian studies at midwestern universities (Greene 1982).

Resistance to public education was particularly apparent in families from rural, peasant backgrounds, whose experiences and values differed from those of the school authorities. For example, there were wide differences between Southern Italian immigrants' cultural values about formal education and dominant American cultural values. Slavic immigrants, who considered the purpose of education to strengthen family and ethnic ties, often resisted formal education for their children. They did not view schooling as a means to advance in the job market; rather they believed that finding employment and working hard was the way to get ahead. As a result, Slavic children had lower educational achievement levels and left school early, a pattern that continued well into the twentieth century (Lazerson 1977, 29–30). These differences had several negative impacts. First, they accentuated the conflict between family loyalties and loyalties to America, whose dominant group now defined schooling in values for an individualistic, routinized work life. Second, with access to good jobs more closely linked to educational attainment, these differences put children of some ethnic groups at an economic disadvantage.

Dominant group educators, especially in the growing school systems in industrial cities, concerned themselves with assimilating European immigrants and gave little attention to African-American education. Few whites joined blacks in their fight for better education, and with no power to control schools, African Americans could not get the white establishment to take progressive steps such as hiring black teachers. Furthermore, educators did not use education to expose and correct racism. Instead, schools were used to "adjust" the African American child to white middle-class norms (Tyack 1974, 220) and to educate an African American elite to aspire to what whites had in a society that denied African Americans dominant group privileges (Woodson 1933). Northern, urban blacks who rejected segregation based on the experience of the South found that integration meant direct domination and degradation in white schools.

Education of Native Americans

From the late eighteenth century and throughout the nineteenth century, the dominant white society encouraged the assimilation of Native Americans.

Even progressive whites maintained that Native American culture would die out in the face of European civilization; they saw Native Americans as either assimilating into the dominant white society or vanishing. Education became an increasingly important part of the push for assimilation.

However, the United States government had little direct involvement in Native American education before the 1880s (Szasz 1974). Instead, missionaries were encouraged to go into areas populated by Native Americans, to enculturate them to European ways, and to convert them to Christianity (Holm 1979). By the late nineteenth and early twentieth centuries, changing popular images and stereotypes about Native Americans resulted in several approaches to Native-American education (Holm 1979). The institutions that were fostered and emphasized at various times included off-reservation industrial boarding schools, day schools on the reservations, public schools (on reservations open to white settlement), and missionary schools.

The Carlisle Indian School in Pennsylvania was the first of the boarding schools to bring Native Americans into white culture, away from their families, to teach them vocational skills. In practice, the young Native Americans were trained for jobs not usually available on the reservations to which they returned.

However, in the early twentieth century some whites rejected the education strategy of enculturating Native American youth, turning away from the idea that they could be assimilated. The prominent stereotypes cast the youth as inferior persons from an inferior culture who needed only limited education (Holm 1979). With this considered, and because day schools were less expensive and were more acceptable by parents, day schools began to replace the boarding schools.

The popular image—"primitivism" leads to art—fueled an emphasis on the arts in schools for Native Americans. Likewise, there emerged a popular image of Native American athletic prowess which was nurtured by outdoor life, focusing attention on Native American student athletes and athletics.

In the 1920s and 1930s an emphasis on educational reform was put into action (Szasz 1974). In the 1930s the Bureau of Indian Affairs' Education Division attempted to be both assimilationist and preservationist, by developing a bilingual education program. Some efforts were made to teach Indian culture, but the values transmitted in the Indian Service schools were still those of the Anglo culture.

Education for Assimilation and for Economic Advancement

Although most educators spoke little about African Americans' involuntary segregated status, they deplored white ethnic groups who preserved their own isolated communities and believed schools should end this isolation (Tyack 1974,

232). And despite their resistance to Americanization, many immigrant parents eventually came to see formal education as the route to upward mobility.

In urban areas, the great migration from Europe brought overwhelming numbers of students into the schools. In New York just after the turn of the century more than two-thirds of all pupils had fathers born abroad (Tyack 1974, 230). Despite misgivings, immigrant parents began to see schooling as the route to new opportunities. In 1909 the literacy rate for children of immigrants was higher than that for children of native-born whites, reflecting increased enrollments of newcomers' children. In addition, for some immigrant families, school employment proved to be a route for socio-economic mobility, with their daughters and sons moving into teaching positions.

Although immigrants' children were successful moving into teaching, school administrators came largely from native-born families. The ward system found in many cities during the nineteenth century gave some power to the immigrant groups that were concentrated in particular neighborhoods. When the system was abolished and school boards were centralized in the name of reform, school administrators were drawn from the upper reaches of the occupational and social structure. However, whether from the dominant, native-born group, or from one of the subordinate white ethnic groups, the great majority of school professionals were ethnocentric in outlook: "In their demands for total assimilation, for Anglo-conformity, many educators went further; nothing less would satisfy them than assaulting all forms of cultural difference, than creating a sense of shame at being 'foreign' " (Tyack 1974, 235).

By the time the United States entered World War 1, despite the growth of Catholic schools and other educational alternatives, the goal of schools had more to do with "monocultural" education than with multicultural education. African Americans were on the outside in most systems, relegated to inferior schools, or, where schools were officially integrated, they were relegated to positions of little influence and had meager representation on teaching staffs. By many measures, including spending per pupil, the position of African Americans in education worsened early in the twentieth century (Berry and Blassingame 1982). The Nativist sentiment that arose during World War 1, which equated patriotism with accepting the complete cultural assimilation of Americanism, ended bilingual or bicultural programs.

The late 1910s and early 1920s were a low point in American tolerance of cultural diversity and multicultural or multiethnic education. The hysteria of World War 1 made ethnic identity suspect; the German language was dropped from many schools' curricula. Racist and Nativist sentiment grew in the years that followed the war; the Klu Klux Klan gained power and members. The economic collapse of the 1930s and the great surge of labor strength in the mid-1930s shifted the focus within intergroup relations to class issues and the workplace rather than the enculturation of children, bilingualism, and better education for African Americans, Native Americans, and women.

Nevertheless, many of the issues that would reemerge in the 1960s and 1970s had become part of the debate over intergroup relations and education: the extent to which education should be bilingual; whether subordinate groups are better served in the opportunity structure by implementing their own distinctive education; the extent to which the formal educational system should usurp the enculturation and socialization of children; and the overlap between cultural and economic issues.

Intercultural Education

In the late 1930s and 1940s the rise of fascism, concerns that Nazi propaganda was affecting people worldwide, and a feeling that ethnic loyalties might be useful in the fight against Nazism supported the development of intercultural education, the first well-defined educational approach to intergroup relations in the United States. With roots in the earlier cultural pluralism approach to intergroup relations, the movement sponsored programs in the nation's schools and included nonformal education efforts such as adult education, community forums, and workshops.

Intercultural education (frequently termed "intergroup education") flourished through the 1940s and into the early 1950s. The movement was basically of the liberal elite, backed strongly by mainstream religious groups, particularly Jewish groups concerned about the spread of Nazism (Glazer 1977). Government, except for school boards, played only a minor role.

Two themes ran through intercultural education: people should not be ashamed of their cultural heritage and people should tolerate racial, religious, and cultural differences. However, tolerance took precedence over the celebration of group differences, and assimilation was more important than pluralism. The intellectual issues behind the movement had largely to do with determining the nature of prejudice, finding effective means to change attitudes, and similar questions (Glazer 1977).

The movement was concerned with individuals and how they should treat one another rather than the study of group conflict and/or the search for equitable resolutions of the intergroup competition that had emerged in the nineteenth century. For the most part, the movement did not recognize or address group political or economic power. Instead, intercultural education advocates were interested in democratic human relations, full citizen rights for minorities, educating young people with the movement's values, and taking action (Cook 1947).

An editorial in a special issue of the *Harvard Educational Review* which was devoted to intercultural education expressed the importance of harmonious intergroup relations to democracy: "We cannot attain the full values of the democratic way of life without intelligent and sensitive cooperation among the diverse groups which compose the American population." This view, it continued, contrasts with that prevailing in Nazi Germany: "In contrast to the authoritarian dogma of a master and subordinate groups, we in the United States are pledged to the dignity and worth of varied cultural groups" (MacCracken 1945, 76–78). Reflecting the movement's themes, the editorial reminded its readers that people do not have to give up their religion, national-origin group, or political party to become an American, and that a coming postwar period of readjustment between groups called for social sensitivity, patience, and social understanding.

By the mid-1940s intercultural education had attracted enough attention that educational journals devoted special issues to it, although the war limited the movement's diffusion into schools. A 1945 review of the movement's literature found almost nothing on either pre-service or in-service teacher training and showed that a third of the educational journals had carried nothing at all on intercultural education in the decade from the mid-1930s to the mid-1940s (Citron, Reynolds, and Taylor 1945).

In the late 1940s intercultural education moved into universities and teacher training institutions, with national organizations completing and publishing major studies. With funding from the National Conference of Christians and Jews, the American Council on Education's Council on Cooperation in Teacher Education carried out two projects to evaluate how various activities influenced attitudes toward others. One study was for elementary and secondary schools; the other, for teacher educators. The latter project, in 1950 reported to be the first project to improve teacher education for intergroup education, showed future teachers at twenty-four institutions the importance of eliminating prejudice in their students and developed techniques and tools to help them do this.[1]

Intercultural Education Distinct from Multicultural Education

A number of factors shaped intercultural education in ways distinct from the forms multicultural education would take in the 1960s and 1970s. These included the rise of fascism and World War 2, concern for the United States' image in the world, the influence of mainstream religious groups, and the growing influence of the social sciences.

As World War 2 approached, Americans were frightened by the power of Nazism, the susceptibility of industrialized societies to anti-Semitism, and the deception of Emperor worship. Proponents of intercultural education felt that they needed to counter Nazi propaganda that was spreading to the United States, that American values were at risk, and that wartime race riots in Detroit showed the fragility of America's intergroup relations. Thus the war effort was a unifying force as the country came together to fight Germany and as schools, churches, and unions became more interested in furthering harmonious intergroup relations.

Intercultural education emphasized group relations and the right to religious freedom among Catholics, Jews, and Protestants. Liberal religious groups supported the movement. Overall, contemporary multicultural education did not focus on organized, mainstream religion. In contrast to later approaches to intergroup relations, little attention was given to religion as a component of ethnicity.

Intercultural education supporters believed that good intergroup relations were a necessary step in keeping the United States strong. As they looked ahead to the post–World War 2 years, some saw that if America were to assume world leadership, the country would need to more fully live up to its democratic ideals. To many involved in the movement, living up to these ideals meant that all groups in America would need to be treated fairly. However, unlike later multicultural education efforts, the intercultural education movement was centered on the European immigrant and did not address structural racism, poverty, or the empowerment of subordinate groups.

Intercultural education did not emphasize control of knowledge and/or the importance of knowledge generated by members of subordinate groups. Instead, intercultural education supporters saw mainstream social sciences, which had just come into their own in the preceding decades, as an important asset to help the movement increase understanding and reduce tensions.

In the view of these supporters psychology could understand bigotry and discrimination. Likewise, anthropology could tell about the nature of culture and provide details on minority peoples who might be discriminated against, and sociology could describe urban problems and race relations. Among the most influential of the social scientists for the movement in the 1940s was Gunner Myrdal, a Swedish sociologist and author of a landmark study of race relations in the United States, *An American Dilemma*.

Intercultural education marshaled the social and biological sciences to provide scientific data to counteract bigoted attitudes and prejudice. At one extreme, intercultural education was pictured as a mental health program to immunize the unguarded against phobias of prejudice and emotion spread by demagogues, such as those who had infected the Germans and Japanese (Miller 1945).

Classroom and Community Activities

Intercultural education was presented to the classroom teacher of the 1940s and 1950s as a means to save cultural resources. The movement portrayed ethnic group arts, crafts, recipes, and other contributions as kinds of "endangered species" to be introduced in the classroom and passed on to more children, lest these species become extinct. The movement's pedagogical materials offered ideas for class activities. A typical activity was described as giving African American children pride and white children "important knowledge," by doing a lesson on African-American history after "George Washington Carver's recipe for peanut butter candy has given them all a happy time together" (DuBois 1945, xiii). Such materials gave little or no attention to how various groups' cultures could alter the dominant group, or to the questions of who determines and defines what counts as knowledge; who determine what knowledge is to be transmitted; and who controls access to educational institutions.

The intercultural education movement's relationship to the community was different from that of later multicultural education efforts primarily because intercultural education proponents came from liberal community and religious groups which had little federal government support or initiative. A plan that originated in 1939 in Springfield, Massachusetts, exemplified this relationship.

The Springfield Plan was developed in a small city which had a comparatively diverse population, a history of educational innovation, and a solid manufacturing economy. Through the school system and communitywide efforts, Springfield's citizens sought to use intercultural education to improve the city's human relations. Leaders described it as parents and civic groups working with schools to develop effective democratic citizenship education (Granrud 1945).

The Springfield model emphasized educating students for democracy, thereby educating them for tolerance. A curriculum committee suggested ways to introduce intercultural education across the curriculum. Tolerance, the contributions and problems of racial and religious groups, and respect for the rights of all, were the guiding principles (Bach 1946). However, the plan did little to challenge the community's political or economic structure or to acknowledge subordinate groups' lack of power.

As manifested in the Springfield Plan and in other attempts, the intercultural education movement was as much a community organization phenomenon as it was a school-based movement. In one respect, the push by mainline liberal community groups (often religious) for cooperation and for racial and religious harmony in the schools is similar to African-American, Latino, feminist, and gay groups' advocacy efforts from the 1960s through the 1990s. These groups also desired to use the schools to advance intergroup relations and mutual respect. However, although the groups were advocating programs in the schools, intercultural education did not call for structural change or power sharing. Moreover, while intercultural education supported diversity to a degree, it appears essentially to have been assimilationist, bringing diverse groups under the umbrella of moderately liberal, middle-class American cultural values.

Movement supporters described themselves as working with their communities' schools to advance intercultural education, assuming that imparting such knowledge would change peoples' behaviors; but they made little mention of groups' economic status and/or how government policy or judicial decisions might contribute to intergroup relations. In particular, the hiring, placement, and other policy decisions of school districts do not seem to have been cause for action. The operations of one community group, the Pittsburgh Council on Intercultural Education, illustrate these points.

The Pittsburgh Council on Intercultural Education

In the first decades of the twentieth century Southern and Eastern Europeans and African Americans migrated to Pittsburgh in large numbers to work in the coal mines, steel mills, and other heavy industry. They were often directly recruited or encouraged to come by employers, particularly in times of labor strife. As a result, of the 1.4 million people in Pennsylvania's Allegheny County in 1940, 12 percent were foreign-born, another 14 percent were children of foreign-born parents, and 6.4 percent were African American (Jackson 1948). The intergroup relations and education issues outlined earlier correspond with the Pittsburgh experience.

A 1936 study of Pittsburgh made recommendations for assimilating ethnic groups more fully into the community. To help carry out these recommendations, the American Service Institute (ASI) was created in 1941. The ASI, along with the Pittsburgh Urban League, the Jewish Community Relations Council, and the Pittsburgh Round Table of Christians and Jews urged public schools to include intercultural education in the curriculum, which the superintendent announced he would do in 1943, based on observations of what had been done in Springfield.

In that year a community support committee of fifteen persons, appointed by the Board of Education, grew into the Pittsburgh Council on Intercultural Education. The council included representatives from ethnic, racial, religious, and socioeconomic groups. Its purpose was to promote adult and community education which supported intercultural education in the schools as part of a goal to encourage the schools to "get some understanding of cultural and racial factors into the school curriculum" (Jackson 1948, 27). The council worked through committees to place positive books on library shelves and to remove books that increased tension, to work with Parent Teacher Associations, to send out speakers, to get coverage from the radio and the press, and to get local universities to include intercultural content in their teacher education courses. The district's director of curriculum linked the board's efforts and those of the council. The group also emphasized in-service teacher education, particularly through summer institutes at major universities. For example, in 1945, twenty teachers attended the University of Chicago with funds from the Frick Educational Commission.

The Pittsburgh case illustrates the relatively successful community approach of many intercultural education efforts as well as the movement's weaknesses. Among the weaknesses was an emphasis on harmony at the expense of justice. The council was dedicated to intergroup understanding in a city where the schools had virtually no African American administrators or teachers, but had to mediate the demands of minority groups who had grievances with the Board of Education. This mediation included convincing the minority press to interpret positively the schools' intercultural education efforts. Such was the case when an African-American newspaper complained about the use of "dialect songs" in the schools' Stephen Foster memorial program. The council brought harmony to the situation by pressuring the newspaper to be more positive but did nothing to change intergroup power relationships between Pittsburgh's white and African-American communities.

In an attempt to get some degree of understanding into the curricula and promote positive books in the library, the council advocated a limited view of cultural pluralism which largely ignored the political and economic barriers faced by Pittsburgh's white ethnic groups and African Americans. The national intercultural education movement was characterized by the same lack of attention to structural issues concerning intergroup relations.

Although the intercultural education movement took an interest in issues of race, that interest, as indicated earlier, was largely stimulated by an event which began in Europe, the rise of Nazism. This focus on the white ethnic experience and its European roots continued the position of the early cultural pluralist writers, such as Horace Kallen, who virtually ignored African Americans in their writing (Glazer 1977; Banks 1979).

Several factors contributed to the end of the intercultural education movement: mainstream educators never internalized the movement's ideology and assumptions nor understood how the movement could contribute to their schools, which, for the most part, educators perceived as virtually free from racial tension; urban racial tensions were subtle in the 1950s; and, intercultural education was based on special programs and funds which dried up, leaving no ongoing effort.

The 1950s: Setting the Stage for Multicultural Education

The concerns about fascism and the desire for interreligious and interracial understanding that drove the intercultural education movement declined in the 1950s, replaced by fear of the Soviet Union and anti-communism. At the same time, white Americans, benefitting from low-cost housing loans and subsidized freeways, began to leave the central cities and move to the suburbs. Manufacturing jobs also left the cities, burdening them with greater numbers of poor people. Despite the 1954 *Brown* v. *Board of Education* Supreme Court decision desegregating schools, African Americans, Hispanics, Native Americans, Asians, and other minority groups were often in legally segregated educational institutions. In the 1960s the civil rights movement and rising ethnic consciousness would challenge and change these conditions, in part with the help of additional favorable court decisions and government intervention in intergroup relations and education.

Housing patterns and economic conditions brought larger numbers of minorities into educational systems in major cities. But these systems, like others around the country, used textbooks and materials that reflected the experience and values of the dominant group, largely Protestant, white, and from professional and upper socio-economic classes. A significant contribution of multicultural education in the 1960s and 1970s was to make materials and textbooks more inclusive; the debate over content and curricula would rage through the 1990s.

During the 1950s and into the 1960s the social sciences provided intergroup relations and education with an intellectual foundation that attempted to make youngsters from minority backgrounds look and act like the dominant group. In response to the perceived deprivation of the subordinate groups, policymakers made extensive efforts to provide groups with programs that would relieve their "cultural poverty" and provide them with the values, discipline, or whatever else it was that the theory defined their cultures as lacking. Multicultural education was based on different assumptions; for example, it examined the implications for student learning of the differences between the culture of the school and the culture of the home. Bilingual and bicultural education became important programmatic manifestations of the new multicultural education approach.

The Rise of Multiethnic and Multicultural Education

In the early 1960s terms like "cultural pluralism" and "diversity" began to appear in the professional literature, although "little was articulated that precisely gave direction and definition to specific concepts and/or approaches that could be applied to educational practice" (Baker 1979, 253). The 1960s and 1970s brought rapid change to intergroup relations and their relationship with education. First came a multiethnic education approach in which the contributions of various ethnic groups were integrated into the curriculum. Beginning as a consolidation of Asian, Black, Hispanic, and Native American studies, this approach ultimately broadened to incorporate white ethnic studies.

By the late 1970s gender and religion were added to the multicultural education concept; the focus shifted from multiethnic education to multicultural education.

While the social and political forces drove the changes in intergroup relations and education, educational organizations issued documents which helped to define the concepts. One important statement was made by the American Association for Colleges of Teacher Education in its publication *No One Model American*. This document defined multicultural education as education that values cultural pluralism, rejecting the view that schools should serve as institutions to eliminate differences. The publication contends that schools should preserve and extend cultural diversity to all students.

Four factors contributed to the rise of multiethnic education and its successor, multicultural education: the civil rights movement, a rise in ethnic consciousness, a more critical analysis of textbooks and other materials, and the loss of belief in theories of cultural deprivation. Each of these factors is discussed below.

The Civil Rights Movement

The civil rights movement—energized by the Montgomery bus boycott, marches, sit-ins and other events; supported after 1960 by court decisions and the federal government; and visible throughout the country on television—brought the issues of intergroup relations—including education—to national attention. The movement demonstrated that these issues did not so much call for fairness and tolerance by the dominant group, as the intercultural education movement had proclaimed, as they called for reconsideration of who held power, how that power was used, and subordinate groups' rights and resources. Desegregation of public schools was an important issue; some of the most dramatic civil rights events, such as the integration of Arkansas' Little Rock Central High School and the integration of southern universities, drew much attention. However, by the mid-1960s the civil rights movement shifted from passive perseverance to political power, self-determination, and cultural consciousness (Gay 1983). One historian of multicultural education locates the birth of this revitalization in the 1965 Watts riot in Los Angeles (Banks 1979).

Cultural Pluralism and Ethnic Consciousness

Cultural pluralism was also revived in the 1960s through the militant, ethnically conscious protests of African Americans who rejected assimilation. Self-determination became a subordinate group goal, and schools became part of the struggle for power, first for African Americans, then for Native Americans, Hispanics, and other minority groups. A multiethnic education movement, and then a multicultural education movement, emerged in response to ethnic revitalization. Battles over education—namely, community control and desegregation—exposed the Anglocentric nature of schools, the bias and racism they passed on, and the terrible poverty produced by conditions existing in the cities (Suzuki 1984). Colleges which historically had educated large numbers of African Americans were one location for the emergence of this ethnic consciousness.

By the mid-1960s the civil rights movement had shifted emphasis from assimilation to Black self-identity. At the same time, many American colleges and university students were growing more rebellious, and African-American students were calling for increased attention to ethnic culture and consciousness.

Among the most striking examples of how college students moved from assimilationism to an emphasis on cultural pride and independence can be seen at Howard University in Washington, D.C. Howard had educated many of the African American elite, including civil rights lawyers and leaders, but in the 1960s its curriculum mirrored that of mainstream white institutions with few courses on African-American culture or history. Beginning in 1966 and for more than a year after that, Howard students argued that their university must become a "Black" university. Their demands culminated in the takeover of a campus building in the spring of 1968. Eventually, after the threat of police intervention and calls from members of Congress (which supplied half of Howard's funding) to end the occupation, the students withdrew. However, the following semester the University hosted the conference "Toward a Black University," marking movement toward the students' goal.

The issues raised at Howard regarding the content of the university's curriculum and whether there should be a distinctively African-American curricula remain at the center of the multicultural education debate today on the nation's campuses.

Multicultural Curricula and Materials

Multicultural education was also promoted by an analysis of curriculum materials. Subordinate group parents and community members found that their children's education in general, and their textbooks and other media in particular, conveyed distortions and inaccuracies about their history and heritage. Over the next decade the nation's education system gave a great deal more attention to inclusive materials and to shaping a curricula that reflected diversity. Even as many educators set about these tasks, for some parents and subordinate group communities, the appropriate response was to initiate more direct action in their local schools.

For these groups, their growing ethnic consciousness was often tied to a desire for control of their children's education. In the Oceanhill-Brownsville community in New York City, the conflict around "Who shall decide what is taught?" mixed with school district politics. African American and Latino parents saw that their children were not achieving their potential and noted 80 percent of the teachers in neighborhood schools were white and 95 percent of the students were African American or Latino, so they demanded community control of local schools. An experimental program funded by the Ford Foundation enabled the local community to set up a community board which met opposition over the issue of transferring teachers. Eventually, the board's refusal to give in (and to let white teachers they had asked to transfer, return) led to a teacher walkout and a citywide teachers' strike. In the Oceanhill-Brownsville schools, which were now controlled by the community board, more emphasis was put on Black culture and history. A new cultural awareness developed. Ultimately, faced with the strike pressures, the central administration suspended the community board, ending one small but significant experiment in multicultural education. However, despite the short-term failure, the events demonstrated that issues of power and control would be central to intergroup relations and education in the 1960s and beyond. Ultimately, multicultural education would focus much more on empowerment and social change.

Rejection of Cultural Deprivation

Another factor in the emergence of multiethnic and then, multicultural, education was the rejection of the deprivation theory. In its place came concepts influenced by anthropology which saw the difficulties subordinate group children faced in schools not from the perspective of cultural deficiency but from the perspective of differences, or conflicts, between the culture of the school (primarily dominant group culture) and the culture of the home. Values, language, and cognitive styles and strategies became a new focus of attention.

Government Involvement in Multicultural Education

Beginning in the 1960s, government at all levels became more involved in multicultural education, particularly in bilingual education. On the federal level, the Civil Rights Act of 1964, Title 9, forbade racial and ethnic discrimination in programs receiving federal funds. Follow-up memoranda prohibited discrimination based on inability to speak English. Most important, the Elementary and Secondary Education Act of 1965 gave funds to public school districts, thus providing a mechanism with which to enforce the 1964 act. The 1972 Ethnic Heritage Studies Act signified a policy under which education voluntarily maintains distinctive cultures. The Lau Supreme Court case (1974) established the principle that cultural factors and related student learning styles should be considered in a school's response to children with different language backgrounds. The 1974 Bilingual Education Act declared that the United States policy was to encourage bilingual education programs where appropriate. In addition to the federal government's involvement, state education authorities and some local school boards mandated the teaching of multiethnic or multicultural education.

By the mid-1970s multicultural education seemed to be becoming a right with a high degree of government support (Glazer 1977). In a relatively short period of time it had progressed from minority studies for the most oppressed; to minority studies, integrated into the curriculum, for all; to bilingual studies; and, finally, to ethnic studies for all.

Current Definitions of Multicultural Education

Over the last several decades the concept "multicultural education" has been given many definitions. Moreover, diverse views of intergroup relations have shaped the concept in different ways. For example, persons who emphasize stratification and equality in intergroup relations define the term in one way; those who view intergroup relations as affirming differences but having integration as an ultimate goal define it in another. In the 1980s and 1990s the definition has generally broadened such that multicultural education encompasses concerns of many additional groups, including women, gays and lesbians, people with special education needs, and people of various age groups, including the very young and the elderly.

However, such a broad definition is not universal. Some have limited it to specific populations, such as ethnic groups. For example, Banks is concerned with multiethnic education and intergroup relations in regard to the relationship of ethnic groups in schools. He describes two extremes, the cultural pluralist ideology and the assimilationist ideology. The cultural pluralist sees ethnic groups as important in the competition for political and economic power. In this argument, the abilities of each member must be developed to aid the group struggle. The pluralist also sees education as culture-specific, stressing its allegiances and attachments, and giving persons skills to continue the group's fight for recognition and resources. In contrast, the assimilationist position sees one universal culture in which the schools' role is to enculturate young people into that culture and socialize them with skills needed for success. Banks (1979) suggests that multiethnic educators must move to a reconciliation which sees a universal culture with ethnic subgroups and subcultures. The emphasis on ideology, understandable in an era of separationism, should be de-emphasized.

In addition to making multicultural education more inclusive, some educators have promoted it as a reform movement for empowering students and changing the schools and society (Sleeter and Grant 1988). The full range of the concept, and related practice, can be seen a comprehensive five-part typology of multicultural education programs offered by Sleeter and Grant (1987, 422) based on their review of its literature through the mid-1980s. Their five categories include:

1. *Teaching the Culturally Different*. Transitions students from various groups into the mainstream.
2. *Human Relations*. Helps students from various groups get along better, but avoids dealing with social stratification and fails to link the practical with the theoretical.
3. *Single Group Studies*. Teaches about specific groups to promote pluralism, but doesn't emphasize social stratification and doesn't attend enough to multiple forms of human diversity.
4. *Multicultural Education*. Reforms the school through appropriate curricula and materials, affirmation of all students' languages, staff changes, and so forth to promote cultural pluralism and social equality.
5. *Education that is Multicultural and Social Reconstructionist*. Prepares students to promote cultural diversity and to challenge structural inequality.

Sleeter and Grant also describe multicultural education in the United States in the mid-1980s as a field without a journal or direct federal support which possesses a literature long on advocacy but short on research: Particularly in North America, England and Australia, the focus is on classroom and classroom teachers, and multicultural educators concerned with providing better education for students of color.

Entering the 1990s, multicultural education programs, in their continued fight for acceptance, face other challenges, one of which is financial. Despite federal and state mandates, individual school districts can only provide what they can afford. They must choose priorities as they allocate resources. In recent years multicultural education advocates have found themselves pitted against other groups in the battle for funds, such as supporters of scholars' programs, or special offerings for "gifted" students.

Another challenge for multicultural education has been the rightist ideology and the related decrease in support on the federal level for the rights of subordinate groups, and decreased interest in the plight of groups lacking political power and economic resources. In the 1980s schools were promoted as institutions for the teaching of vocational skills and for passing on "family" values rather than institutions for the teaching of diversity or social justice.

Conclusion

This chapter began with a discussion of multiculturalism and education by tracing the history of education and intergroup relations in the United States, noting the formation of the dominant group views in the nineteenth century and the exclusion of subordinate groups from any meaningful say in educational institutions and policy. We showed how concepts such as "melting pot," developed in the early twentieth century, continue to describe American approaches to intergroup relations and education; how the intercultural education movement of the 1940s differed from later multicultural and multiethnic education efforts; and how the civil rights movement, social science rejection of cultural deprivation, and the federal government influenced multicultural education through the 1980s. We concluded with a brief overview of the diversity of contemporary multicultural education efforts and the continued efforts to include more groups under the multicultural education umbrella.

The following chapters will reveal that multicultural education is only part of the story of the relationship between groups and education. The broader consideration is not limited to the classroom; it intersects issues related to group power, how groups have a say in what is taught and who teaches, and what counts as knowledge in societies around the world.

CHAPTER 2

Multiculturalism: The Controversy and Context

Multiculturalism, particularly multiculturalism as it relates to formal education, has generated great interest and controversy during the past decade. Of concern have been areas such as multicultural education in public schools, the establishment of ethnic studies courses or programs in universities, textbook revisions, and the addition of non-Western readings to the curriculum at all levels. In the 1990s multiculturalism and its place in educational institutions has become a topic of intense public debate.

A controversy surrounding Christopher Columbus demonstrates the degree to which multiculturalism currently impacts education and how it has entered public discussion in the United States. At its most basic, the controversy centers on the question: "What story should children hear in school, if anything, about Christopher Columbus?" The approach of the 500th anniversary of Columbus's 1492 Atlantic expedition precipitated a rancorous debate throughout the country that included individual teachers, school boards, and various national educational and scholarly organizations. For some, Columbus was the perpetrator of Native American genocide, and his voyages opened the door for black slavery. For others, he was a person of the Renaissance whose vision and daring changed history decisively and positively. For many, he was somewhere in between, entangled with their childhood images, learned in school or remembered from celebrations and parades.

The positions taken in this debate over what to present in the classroom often depended on the advocates' group membership: ethnic, racial, or cultural. Moreover, the intensity of the debate showed that more was at stake than a single history lesson—the rancor revealed deep conflicts between dominant and subordinate groups in the United States.

Controversy about multiculturalism is of international interest and concern. In Britain the debates over multiculturalism and education have centered around the country's growing immigrant population. In Singapore, as in many other societies, the language of instruction has been closely linked to discussions of multiculturalism and education. In Canada, where multiculturalism is a

29

national policy, bilingualism is just one of a number of issues related to immigration, tensions between French and English-speaking populations, and the education of native peoples.

Underlying multiculturalism and education debates in many societies are questions such as:

• Which group(s) determines and defines what counts as knowledge?
• Which group(s) should determine what knowledge is to be transmitted through educational institutions?
• Which group(s) controls access to formal education institutions and the certification they offer which is crucial to upward mobility in the job market?

Attempts to answer these questions and resolve these debates have affected both the goals and the practice of education.

Much of the recent public debate about multiculturalism in the United States has centered on efforts by minority ethnic and racial groups to gain greater power in answering these questions. Although the debates have focused on education, at their core is the relationship between and among groups, each of which wields a greater or lesser degree of political and economic power in relation to the other groups.

Frameworks for Understanding Multiculturalism and Education

Several frameworks can help clarify and explain the issues that prompt the debates such as the one over Christopher Columbus and the competition among dominant and subordinate groups that underlies them. These frameworks are useful for understanding current controversies related to education and for understanding multiculturalism (broadly defined) within the societies in which these debates are taking place.

Multiculturalism is a concept that reflects intergroup relations. In this view contemporary debates and controversies around multiculturalism represent not a problem of communication or a lack of mutual understanding but an issue of intergroup competition and conflict. The competition and conflict not only allocate power and resources to various groups, but also clarify their identities.

In describing this interplay, we give particular attention to those groups defined by ethnicity, race, and social class. Intergroup relations are so closely tied to economic issues that multiculturalism must include social class. Some approaches to multiculturalism include ethnicity and race but exclude social class. For example, Lambert and Taylor (1990) suggest that multiculturalism can refer to ethnic pluralism, or the coexistence of ethnic, racial, or cultural subgroups in a society. They maintain that multiculturalism is descriptive of an ideology about ethnic diversity.

Yet in many arenas of public life and policy, including education, multiculturalism has been used to encompass more than ethnicity, race, or socioeconomic status. Under the rubric of multiculturalism, groups based on gender, religion, and other characteristics, including sexual orientation, disability, and age, have staked claims to power around the questions discussed above.

By including economic issues, this framework addresses both structural and cultural analyses applied to education. The structural arguments are about whether education does or does not lead to more opportunity for higher status and better jobs. In these arguments, values and beliefs take a secondary role (see discussion of Atlanta later in this chapter). From a different perspective, the cultural arguments are about which values dominate a society and its formal education system. This argument is exemplified by the debate between advocates and critics of Afrocentrism.

In the real world of group competition and conflict, structural and cultural issues are thoroughly entangled. Groups who argue for a greater voice in determining what should be written in textbooks may very well be the same groups concerned with whether better access to education can reward them with higher status and better jobs. The framework helps us understand how the structural and cultural interact and how education relates to that process.

Control of ideas and information is important to a group's relative strength or weakness and has become increasingly so in the last one hundred years. Particularly in societies lacking a high degree of centralized control, such as the industrial democracies of North America and Western Europe, groups struggle over which ideas should be presented to the public through schools, nonformal education, and the media (Spring 1990). A recent U.S. debate over textbooks illustrates how dominant and subordinate segments of society fight for this control.

In 1987 California's State Board of Education mandated a new history and social studies curriculum and sought textbooks based on this new curriculum. California, as the nation's most populous and diverse state, is the key market for textbook adoption. Publishers estimated this new series was worth over $50 million in sales. Despite efforts by the textbook developers to make the series they proposed for adoption inclusive and fair to all groups, the adoption and review process was filled with protests. Some critics described the books as racist. The Oakland School District, which is 57 percent African American and 91 percent minority, did not adopt the texts. Instead, it opted to develop its own materials. Native Americans, Hispanics, African Americans, and others found portions of the books—or even the whole approach—lacking. Religious groups also protested the series. Jewish and Muslim groups found fault in how material about their faiths was presented. Other critics charged that the series distorted and devalued the experiences of groups—including African Americans and Hispanics—whose history differed from those who came as part of the immigration from Europe (Reinhold 1991).

A bitter debate around multiculturalism and education has centered on whether or not the curricula in public schools and higher education should be more diverse. In one sense, the "melting pot" concept appears to have won the day. Even relatively conservative educators grant that in a diverse society, the contributions and historical achievements of various ethnic groups, women as well as men, and racial minorities, should be noted.

The debate over multiculturalism is somewhat different in higher education than in public schools. Public schools usually involve a district or statewide curriculum or textbook adoption which requires specific, concrete outlines or lists aired widely in public. The question is "Which version (or Whose version) of history will be taught?" (Coughlin 1991). The problem is most acute when the question has to be translated into curricula or into a textbook, as the California textbook example demonstrates.

However, for many, multiculturalism clearly is limited and does not include reallocation of power between groups nor the abdication by the dominant group of its superordinate cultural, economic, or political position. These critics raise the fear that multiculturalism will promote social fragmentation.

Among the questions driving the debate are:

- Does the United States have a common cultural history or does each group have a separate (and irreconcilable one)?
- Is there a common narrative, built from many other narratives, many of which have been inadequately told, or are there only a whole series of specific group narratives?
- Should the defining feature of education in a diverse society be the highlighting of individual group characteristics, achievements, and values, or should it be the transmission of a common set of beliefs and values?
- Should school curricula highlight the differences or the similarities among groups?

Those who question multicultural education maintain that a society needs common values and history. While acknowledging that in the past ethnic and racial minorities, women, and other groups have not been adequately represented in the curriculum, those who question wider application of multicultural education point out that America's system of government, political ideas, and language derive, in large part, from actions and ideals of British males. They argue that these ideas, ideals, and institutions (pluralism and democracy, for example) are truly valuable.

Arthur Schlesinger, Jr. and Diane Ravitch are representative of those who support diversity, but are cautious about the ramifications of multiculturalism and multicultural education. Schlesinger (1991) argues that an ethnic interpretation of American history reverses the approach to history that has allowed the United States to become the world's most successful large multiethnic nation: the creation of a new identity and a new national culture. A common language, ideas about democracy and human rights, and a commitment to including various cultures have contributed to America's success. In his view, immigrants came to something they viewed as positive. They desired to escape their pasts and were willing to integrate into a new culture. From Schlesinger's perspective, education should enable children to understand, to contribute to, and to change, this common American culture.

Ravitch (1990) maintains that the ethnic revival of the 1960s brought attention to race, ethnicity, and gender in American education. With this new attention, previously ignored or distorted roles and contributions of Blacks, Hispanics, Asians, Native Americans, women, and white ethnic groups were built into the curriculum. A "pluralistic" multiculturalism has become an organizing principal of American society and children today learn that cultural diversity is positive.

However, Ravitch believes that in the 1980s ethnic interest groups began to politicize the curriculum. Groups demanding the removal of myths and fables now vie with creationists for the attention of school boards. Advocates of what she labels "particularistic" multiculturalism declare that biology controls a person's culture and that teaching Afrocentric or other multicultural models will raise children's self-esteem and school performance. Particularistic multiculturalism, she says, rejects interactions between groups that might blur distinctions between them. It ignores class, gender, sexual orientation, and religious links that might bind groups. It is a political movement and a kind of cultural predestination. Its supporters' specific proposals for change in the curriculum are primarily weapons to criticize existing universities, educational systems, and disciplines.

For Ravitch, that American schools and education have strong ties with Europe is not surprising—nearly 80 percent of Americans are of European descent, and Europeans and their ideas created many of the nation's institutions. However, Ravitch believes that today education is not so much Eurocentric as it is "Americanicentric," leaving many students unknowing and unconcerned about the larger world. Preserving a sense of American community is important to her; she argues that while multiculturalism can be a source of debate and discussion; it should not be a source of discord and fragmentation.

In contrast to Schlesinger and Ravitch are those who advocate a multiculturalism which promotes and empowers groups which have not previously had access to decisions about what is appropriate knowledge and how it should be transmitted. Afrocentrism and the related Afrocentric education are examples of such groups.

Afrocentrism's roots go back seventy-five years to the writings of Marcus Garvey, who used his knowledge of African and Egyptian history to assist in the struggle for Black freedom. Afrocentrism stands for infusing more about Africa, Africans, and African-Americans and their experiences into curricula in the United States, curricula which its advocates maintain is dominated by European knowledge and which excludes information about Africa and the role African peoples have played in American history. Afrocentrism offers African American scholars alternatives to what one of its proponents, Molefi Kete Asante (1991), terms "Eurocentric frames of reference."

Many of Afrocentrism's advocates emphasize Egypt's importance in the development of civilization, its influence over the Greeks, and its status as an African society and culture. Many come from urban school districts with large African American student populations and believe students should hear history that can build their pride and self-esteem.

Afrocentrists argue that racism among history and classics scholars has distorted history, de-emphasizing, for example, Egypt's important role in the development of civilization and in the diffusion of African culture across the world (Bernal 1987; Diop 1991; James 1976).

Those who challenge Afrocentrism often disagree with such specific tenets as Greek legends have their origins in Egypt. Others seek to modify these tenets, saying that to show influence is not to show origins, acknowledging Egyptian contributions but also pointing to the influence of other Mediterranean cultures (Lefkowitz 1992). The debate has raised questions about historical truth and myth. The often complex and technical arguments about historical accuracy demonstrate the importance of group identity and the desire for groups to shape and control the knowledge that is passed on to their children.

Much of the Afrocentrists' effort has been to infuse material into the curriculum in history and the humanities. Some school districts have also tried to add Afrocentric perspectives into the teaching of science and mathematics. These efforts have, on occasion, led to controversy in districts where those who do not accept the Afrocentrist viewpoint have challenged specific readings (West 1992).

Demographics and Approaches to Intergroup Relations

While the debate about multiculturalism in education is concerned with minority groups determining what counts as knowledge, what knowledge should be submitted, and who controls access to education, the core of the debates is the greater or lesser degree of political power any one group holds in relation to others. In order to more fully understand the importance of group power and education, we describe in some detail recent demographic changes and summarize various conceptual approaches to intergroup relations.

First, we describe how demographic changes in the United States, like changes in Europe, Japan, and elsewhere, are altering the total population and its student population. Perhaps more than any other factor, these demographic changes chart pressures for shifts in group relationships and prompt the debates about multiculturalism and education.

Second, we briefly summarize the efforts by social scientists and educators over the past century to describe the relationship of dominant and subordinate groups with educational goals and practice. We illustrate these efforts by examining evolving attitudes toward immigration, particularly the drive to "Americanize" immigrants, which began in the early twentieth century.

Changing Demographics

During the last two decades demographic changes have affected many countries. In addition to general growth, populations have moved. International migration for employment, once viewed as primarily a phenomenon directed toward Western Europe, North America, or Europe, is expanding. Asia's four main labor importers (Japan, Hong Kong, Malaysia, and Singapore) are increasing the number of workers they take in. The number of foreign workers in Japan more than doubled between 1980 and 1988 (Martin 1991). In Europe countries such as Spain, which until recently sent emigrants to wealthier northern neighbors, are now themselves the destination of immigrants. Some estimate that by the end of the 1990s a third of the people under thirty-five in Europe's urban areas will be immigrants (Suarez-Orozco 1991). Such migration, which typically involves groups with low socioeconomic status, and often of ethnicity, race, and/or religion different from that of the dominant population in a receiving country, guarantees further demographic changes and major intergroup competition and potential conflict.

The United States illustrates these large-scale demographic changes. In the 1970s and 1980s the demographic composition of the United States changed more rapidly than it had during any period since the great European immigrations in the late nineteenth and early twentieth century. These changes have continued into the 1990s. Increased immigration, particularly from Latin America and Asia, has added both to the size of various groups and to their diversity. The demographic changes have also been tied to geography and are most pronounced in younger age groups. Here we examine this demographic shift, with particular reference to the school-age population.

Among the most significant demographic changes for inter-group relations has been the steady rise in the nonwhite proportion of the American population.

In 1960, 11 percent of the persons living in the United States were nonwhite; by 1985 this number had risen to 15 percent; and the U.S. Bureau of the Census estimates that by 2000 the figure will be 17 percent (U.S. Bureau of the Census 1991, No. 16). Most of this nonwhite group is African American, although North America's Asian population has grown faster than any other major group in recent decades.

Even more significant, when Hispanics are counted among the minority groups (census figures describe them as being of any race), the demographic changes become more dramatic. At the end of the 1970s, one in five residents of the United States was a member of a group that was not the majority; at the end of the 1980s the figure was one in four.

Within groups such as Hispanics and Asians, population growth has not been equally large across national groups. For example, within the United States' Hispanic population, growth has been greatest among Mexican Americans, with large increases also in the Central American population. The Cuban and Puerto Rican populations have grown less rapidly.

The Asian population, while growing faster than the Hispanic, has had less impact on the overall population size because it has had much lower absolute numbers. However, Asians have shown a similar pattern to Hispanics in that various Asian nationality groups have grown at different rates. The Korean population, for example, has grown much more rapidly than has the Japanese.

Immigration

Immigration to the United States during the last two decades has been significantly greater than it was during the 1930s through the 1950s. Fewer of the recent immigrants have come from Europe; more have come from Latin America and Asia. The size and length of the influx mark it as a third great wave of immigration, as significant in numbers and implications for intergroup relations in the United States as were the immigrations of the mid-nineteenth century and those of the late nineteenth and early twentieth centuries (Marger 1991).

In recent years immigration has accounted for a significant part of U.S. population growth. After decades of decline in the foreign-born population—reaching as low as 4.7 percent of the total population in 1970—the foreign-born population began to increase in the 1970s. By 1980 it had increased to 6.2 percent (U.S. Bureau of the Census 1991, No. 46).

Between 1970 and 1980 the growth in the foreign-born population accounted for 19.1 percent of the country's total population growth. This is the highest proportion of total growth accounted for by immigration since between 1900 and 1920. In absolute numbers, the increase in the foreign-born population in the 1970s (4.46 million) was the highest since the 1850s (Jasso and Rosenzweig 1990).

The numbers of persons who arrive through immigration should continue to increase, continuing the trend of the last several decades, when the numbers of legal immigrants increased from 3.2 million in the 1960s to 6.0 million during the 1980s. New legislation passed in 1990 will raise the number of legal immigrants in the 1990s, with particularly large increases in immigrants with high incomes or specialized job skills (Riche 1991).

Legal immigration is only part of the influx since many persons come to the United States illegally; the most recent group being persons from the former Soviet Union who entered the country on visitor visas and then stayed, integrating into the communities of Soviet immigrants who preceded them. Estimates of illegal immigrants vary considerably, complicated by lack of data and by immigrants' movement back and forth to particular countries of origin, especially Mexico.

A popular American belief is that large numbers of illegal immigrants are responsible for the current shift to a more diverse society. In fact, demographers and immigration specialists have suggested that the actual increase in resident population due to illegal immigration may be smaller than previously thought. Given the large numbers of persons who return to the country from which they emigrated (some going back and forth more than once), estimates of 2 to 6 million illegal aliens given frequently in the 1970s and 1980s may have greatly overestimated the size of the permanent illegal population (Jasso and Rosensweig 1990).

The size of recent demographic changes is only part of the story. For intergroup relations, equally important factors are the new arrivals' origins and destinations. Both factors exhibit patterns very different from the large-scale immigrations of the past. The foreign-born populations' countries of origin have changed dramatically, with global political and economic events affecting the flow of immigrants to the United States. In 1989, of over one million immigrants admitted to the United States, the largest numbers were from Mexico (405,000), El Salvador (58,000), Philippines (57,000), Vietnam (38,000), Korea (37,000), (Mainland) China (32,000), India (31,000), the Dominican Republic (27,000), and Jamaica (25,000) (U.S. Bureau of the Census 1991, No. 9).

Several of these populations represent groups who have come as refugees in large numbers over a short period of time. Among refugees, several groups previously had very few members in this country. For example, in 1980, 90 percent of the Vietnamese and 72 percent of the Iranians had come to the United States in the preceding five years. In contrast, more than 80 percent of immigrants from Norway, Sweden, and Austria had come before 1960 (U.S. Bureau of the Census 1991, No. 47).

The long border with Mexico and the economic disparity between Mexico and the United States are two factors which account for the large number of Mexican immigrants. International events, such as the guerilla wars in Central

America, the conflict in Vietnam, and the Islamic revolution in Iran have accounted for the arrival of other large groups. The liberalization and then breakup of the Soviet Union has increased the numbers of persons from the former USSR coming to the United States and then staying after their visas expire; one estimate put that number at 30,000 at the beginning of 1992 (Mydans 1992). Many persons from Korea and the Philippines arrive because of America's military presence in those countries—foreign bases mean marriages to foreign nationals, particularly in countries with standards of living well below that of the United States.

Also important for intergroup relations is the concentration of new immigrant groups in particular cities and states. The great majority of these new arrivals head for just a few urban areas of the country, primarily in California and New York. Many also go to cities in Texas, Illinois, Florida, and New Jersey, and in a few other East Coast states. This phenomenon has great implications for education, as well.

Issues of multiculturalism become particularly acute in these centers. In some cases, where immigrants from the same country locate in geographically defined areas, they may come to dominate a particular niche in the economy. In one such case Caribbean immigrants to New York City have come into conflict with the dominant group over issues of transportation. Fleets of unlicensed private vans, offering cheaper fares and more frequent service along established bus lines and subway feeder routes, have cut into the public transportation authority's revenues. The city has retaliated by introducing fines against those whose entrepreneurship challenged the status quo. In other areas of the country the knowledge and skills of immigrants have challenged economic control by existing populations in fishing, agriculture, and urban small businesses.

Age Distribution by Group

While immigration accounts for changes in the relative size of the various groups in American society, future trends are determined by groups' current age makeup. Overall, the population is getting older. In 1989, 12.5 percent of the population was sixty-five years of age and older as compared to 11.3 percent ten years earlier. During the same time period, the portion of the population age nine and under increased from 14.0 percent to 14.8 percent (Statistical Abstract 1991, No. 13).

There is a marked difference in the age distribution of various racial and ethnic groups. Most minority groups are relatively young compared to non-Hispanic whites. For example, in 1988 Hispanics had a median age of 24.0 years, African Americans, 25.6, and non-Hispanic whites, 31.4 years (Riche 1991). Among children up to nine years old, 74.8 percent are white; whereas among persons over eighty, 90.4 percent are white. These differences in age groups not only have an immediate impact on the education system but also indicate future changes. Groups with a larger percentage of their population yet to reach childbearing age will grow more in the future than will the older majority population.

Geographical Concentration

Just as immigrants have tended to move to certain areas more than to others, the overall increase in racial and ethnic diversity in the United States is not uniformly distributed. As with other factors, the concentration of minority groups in specific geographic regions means that intergroup relations and their effects on government, commerce, and education in these areas become particularly important. The 1990 census, for example, found that of the more than 14.5 million people in the Los Angeles Metropolitan Area, more than 51 percent are nonwhite (U.S. Bureau of the Census 1991, No. 38). Miami is another metropolitan area where minority groups are now the numerical majority, with Cuban Americans emerging as the dominant political and economic group.

The area of the United States that is most diverse constitutes a large arc stretching south from New England down the East Coast, across the South, Texas, the Southwest, and into California. Other areas of diversity include urban centers with large concentrations of African Americans and Hispanics, as well as rural areas with Native American populations. However, large areas of the United States are not particularly diverse, including much of the Northwest, Midwest, and northern New England; many of these locales have a less than five percent minority population.

Although cities are generally the destination of most immigrants and the residence of many minority groups, in some areas the suburbs are also becoming increasingly multicultural. Prince George's County, bordering Washington, D.C., is representative of the growing number of suburbs in which racial minorities constitute the majority: in 1990, 57 percent of the population was nonwhite and 9,000 of the county's 25,000 businesses were minority-owned (The Rainbow Comes 1991). However, in other cases, such as Atlanta and Detroit, suburbs have remained overwhelmingly white, and to the detriment of minorities and the underclass, businesses have left central cities for emerging satellite districts.

School-Age Population

The demographic shift in the school-age population has been even more rapid than the shift in the overall population. Growth in minority populations over the last several decades has changed the ethnic and racial composition of American schools. Between 1976 and 1986 public school minority enrollment went from 24 percent to nearly 30 percent. In 1986 African American enrollment was 16 percent; Hispanic, 10 percent; Asian-Pacific Islander, 3 percent; and

American Indian/Native American, 1 percent. The largest growth during those ten years was among Asian-Pacific Islanders, whose numbers increased by 116 percent (U.S. Department of Education 1991).

The degree of diversity of the school-age population, like that of the population at large, varies widely according to geography. Where this diversity is most pronounced, the shifts in intergroup relations will be dramatic, with groups now labeled "minority" in the majority. By the mid-1990s California, the District of Columbia, Hawaii, Mississippi, and New Mexico will all graduate more nonwhite students than white students. By the mid-1990s, for the nation as a whole, whites will account for 66 percent of the elementary and secondary school enrollment, a drop of five percent since the mid-1980s (Pitsch 1991).

The unequal distribution of minority groups across the country is related to continued segregation in the nation's schools. Despite legal efforts to eliminate it, segregation of Hispanics increased in the 1980s and segregation faced by African Americans has shown little improvement since 1972. In 1988–89, three out of four Hispanic students attended schools with predominant minority enrollments. Residential segregation is the primary reason for this segregation (Schmidt 1992).

A study by the Knight-Ridder newspaper chain which compared racial segregation in 1980 and 1990 found little reduction in residential segregation at the neighborhood level. Northern metropolitan areas (Chicago, Cleveland, Detroit) showed the greatest degree of black residential isolation (defined as living in a block with at least 90 percent of people of the same race) in 1990. Cities such as Atlanta (43 percent) and Pittsburgh (32 percent) were near average for the country's fifty largest metropolitan areas. Cities in Florida (Orlando) and Texas (Houston) showed the greatest decreases in black residential isolation in the 1980s (Gillmoor & Doig 1992).

Economic Changes

The changes in population are not just related to race and ethnicity. The United States' changing demographics parallels sharp economic changes. During the 1980s and early 1990s group variations in economic resources widened as income grew for the wealthiest segment of the population but remained the same or decreased for working-class families. For example, in the 1980s the wealthiest 20 percent of the population increased its share of all household income from 44 to 47 percent. In part, education and the entry of more women into the work force accounted for this shift, with college-educated, dual-career couples gaining economic advantage (Waldrop and Exeter 1991).

The economic status of various groups continues to show wide disparity in income distribution by race and ethnicity. In 1989 the median family income for whites was $33,915 (in 1988 dollars), for African Americans, $19,329, and for Hispanics, $21,769 (U.S. Bureau of the Census 1991, No. 45).

Children have been affected particularly hard by such income changes. Over the last two decades, the percentage of children under eighteen in poverty has grown from 14.9 percent (1970) to 19.2 percent (1990). Childhood poverty demonstrates that issues of ethnicity, race, and poverty are intertwined. While just over 14 percent of white children lived in poverty in 1988, nearly 44 percent of African American children lived in poverty. For Hispanics, the figure was close to 38 percent (U.S. Department of Education 1991).

Educational Achievement

Educational achievement is related to income, social status, and good jobs. On average, those who complete the most years of formal schooling earn the highest incomes. In fact, in the United States, the strength of this relationship is growing as the economy loses well-paying manufacturing jobs that do not require high levels of formal education. Census Bureau figures (adjusted for inflation) show that during the 1980s the median income for men with some high school education *decreased* from $18,343 to $14,439; for men with college diplomas, median income *increased* from $35,933 to $37,553. For women, there was a slight increase (2 percent) for those with some high school education but a large increase, from $16,602 to $21,659 (30 percent), for those with college education (Waldrop and Exeter 1991).

In the competition for these higher wages and the education related to them, race and ethnicity mix with social class. The farther one moves up the formal education system, the greater the disparity between majority and minority groups completing a given educational level. In 1989, 21.6 percent of whites, 35.4 percent of African Americans, and 49.1 percent of Hispanics twenty-five years of age and older had not completed high school. In the same year 21.8 percent of whites had completed four or more years of college. For African Americans the figure was 11.8 percent and for Hispanics, 9.9 percent (U.S. Bureau of the Census 1991, No. 224).

Given the relationship between years of education completed to income, these figures demonstrate not only unequal access to education between dominant and subordinate groups but also offer one explanation for why African Americans and Hispanics lag in getting their share of better-paying jobs. The figures also demonstrate why group competition and conflict over definitions of knowledge, decisions about what knowledge institutions should transmit, and the control of access and certification functions of these institutions relate not just to schooling itself but to group maintenance of political and economic power, as well.

Moreover, unequal access is not confined to formal education institutions. Poverty affects access not only to formal education but also to nonformal education. The National Commission on Children has found that nonformal education programs are less available to poor urban children than they are to nonpoor children (National Commission on Children 1991). For example, only 52 percent of poor urban children have access to organizations such as Scouts and Boys' and Girls' Clubs, compared to 79 percent of nonpoor children. For organized sports the comparable figures were 49 percent and 74 percent. This inequality is particularly striking given the important role that clubs, out-of-school classes, youth organizations, and other youth activities play in socializing future generations.

Intergroup Relations and Education in Atlanta

The experience of Atlanta during the 1970s and 1980s demonstrates intergroup competition and conflict and how race and class are intertwined. During these two decades Atlanta experienced some of the demographic changes detailed above: increased minority school enrollment, white movement to the suburbs, and increased job opportunities and income for dual-wage earning, professional families. However, the Atlanta case is most instructive because it demonstrates that even a school system over which African Americans had some degree of control and in which schools received reasonable amounts of funding could not provide genuine equal opportunity in preparing youth for higher education or higher-paying jobs when faced with racial and economic separation (Orfield and Ashkinaze 1991).

Atlanta schools became more segregated in the 1980s (93 percent African American), a decade after a compromise effort to avoid busing was made by African American leaders and white business leaders. In return for accepting virtually segregated schools, African Americans committed to improving education and basic skills assumed control of the Atlanta schools in the 1970s. However, as whites moved to suburbs outside Atlanta, inequality remained, linked to class and class differences among schools. Despite the movement of middle-class African Americans to certain suburbs, they remained largely white. Several counties had less than five percent African American enrollment (Orfield and Ashkinaze 1991).

Access to higher education for Atlanta's minorities, especially African American males, declined during the 1980s, while access increased for whites. Lower African American family wealth compared to whites, combined with increased tuition, lower financial aid, and reduced support systems also contributed to the decline, which reversed the progress made from the mid-1960s through the 1970s. The decline in African American college enrollment was particularly troublesome in Atlanta, where economic growth and an increased entrance of highly educated women to the work force created higher educational requirements for specific jobs. Lack of enforcement of civil rights regulations, increased use of tests, and higher admission standards were also contributing factors (Orfield and Ashkinaze 1991).

The Atlanta case demonstrates how intergroup competition for resources resists outside intervention. Faced with growing African American enrollment and challenges to school segregation, the dominant group ceded control of the central school district to the subordinate group, and using its economic muscle, moved to the suburbs.

While the Atlanta case illustrates the contemporary inter-group conflict between African Americans and whites in large urban areas, conflict between persons who were already living in the United States and immigrants from Southern and Eastern Europe who were entering the United States in the early twentieth century *defined* issues related to the integration of subordinate groups into a society. This earlier public debate dealt with how schools should be used to integrate immigrants into the receiving country versus the desires of immigrant parents for control over their children's education.

Historical Perspectives on the Relationship Between Dominant and Subordinate Groups in the United States

Race, ethnicity, and social class have long influenced American educational goals and practice. However, the growth of public schooling in the second half of the nineteenth century, combined with the arrival of large numbers of immigrants different from the Protestant Northern Europeans who constituted America's dominant group, brought schooling and education to the center of intergroup relations. Public schooling's attractiveness to those concerned with growing immigration was its potential to reach all young people, as well as many other persons through adult education.

There exist various interpretations of early twentieth century schooling, both cultural and structural, which illustrate the complexity of group relationships to education. One view emphasizes the power of the state and the power of reformers bent on progressive social engineering. From this perspective, schools were ideal institutions for enculturating newcomers to American values and norms. The immigrants' home cultures can be studied to see how they affect their assimilation (Weiss 1982). Another view emphasizes how elites used education to ensure docile workers, or how education was the scene of struggles between workers and elites (Spring 1990). In this view schools reflect values of the economic elite, who use schools to inculcate values that strengthen social control.

By the early twentieth century several approaches to the relations among receivers and immigrants, based primarily on the immigrant experience and the reaction to it, were being articulated in the United States. These approaches shaped intergroup relations theory and educational goals and practice throughout the century. Interestingly, ideas related to these approaches are at the center of the contemporary debate about multiculturalism and education. Such issues involve interpretation and the degree to which new subordinate groups entering a society should surrender their values, take on new values, or attempt to influence existing values.

Postiglione (1983) proposes five models to describe what happens when groups come together, three of which parallel concepts that emerged in the early twentieth century and which could be used to categorize much of the contemporary debate over multiculturalism.

The first model, "Anglo-conformity" (popularized as "Americanization"), originated in an ideology of Northern and Western European superiority which maintained that groups not from these areas threatened American society and should either be restricted from immigrating to the United States or be compelled to conform. The dominant group's values were accepted as the values everyone should assume, so the burden for change rested with the immigrant group (Cubberly 1929). Often referred to as the "melting pot theory," the second model was common during the great migrations of the late nineteenth and early twentieth centuries and was intended to ensure that the "best" traits of various groups were merged into a common American character, frequently in the crucible of the American frontier. No single set of immigrant group values were expected to dominate, because it was expected that subordinate groups would reduce their values and norms to a kind of lowest common denominator. The third model, "cultural pluralism," was not as widespread as the Americanization and melting pot concepts and emphasized the contributions each culture made to American society and the value of each ethnic group.

Two later models are derived less from early twentieth century practical experience and more from recent scholarship: "Emerging culture" views the larger American society modified in some way by the arrival of each new group who themselves are modified as they become Haitian Americans, Vietnamese Americans, or other acculturated group members. The final model, "impact-integration," focuses on inter- and intra-group dynamics, viewing cultural groups, both the new group and the old group, "colliding" and integrating with each other. Conflicts between groups led to a synthesis which contributes meaning and importance to the society (Glazer and Moynihan 1970; Greeley 1974; Novak 1972).

Of these models Anglo-conformity, or the Americanization movement, was a powerful force in shaping the behavior of immigrants and receivers during the first part of the twentieth century. We turn to a more detailed discussion of this movement as it illustrates important points about how groups were brought together in shaping the future of the country.

Americanization

In the mid-19th century large-scale immigration from Europe (three million persons came between 1846 and 1855) raised concerns about the culturally, religiously, and linguistically different who, the dominant group feared, might bring radical ideologies with them. These concerns strengthened the arguments of persons and groups advocating the establishment of public schools which their supporters believed could inculcate newcomers' children with American values and the English language (Rippa 1988). Public schools became a focal point for forced assimilation of immigrants, just as they did for assimilation of Native Americans.

Americanization reached its greatest frenzy and had its greatest impact when millions of Eastern and Southern European immigrants arrived in the United States between 1880 and the beginning of World War 1. The immigrants settled close to industrial jobs in urban neighborhoods defined by ethnic or nationality group membership. In 1909 up to three quarters of the children enrolled in public schools in some large cities were immigrants. As the problems of urban America were more and more attributed to characteristics of immigrant groups, many educators and other public officials advocated divesting immigrants of their culture and ethnicity.

Through the Bureau of Naturalization, which pressed for the education of immigrants in public schools, the federal government became involved with Americanization: immigrant education was to be complete, even teaching people how to brush their teeth and how and what to cook. Immigrants were to completely repudiate their culture (McClymer 1982).

The Americanization approach toward immigrants was not fostered by persons who claimed to despise foreigners. To the contrary, it was a movement with widespread support among liberals and progressives who viewed Americanization as a social improvement. Even some ethnic organizations took it on as a way to ease their members' transition into a new society. Progressives believed that public education should be responsible for bringing diverse aspects of life such as health and vocational training to all classes and cultures of peoples; they took for granted that the norms and values which education brought were those of the dominant American culture (Cremin 1962).

The United States' entry into World War 1 further aided the Americanization movement and supported a more negative view of immigrants. The war heightened the perception of immigrants as cultural aliens. To superimpose a new system of values on immigrant children soon became an expected role of education (Rippa 1988) and compulsory school attendance laws aided these efforts.

However, these new subordinate groups, whose members were often differentiated from the dominant group by religion, dress, language, and other cultural behavior, recognized the importance of education for achieving social mobility and status and established parochial schools to resist efforts to Americanize their children through public schools (whose formal efforts at the turn of the century were largely confined to teaching immigrants English). Native-language newspapers, fraternal organizations, and other mechanisms to help immigrants reinforce their backgrounds also helped them resist acculturation. From this perspective, efforts to establish parochial school systems by Catholic immigrants in Pittsburgh, Chicago, and Buffalo (among other cities) can be seen as efforts to determine and define what constitutes knowledge and what knowledge should be transmitted through educational institutions. These efforts, and their importance to group identity and autonomy, are not dissimilar from Native Americans' development during the 1980s of tribal colleges over which they would have control and which would foster Native American self-identity (Marriott 1992).

In 1924 an immigration act limited the number of immigrants permitted to enter the United States. From the mid-1920s until the 1980s, the number of immigrants was lower than it had been in the preceding century. During the early part of this period fears of fueling nativist sentiment and opposition on the part of those who wished to limit the number of immigrants were so strong that they prevented changes or exceptions in quotas that would have admitted persons persecuted by the Nazis.

However, external political factors did, at times, influence immigration policy. For example, in 1943 Congress responded to the United States' wartime alliance with China, by lifting the restriction on Chinese immigration. This act began a more than twenty-year legislative process which substituted ideology and class, rather than race and ethnicity, as immigration and naturalization criteria (Daniels 1986). A prime example of this shift is the legislation passed in the 1950s which gave admission preference to persons from countries with communist governments.

The nativism fueled by World War 1 reappeared in the 1980s with verbal bashing against Japan, the beating of a Chinese American man in Michigan by an unemployed auto worker who thought the man was Japanese, and violence against Vietnamese immigrants in the fishing industry in Texas. Another phenomenon with roots in Americanization, is the "English-only" movement. Like those in the early twentieth century who advocated enculturating immigrants, those who support the exclusive use of English argue that there is one standard—that of the dominant group—to which subordinate groups should adhere.

Conclusion

The immigrant experience of the late nineteenth and early twentieth centuries was an important era in education and intergroup relations and for the development of conceptual approaches to these relations. In the 1980s and 1990s changing demographics, including increases in immigration, have helped renew interest in the questions concerning which groups control and define knowledge and determine what should be taught in schools. Immigrant groups, as well as residents for many generations, have renewed claims to have a say in educational institutions, just as immigrant parents did a century ago.

In some instances, these claims have taken the form of court cases, such as the landmark *Lau* v. *Nichols* (1974) in which a class action suit brought on behalf of Chinese children in San Francisco resulted in a ruling which secured non-English-speaking children a right to an education that meets their linguistic and cultural needs. The case has had significant impact on the way in which educational institutions respond to immigrant children.

In other cases the claims have been part of long-term struggles, often against local and state education agencies and boards. For Mexican Americans in Texas the struggle has required multiple approaches, including fighting to eliminate segregated school facilities through the mid-1970s, and battling for bilingual education during the 1970s and 1980s (San Miguel 1987). The Texas case represents the long-term struggles for power of subordinate groups in determining what is worth teaching, what gets taught, and who does the teaching.

The first section traced the historical development of multicultural education. Chapter 2 considered multiculturalism and education, first by describing the recent demographic changes in the United States that have been part of the reason for renewed interest in intergroup relations and education, and second by giving a brief overview of various ways in which social scientists have described the relationship between dominant and subordinate groups. The next section considers in more detail the conceptual framework that helps us understand intergroup relations, taking into account both cultural and structural factors.

Part 2

Nation, State, Community, and Family in Multiculturalism and Education

CHAPTER 3

The Nation-State and
Multicultural Identities

Answers to the questions, "Who determines what counts as knowledge?" "What knowledge will be transmitted through educational institutions?" "Who has access to those institutions?" are rooted in the power, influence, and relationships among socioeconomic, ethnic, and racial groups. While indicators of group membership are often difficult to determine, individuals and groups may be distinguished through some of the following: heritage, identity, values and belief systems, behaviors, physical appearance, and levels of resources and political power. Age and gender often confound and complicate these other characteristics.

Segments or groups based on some or all of these distinctions emerge in all societies. Schooling is important to these groups as each expresses its vision of how they and their children can use education to secure an appropriate place in society. Educational institutions become natural arenas for potentially compatible—but more likely contentious—intergroup relations as each group attempts to achieve its goals through the support of particular educational policies and practices. The educational decisions that must be made and the issues around which there is often disagreement include: how an institution is governed; how access to programs or levels is determined (e.g., tests, residence, sponsorship); how the various educational levels and programs articulate with each other; who determines (e.g., teachers, parents, elected or appointed school boards) the curriculum and individual courses of study; who does the teaching and who administers the institution (e.g., chosen by ethnicity, gender, or other); and what language is used as the medium of instruction.

We believe that the tension among groups vis-á-vis influencing educational policy and practice, results from the interplay of groups whose members act on certain concerns or needs which they believe do or should involve schooling. An institution's educational philosophy and the way it gets implemented is typically not neutral but rather represents certain group interests and works against others. The disparities in the educational systems of the Catholics and Protestants in Northern Ireland, the Jews and Arabs in the Middle East, blacks and whites in South Africa, or the Indians and mestizos of Peru and Bolivia provide evidence of the biases which are reflected in all levels of schooling. In effect, much that passes for truth in education is influenced heavily by the desires of particular groups as they enter education as a social action arena. Thus what knowledge is worth most and what knowledge should be transmitted, as well as who should have access to education, are determined by ongoing interactions among groups of people differentiated by political, social, and economic power.

When new populations enter a society (like contemporary immigrations of large numbers of Asians and Hispanics to the United States), or as a society goes through changing relationships among groups, challenges to what knowledge is produced, transmitted, and tested are often posed. Examples can be seen in the Asian-American, African-American, Hispanic-American, and Native-American Studies programs in the United States, all of which are a direct result of the challenges posed by new groups entering educational institutions in larger numbers. The interests of these groups in protecting and disseminating their perspectives on truth and objectivity were typically rejected by traditional university departments in the 1970s; the studies programs often only served as student or community outreach centers and institutes. One of the reasons for the lack of academic integration of these programs was that university colleagues considered the available knowledge too shallow to legitimate such programs as fields of teaching and scholarship. Other reasons included the general lack of depth characteristic of interdisciplinary study, the fragile connection with other fields of study, and the difficulty in identifying careers for which these programs might prepare students. These issues were exacerbated by the fact that being a member of the identified ethnic group often determined who could contribute to or criticize the field of study. While such programs continue to struggle for legitimacy and resources and to overcome some of these issues, they also appear to have secured a lasting place in the college curriculum.

While educational programs like ethnic studies may be partially designed to better the relationships among social segments in the United States and many other societies, social class, ethnicity, and race also form a basis for violence and conflict over educational interests in several countries. Contemporary strife in Eastern Europe, the Middle East, the Caribbean, and South Africa provide examples. In these societies can be found intense, long-term discrimination; bias; hatred; and sometimes war, usually precipitated by one race, ethnic, or social class group toward another. The dismantling of apartheid in South Africa; the persecution of the Kurds in Iran, Iraq, and Turkey; and the killing of Croatians and Muslims and the destruction of their communities by neighboring Serbs in Eastern Europe are examples of such conflicts. To varying degrees schooling issues such as language of instruction, who gets into institutions, and what is to be studied have been present during stages of these conflicts.

By means of evolving change processes and more violent upheavals associated with group interests, it is now common to find educational planners, administrators, and practitioners in many countries attending to the interests and demands of ethnic, racial, class, caste, and other minority or subordinate groups for greater access and participation in educational institutions. Women, the disabled, the elderly, and the gay and lesbian communities have extended the list of these interest groups. In most societies such segmentation reflects the importance of gender, blood relatives, language, religion, and historical tradition in shaping personal and group identification.

Not surprisingly, such identities exist even in the face of totalitarianism and repression. Educational institutions are important in this interplay among groups because they are perceived as ways to at once achieve change and maintain the status quo. From the perspective of a subordinate group, formal education offers a way to reinforce cultural identity and enable members to become involved in new ways socioeconomically in the wider society. From the dominant group's perspective educational institutions are important because they are among the principal mechanisms for maintaining and shaping the nature of the relationship between groups and for slowing the rate of change in a given society. Sometimes this means increasing control and pressing for the assimilation of subordinate groups. In other instances, even though the dominant group may impose its values and behaviors, the subordinates may seek their own identity and independence. Short of such polarization in goals, it is common to find many minority populations desiring to hold onto some aspects of their ethnic heritage through family structures, language, food, dress, and similar avenues of expression. This often happens, even if minority groups coalesce into broader "panethnic" identities (e.g., West Indians, Native Americans, Asian Americans).

This chapter demonstrates that all countries must face the challenge of segmentation and that educational policies can be influential in shaping national identity as well as individual ethnic, racial, socioeconomic, and other group identities. While most cases of intergroup relationships fail to be adequate models, all provide insight into the ways in which multisegmented societies approach societal integration and how they use education to achieve their goals. The examples also demonstrate that it is possible for nations not only to exist but to thrive on the presence of minority groups whose goals include preserving their respective heritage and identities. Our discussion will focus primarily on ethnic, racial, and socioeconomic populations.

Education and its Relationship to Ethnicity and Social Class

To begin our discussion, it is important to realize that all nations are characterized by ethnic groups which cut horizontally across a society and the social classes that divide its population (including ethnic groups) vertically from top to bottom. The horizontal, or ethnic group, segments reflect the preservation of such characteristics as language, values, food, and traditional dress, while those at the top are differentiated from those at the bottom by wealth or political power. Combinations of ethnicity and class provide frames of reference for the individuals who traditionally identify with them. Sometimes such identities become the basis for group stereotypes about food and dress, vocational pursuits, or occupations.

The ethnic groups represent a common ancestry, memories of a historical past, or ways of behaving which help define members as a distinct population (Schermerhorn 1970, 12). While a group may or may not objectively describe itself, it may also be assigned valid and invalid characteristics by others. For example, it is common for a group to build an image of itself which exaggerates its historical importance. At the same time, outsiders may negatively stereotype that same group's history based upon the food consumed, the language spoken, habits of personal hygiene, or other behaviors which are different from those that prevail in the wider society. This difference between self-identity and perception by others has often been encountered by new immigrant groups in the United States. European immigrants in the early years of this century, as well as Hispanic Americans and Southeast Asians in the 1980s and 1990s, have suffered some level of negative stereotyping and have had to adjust their own identities in accordance with their immigrant status. This interplay of cultural self-perception and perception by others combines to provide a foundation for an ethnic group's internal relationships as well as for its relationship to other groups in society.

Social classes on the other hand are based on a group's relative access to, or possession of, political and economic power, or resources. Here the focus is on how this power and resource base gets played out in (among others) governmental, educational, and occupational pursuits. Some argue that it is socioeconomic status, not ethnicity, that is central to group identity and intergroup relations. From this perspective such intergroup relations are not likely to be improved through legal means, like ethnically or racially based affirmative action, court-ordered busing, or anti-discrimination lawsuits. Instead, to improve equity and equal opportunity among groups, some would emphasize race-and ethnic-neutral programs such as full-employment strategies, job skills training, comprehensive health care, public school reform, increased childcare, and prevention of crime and drug abuse. From the social class perspective some would emphasize building political coalitions which link individuals from various ethnic and racial groups to economic issues (see chapter 7).

Although it may be promising to separate ethnic from social class characteristics, it is apparent that they overlap in shaping group members' behavior as well as others' perceptions of that group. Thus group characteristics and attributes are often found to be intertwined in such a way that certain well-defined groups occupy either higher or lower class positions relative to other groups in society. In the United States, for example, African Americans, Hispanic Americans, and Native Americans, as members of ethnic groups, are more likely also to be among the economically poor or subordinate segments of the society, while those who are Caucasian and who trace their roots to Northern and Western Europe are more likely to be members of the dominant group. Thus ethnic and racial discrimination by some is often argued to be at the core of socioeconomic inequality and poverty. The results restrain members of certain groups from participating in society in accordance with their ethnic and social class relationships.

It should also be noted that there are other dimensions which can be used both to refine and crosscut these ethnic and socioeconomic groups. Gender, for example, is sometimes the basis for the organization of social action groups. In this regard, women's rights advocates have demonstrated the underrepresentation of women in higher wage-earning positions and in corporate executive positions. Concerns over women's rights can also be seen in education through the women's studies movement. In higher education Women's Studies has taken on many of the characteristics of ethnic studies as it seeks to develop a knowledge base and a place in the curriculum and organization of schools and colleges. Other crosscutting dimensions include sexual orientation, age, disability, and special needs, all of which may be represented by socially active groups in the educational process.

Education, Certification, and Socioeconomic Mobility

The interaction of groups through educational institutions is often mediated by the ways schools and universities shape access to occupations—roles and statuses—in the wider society. In the United States, and now more common throughout the world, certificates and diplomas have become necessary to gain access to particular jobs and thus to gain greater status in society. One way to grasp the significance of this is to differentiate among types of education. For our purposes we can say that in all societies there are three major functions of educational processes: socialization, skills training, and certification. Although socialization and skills training are likely to occur both inside and outside school, certification—the distribution of grades, diplomas and certificates—for access to jobs and other schooling has increasingly become a function reserved for educational institutions alone. It is this power over certification that gives educational institutions (for better or worse) a preeminence in discussions of the purposes of "education," or even "learning," both in industrial and in so-called developing countries.

Because formal education functions as such an important sorting institution, i.e., a gate keeper, the critical issue for educators and scholars concerns the interaction between the schools' general purposes and the ethnic and social class divisions in a society; specifically, the extent to which educational institutions act to maintain and perpetuate inequality through these divisions, or act to reduce and ameliorate that inequality.

One argument is that schooling can help subordinate groups achieve status and income on a roughly equal basis with society's more privileged groups. The teaching of work-related skills, for example, is a function schools can perform which places individuals of disparate backgrounds in similar wage-earning positions. In general, this approach to mobility through schooling assumes that income and social status are acquired by those who are most intelligent and skillful without regard for their background characteristics. From this viewpoint the lesson for those who wish to succeed is: work hard, sacrifice as necessary, and place a high priority on school achievement. Social class background and ethnicity are therefore accorded little or no importance in explaining school or societal success.

The opposing line of argument says that the school can either reinforce or conflict with ethnic and social class characteristics brought to school by children. Therefore certain groups will be advantaged by virtue of their skills, values, and knowledge—what they have learned in the family and neighborhood. Similarly, other students will be disadvantaged because of the way in which school operations and expectations conflict with the social class and ethnic background of the students. When such conflicts affect a substantial number of a particular class or ethnic group, it may be argued that schools exacerbate social and cultural distinctions in society.

While both of these arguments can be justified, schooling which occurs across social class and ethnic group boundaries often supports unequal outcomes. This is most likely to happen when dominant ethnic groups purposely provide inferior schooling to subordinate racial and ethnic groups and thereby limit their access to the rewards of schooling in later life. Consequently, the ethnic minorities adapt their child-rearing practices and their expectations for the future to their assigned status in society, thereby perpetuating the group's socioeconomic position (often at the lower level).

John Ogbu (1978) argues this way when he seeks to explain why low socioeconomic status minority group children in the United States as well as their counterparts in other countries do poorly in school. Ogbu labels the minority populations who reside in a given country either voluntary or involuntary. Voluntary minorities are those who chose to settle in a country on their own initiative. Involuntary minorities are those whose migration was forced (e.g., African Americans), or whose territory was acquired by force (e.g., Native Americans, Mexican Americans), and who are typically distinguished from the majority by physical features resulting in caste or caste-like status. By caste or caste-like, he means the positions they occupy are hereditary, the groups are endogamous, and the societies in which they live are characterized by rigid stratification systems. Ogbu argues that for these involuntary populations there is a social and occupational ceiling on their opportunities, channeling them into certain jobs whose status and income is typically less. The psychological consequences of this caste-like experience for members of these involuntary minority groups are often overwhelming, and the adaptation such groups make is often self-defeating. For example, Ogbu argues that members of such groups succumb to the dominant group stereotypes which label them inferior; that they do not have enough confidence in themselves to succeed in schooling and in careers; and that they believe they cannot be academically successful and also carry forward their cultural identity and traditions.

The implication of this process of ethnic group socialization and the struggle for school diplomas is only members of the dominant group are automatically successful in "cashing in" their educational experiences for access to the highest paying, and most prestigious jobs. Thus schooling reinforces the racial and/or ethnic characteristics which are brought to school and which form the basis for social interaction between groups.

The use of social class and ethnicity to assess the ways schools function to promote equality and inequality can be seen in a recent case study of the city of Atlanta. Gary Orfield and Carole Ashkinaze (1991) studied relationships among the economy, politics, and African Americans in the 1980s. Despite improvements in general economic conditions and increased African-American control over the local political structures during the decade, they found that the quality of education, housing, and jobs deteriorated for African Americans and that their relative level of income did not increase. They also found that suburbanization for most African Americans did not mean crossing the color line; instead it meant the color line was being extended, i.e., whites were moving further away from the city. In this way, white suburbs remained the center of resistance for school integration, mass transit links, and zoning for affordable housing, thereby reinforcing the social and physical distance among and between groups.

As is evident in case studies like this one, the role and function of formal education in a segmented area like Atlanta can best be analyzed by considering *both* social class and ethnicity and by paying attention to *both* dominant and subordinate group perspectives. In other words, it cannot be assumed that any level of educational institution in a given society will attend to ethnicity or social class exclusively, nor can it be assumed that formal education will serve only to suppress subordinate groups. What is needed instead of these more abstract perspectives is a contextual approach which looks at particular cases and weighs the interaction of ethnicity and social class. A key to such an analysis depends on the particular integrative processes by which groups interact in society and the educational policies which are intended to shape some of those interactions.

Societal Integration

How various groups interact within the bounds of a single society or political entity can be broadly placed under the term "integration." Drawing on Schermerhorn (1970), we would emphasize the *dynamic* nature of integration; it is not a state of being, but rather a process involving negotiation, adaptation, and in some instances, conflict. Schermerhorn argues that the dominant group in a society sets the tone and determines the nature of the integration activities and objectives. This does not mean that Schermerhorn fails to recognize the importance of a society's subordinate groups as they challenge and work to secure greater access to societal resources. Nevertheless, it is usually the dominant group in a society which sets the integrative agenda and typically determines the desirable long-range goals for the subordinate group(s) as well as for itself. As such, educational policy statements and policy implementation—even in a multigroup setting—are oftentimes the monopoly of the dominant group.

We are interested in how the particular social institution, formal education, functions in this process of integration in societies with different patterns of segmentation *both* along ethnic lines and along social class lines. By examining approaches to integration through educational policies, we should be able to see how the "same" policy—e.g., bilingual education, vocational training, separate educational facilities, and so forth—may have very different implications according to the particular dominant-subordinate relationships between two or more groups.

The integration process typically involves an ongoing negotiation process. At times the groups agree to common goals and activities, and at other times they disagree and seek greater autonomy and independence. If a multigroup society, for example, chooses to have one official language, like in the United States, rather than two, like in Canada, or several like in Switzerland, the policy chosen reflects the interests, power, and influence of the various groups in the society. Usually, the results demonstrate the extent to which the dominant group values homogeneity or is willing to tolerate differences.

Schermerhorn indicates that each society is typically characterized either by common, society-wide lifestyles and institutional participation or by differences in those lifestyles and patterns. If they differ, there is a tendency for each group to retain and preserve unique cultural attributes as well as to seek greater autonomy politically and economically. We can think of these opposing orientations as either pulling together, increasing homogeneity and centralization or as pulling apart, increasing heterogeneity and decentralization thereby giving groups greater autonomy.

If the dominant and subordinate groups agree to support common goals and policies or to encourage greater group autonomy and differences, a shared form of integration can occur. If the groups differ, however—one group seeking closer ties and commonality and the other seeking autonomy to preserve separateness—the integrative process is likely to be conflictual. It is the tendency of *both* groups—the desire for commonality or separateness—that must be taken into account. And when the groups pull in opposite directions, integration may exist only because the dominant group uses force to achieve its goals and maintain stability.

Building on Schermerhorn's outline, we would suggest that the process of integration may find a single group's socioeconomic and ethnic interests contradictory. For example, in the United States there is general support for English to be the single, national language. Yet at various levels the government supports the views of many minority groups who seek native language and bilingual instruction in preschools and elementary schools. Although such a policy appears on its surface, contradictory, it is assumed from the dominant group's perspective that native-language and bilingual instruction will actually speed a minority ethnic group's acquisition and usage of English. Some members of ethnic minority groups of various social class levels who receive bilingual instruction or instruction in the native language are also, however, the loudest protestors of such programs. They protest because they perceive such programs to be remedial, and they do not connect such instruction with the learning of English, something they value as a means of gaining access to jobs and other forms of participation in the wider society. Their desire to acquire English, however, doesn't necessarily mean that these parents would be willing to have their children give up their native language capability and thereby cut themselves off from their ethnic heritage.

Another example of educational policies which appear simultaneously to support commonality and autonomy and which are thus contradictory involves the use of standardized achievement tests. The use of such tests, and recent efforts to implement nationally sanctioned examinations at various levels of schooling in the United States, reflect the dominant group's desire for commonality. At the same time, however, because control over schools is at the state and local levels, decisions regarding what is studied may be in opposition to national efforts. Again, such policies indicate the push and pull which often goes on between local and regional or state and national levels as dominant and subordinate groups struggle to incorporate the school and its participants into either or both the local and the nation-state's economic, political, and cultural norms.

Educational Case Studies

The following discussion provides examples of how integration occurs in a number of different societies and how dominant and subordinate groups attempt to use education to achieve their particular goals (Hawkins and La Belle 1985). To assist in organizing the discussion, we will borrow Barth and Noel's (1972) concepts of coercion, consensus, and interdependence as ways the integration process occurs. The first example is South Africa, where dominant and subordinate groups differ on how integration should occur. In South Africa dominant group coercion has been used to force black compliance with white goals. The recent realignment of dominant and subordinate groups in the former Soviet Union serves as a second example. Again, this case documents how dominant and subordinate groups differ on goals and how coercion was used historically to maintain the viability of the nation. We then turn to the United States, Britain, and certain other countries where the possibility for all groups to satisfy their particular needs appears to be an oftentimes fragile basis for integration. In these instances, there is general agreement on stated goals for dominant and subordinate group integration, even though in reality there is considerable inequality among groups. The third and final example is drawn from India and Switzerland, where interdependence among and between groups helps explain the nature of integration. In these instances, again we find general consensus concerning the nature of the integration that should occur, even though many intergroup relations' goals have not yet been realized.

Before presenting these examples, it is important to provide an introduction to *coercion, consensus,* and *interdependence* as ways in which the integration process in various countries is sustained. We believe that these three mechanisms reflect the general approaches employed by dominant groups in interaction with subordinates to implement their definition of societal integration.

Coercion

The first approach to integration involves dominant group actions that rely on the application of military or police forces for survival. Coercion usually takes place in cases where the ethnic groups or social classes are oriented toward the attainment of incompatible or mutually exclusive goals. The incompatibility is often reflected in group attempts to pull the country toward either a common or a separate identity. For example, a subordinate group may want greater access to economic and political power, while the dominant group may wish to determine if and how that is to occur. Similarly, the subordinate group may want greater autonomy in its language and religion, while the dominant group may desire greater uniformity (Paulston 1976).

Consensus

The second approach to integration involves the establishment of agreement among all of the various groups into which the society is divided. Consensus is often seen as the natural outcome of a set common values (cultural, economic, political, etc), which sometimes only verbally stated goals agreed upon by two or more groups. These similarities are assumed to provide the basis for general agreement on the direction of the total society. In many cases, the shared values in this kind of society have grown out of long-standing religious, commercial, or linguistic ties between groups and as such are considered almost "natural" by the groups themselves.

Interdependence

The third approach to integration essentially recognizes that only together, through mutual dependence and contributions, can the groups function as a whole. This interdependence is usually based on socioeconomic rather than ethnic interests. Thus, for example, a dominant group may control the means of production while also being aware of the importance of the labor provided by lower socioeconomic and minority ethnic populations. Such strong economic ties may not, however, lead to sharing language, religion, political views, or anything else across group lines. Over time, however, once there is a mutual dependence in the factory or marketplace, such interdependence may also develop through cultural activities.

Turning now to examples of each approach, coercion can be seen in South Africa, where whites force behavioral compliance on the subordinate blacks. In this case the whites and blacks are separated horizontally based on racial and cultural heritage. They are also separated socioeconomically: the white population holds a virtual political and economic monopoly while blacks occupy the lowest occupational and social positions. Horizontally therefore, race and social class coincide to divide the populations. A legal framework called apartheid exists to maintain the divisions. As evidenced by the struggle for greater freedom carried on by blacks over the past several decades, whites have maintained power primarily through the police and armed forces. These coercive mechanisms have limited the extent to which blacks can seek access to economic and political resources and have forced them to maintain separation.

Formal education in South Africa under apartheid has been highly centralized nationally; access to schools often coincides with race and provides little if any opportunity for blacks to compete successfully with whites. Under apartheid, curricula and the language of instruction in South African schools have reflected a strong bias toward Afrikans and English and away from indigenous languages. This means that acculturation is forced and limited and that assimilation is nearly impossible since most of the subordinate blacks are kept out of schools or are led through schools for basic literacy and other skills. Such policies have served to standardize behavior for access to economic and political resources while maintaining distance between the groups.

This case shows how in the cultural sphere the whites foster separateness through parallel schools while simultaneously fostering minimal cultural commonality through language policies emphasizing Afrikans and English. Socioeconomically however, whites use education to prepare blacks for participation in an economy dominated by whites but limit that involvement to lower levels of the labor force. Again, language is important here because some minimal knowledge of Afrikans or English must be learned to foster that economic participation. Like bilingual education in the United States, such seemingly crosscutting goals may seem contradictory to some. The issue that may be most important, however, is the relationship between the goals of the dominant whites as opposed to the goals of blacks with regard to these issues. Whether both groups share rather than differ in their orientations will not affect integration per se; the important difference between agreed-upon and conflictual types of integration is that the former carries greater ease. That is, in either case there will be coordinated compliance with objectives of the dominant group, but where that compliance is voluntary, it will also be somewhat more predictable over time and will require less governmental effort to maintain. The situation in South Africa obviously does not reflect this consensus-oriented system of relationships between dominant and subordinate groups.

Another example of coercion can be see in the former Soviet Union, and it may provide some lessons for a nation like South Africa should the system of apartheid ultimately crumble. The division of the Soviet Union is assumed to have occurred principally because the government was unable to satisfactorily demonstrate its ability to reflect a concern for ethnic and socioeconomic goals among subordinate groups. Although this issue was apparent to those who knew the country, it was not until the late 1980s that the problems in Armenia between Armenians and Azerbaijanis (from the Azerbijan Republic) taught the world of the divisiveness present and ultimately became the lightening rod for the events that followed. Armenia was a case where territorial conflict had been present and where such issues as Armenian control over their schools for curricular and language integrity was a major policy issue to be resolved. Placed in context, the Azerbaijani-Armenian conflict provided the entry point into the other conflicts that subsequently occurred in the Soviet Union. All of them, however, were preceded by years of coercive efforts to force assimilation on separate ethnic groups.

Within the Soviet Union, prior to the Russian revolution, assimilationist policies were perhaps most evident through language-of-instruction policies. At that time, Russian was already in place as the preferred language of the dominant Bolsheviks. In 1917, at the time of the revolution, non-Russians were promised equal educational opportunity, including the use of their native language in schools. Ultimately, however, the promise was disregarded; instead, the Russians favored a single ethnic group in a given locale and used the language of that group for schooling. In effect, the Bolsheviks wanted to make sure that their view of history was taught, including their history of any given ethnic group. Lenin promised to end this Russification process, but acculturation ultimately became the rule for some one hundred ethnic groups in the country. By the 1930s considerable pressure was exerted on local groups to discourage the development of local languages.

In contradistinction to South Africa and the former Soviet Union are countries where consensus rather than coercion tends to dominate the approach to intergroup relations. A place where consensus seems to have found some acceptance is found in our next case study, the United States. Although often tenuous and tension-filled, consensus in the United States is based on the promise of eventual equality and enhanced social and economic status for subordinates. It exists because of a general acceptance of stated values and goals and because certain governmental policies (e.g., affirmative action) are intended to assist in achieving such goals. In reality, however, typical behavior and government actions are oftentimes paternalistic and policies providing health, education, and other services are employed to legitimate dominant group goals. While clearly there is subordinate status associated with ethnic and racial membership for large numbers of African Americans, Hispanic Americans, Native Americans and Asian Americans in the United States, occupational roles are not completely contingent upon ethnic and racial group boundaries as in a place like South Africa. This means that some individuals from these subordinate groups may be in high-status positions in the United States. Nevertheless, the dominant group protects its prerogatives, and the majority of the subordinate group remains in lower status positions.

Access to schools in the United States seems broad for all groups, where success depends upon accommodation via standardized tests and grade point averages and other dominant group criteria. Those who do not succeed are more likely to be tracked into vocational and trade streams. In the United States the curricula in schools tends to reflect the heritage and background of the dominant group, providing minimal exposure to minority populations through symbolic or token attention to traditional foods, dress, or other behaviors. Language policies in the United States are also homogenizing, since English is the language of most instruction. As mentioned earlier, this has been tempered somewhat by offering bilingual education at younger ages, through which children may receive some exposure to the mother language, and by offering secondary school electives. Basically, such language exposure should not interfere with the acquisition of English; thus, other language learning must be justified transitional or facilitative of this objective. In the case of the United

States it is interesting to note the paradox of bilingual education, serving at once exclusionary and egalitarian ends. Overall, however, the dominant group in the United States determines what values and appropriate behaviors need to be followed for successful acculturation and assimilation.

Consensus in modern multiethnic states of the post–World War 1 and –World War 2 periods provides other examples in which conscious, planned attempts have been made to forge between-group ties that were never before considered, or to strengthen ties that were dormant. The critical role of language and other traditions in twentieth-century Balkan and Eastern European nationalist movements, religion in pan-Arabist movements, socialism in the Soviet Union and China, and economic development and pluralist democracy in India can all be considered dominant group approaches to consensus building. We would also point out that consensus can exist where *no* values are held in common. In extreme cases, two or more groups might even share the territory of a single political entity yet be so divergent in every other respect as to seek autonomy; convenience alone could be the binding tie and consensus could consist of little more than an "agreement to disagree."

Another example of a society in which consensus predominates as a strategy for societal integration is Britain, where like in the United States, there is a general assumption that the society will ultimately have in place the policies needed for equality and enhanced socioeconomic status for ethnic group membership. This can be seen with the Black West Indian immigrants to Britain. Because consensus is a fragile approach to integration, its use often depends on the relatively larger size of the dominant group and its control over the important levers of social control. While in Britain there clearly are problems with discriminatory hiring practices, housing patterns, school access, and retention between the dominant population and the lower status West Indians, there are sufficient "openings" to some of the benefits of the dominant group to provide hope and legitimacy for the established system.

Consensus as a basis for national integration is, of course, a variable, not a single, well-defined state of being. Just as consensus can be oriented toward commonality or separateness, it also interacts with ethnicity and social class. For example, groups that participate in a common religion may still differ in other ways that prevent full societal integration. Thus, although religious strife might be avoided, political, linguistic, socioeconomic, or other differences would create a basis for conflict. In much the same way, culturally distinct groups could share a set of political or economic values, like socialism, but such an orientation would be insufficient to establish consensus around such educational policies as which language to teach in schools. Consensus, like other strategies for integration, must be examined within its particular sociocultural setting: the degree to which it is employed successfully will vary widely from one intergroup relationship to another.

La Belle and White (1980) argue that interdependence can be the dominant mode of societal integration in very different societies, such as India and Switzerland. India represents a tremendously long history of complex relationships among a large number of ethnic groups, most of which are tied to particular geographic areas. Such characteristics work against consensus but provide an opportunity for all groups to demonstrate some form of contribution to support a unified nation. In many respects no single ethnic group in India enjoys a complete monopoly of political, economic power or cultural, social prestige. It is the sharp distinctions along caste and class lines within each group—cutting across ethnic differences—which give the Indian situation unique features. In this regard, there is a tendency toward a division between the elite and the masses that places the upper soeioeconomic strata of each ethnic group together for purposes of political and economic eontrol. Because these class and caste lines cut across the ethnic groups, both the upper and lower strata retain their cultural and linguistic identities.

The policies governing education in India provide insight into the ways in which ethnic and social class groups come together as well as seek some modicum of separation. At the lower levels of the educational system, there is considerable flexibility for each ethnic group to have relative autonomy in perpetuating their separate, unique identities. In some instances this means separate and parallel school systems in accordance with ethnic group and socioeconomic status differences. In the public sector there is regional decentralization of certain aspects of educational decision making, while at the national level there is overall supervision and coordination. Language-of-instruction policies enable primary education to be conducted in the mother-tongue, but secondary education must give way to more common regional languages. This is one way the system reflects the interests of groups in order to come together for the survival of the nation and weave local interests into intergroup relationships. It is also the inherent bias against lower castes which perpetuates the assumption that acculturation to elite life ways is the ultimate goal.

Another example of a country much different from India which also shows the use of interdependence as a strategy for integration is Switzerland, which is composed of several ethnic groups roughly equal in prestige, political power, and economic power and who, although concentrated in different geographic areas, participate in a single structural system of roles and positions. A balance among groups rather than parity in each aspect of national life is common in Switzerland, for every group has enough leverage in at least one dimension to be able to substantially modify or veto the initiatives of the other group(s). Occupational categories are not defined by ethnicity because there are few, if any, economic units which operate in isolation from the wider economy's system of supply, demand, and control. Educational policy in Switzerland involves shared governance in which the decentralization of decision making closely follows ethnic group boundaries. At the same time there is central government intervention which provides common ideology and national goals and usually holds final authority in many areas of the curricula. As with the Indian case, more flexibility is given to states and regions for group-specific language-of-instruction and other practices at the elementary level, while more common international content and purposes are implemented nationally at the higher levels. In general, ethnic parity and lessened socioeconomic competition among groups in Switzerland are more likely to support educational policies for equality rather than inequality.

Because of its primary orientation to the socioeconomic aspect of intergroup relations, interdependence as an integrative mechanism is more directly manipulable by dominant groups. The creation of a broad infrastructure—containing roads, telecommunications, industrial centers, schools, and so forth—which includes subordinate groups even against the wishes of the latter is, at first, a technical matter of planning and investments; there is no initial need to assure subordinate group agreement, only acquiescence. As such, interdependence is useful where cultural differences between groups are great—a gap consensus cannot always bridge. Further, interdependence for integration may be equally applicable across a whole range of structural relationships, from sharp inequality between groups to situations in which groups are equal in power and guard their cultural prerogatives.

The discussion of these case studies across coercion, consensus, and interdependence approaches to integration suggests formal education is a vehicle through which integrative mechanisms take concrete form. Thus such mechanisms cannot automatically be assumed to be agents of subordinate group acculturation or assimilation. As we have suggested, dominant groups are as likely to employ education for purposes of building commonality at a regional or national level as for purposes of building individual group autonomy; indeed, acculturation rather than assimilation appears to be a more common strategy, even where homogenizing tendencies are the mode. Hence attention should be directed to educational policies as the expression (within particular relationships between groups) of the tendencies and mechanisms that shape societal integration in multigroup settings.

Conclusion

We have tried to show that multiculturalism is expressed through formal education institutions as groups interact to further their own special interests, usually tied to constructing a society which reflects separate group values and beliefs. A complex interplay of goals, strategies, and means are employed in this process, often making it difficult to characterize a single aspect as reflective of overall policy and practice. We have also tried to demonstrate that all societies face a natural tension between national- and group-specific interests and that education is a common arena within which to see them carried out.

We conclude that there is nothing inherently detrimental for a society to be simultaneously pulled in centralized and decentralized directions. Instead, we believe that balancing the interests of the nation-state with those of the separate social class, ethnic, and racial groups is a necessary political process that must go on and that can strengthen the overall societal health of a given country. To maintain such a balance, both socioeconomic and ethnic interests must be on the forefront of the political agenda; and in order for there to be successful integrative processes and outcomes, both consensus and interdependence need to find their ways into the ongoing interactions.

In effect, the survival of a nation over time depends to some extent on the ability of the dominant group to reflect the ethnic-cultural identity of the total population and to ensure that the socioeconomic needs and interests of the various groups are being met. Individuals and groups must be able to connect or link with the nation as well as with their own ethnic group or social class. They must be able to internalize local and national values, represent various group symbols, and demonstrate some level of commitment both to local identities and to the state's authority.

They must also believe that the system is a vehicle for achieving their needs and interests. It is clear that in many societies these attachments are not firm enough to avoid coercion, nor are they firm enought to ensure long-term survival of the political and economic structures.

Gaps between rich and poor and the needs of the dominant group to foster more commonality than is needed for integration remain central challenges in most societies. The group of most concern is often the one which remains socially and economically isolated from the mainstream and constitutes an underclass in society. Even though under some circumstances the condition of the economy may provide the most powerful explanation for the existence of continued poverty or the stability of a gap between social classes, economic interventions through job training and placement have not always proved salient in fostering change. Similarly, affirmative action efforts may facilitate mobility, but successful educational interventions demonstrate the need to link communities and schools and design teaching and learning strategies which acknowledge and build on, rather than deride or ignore, differences in social class and ethnic backgrounds. It is to those issues we now turn.

CHAPTER 4

The State, Community, Family, and Formal Education in Societal Integration

The stability and long-term survival of a culturally and socially diverse society necessitates a close working relationship among and between institutions, including families, communities, and schools. Thus those of us interested in multiculturalism and education must be concerned with how these institutions relate to one another and how they serve the students who attend them. This chapter discusses the role and contributions schools make to a nation and how youngsters learn to be citizens of a country and members of a community and family. It also points to the relationships between child-rearing practices and schooling as they affect educational achievement. Overall, the chapter attempts to place what goes on in schools into a broader societal context as it discusses the ways families, communities, and schools seek to increase both their independent existence as well as their collective viability.

National Interests in Schools

A government's primary motivation for the support of schools is to ensure a productive and compliant citizenry which has the skills and knowledge to prosper as well as the allegiances to support national values. Schools, as extra-family institutions, become most important in the history of nations as communities become larger, more ethnically and socially diverse, more complex, and as specialized knowledge is needed for the use of technology and the organization and administration of society's business. Further, as societies reach this point in their development, there is a need to bring the orientations of the larger social entities (beyond the family) to each new generation. Both schooling, i.e., formal education and that which is systematic but goes on outside of schools, i.e., nonformal education, take shape to complement and at times compete with families for the allegiance of the new generation.

Schools, like families, have their own social and cultural characteristics (ideas, feelings, practices) which children learn and which arise in part from the unique traditions of the institution. In the area of multiculturalism this means that the climate of schools might support respect for individual and cultural difference, or might support racism or bigotry. Influencing these school-based traditions are the groups and institutions—political, religious, and special interests—in the community, region, and nation which expect from schools certain values, programs, and outcomes. Oftentimes, it is the more economically and politically powerful of these external groups which determine what kind of climate a school will sustain. Additionally, because schools need to satisfy state-sanctioned guidelines for health, safety, curricula, and teacher certification, they are tied to the regulatory bodies of the government and accrediting agencies. Thus whether secular or religious, private or public, schools must show allegiance and ultimately be accountable to those who dominate decision making in the larger society.

Given these ties between schools and outside groups and the controls outsiders have over schooling, schools are expected to support selected values of the wider society and the political and economic structure. It is therefore assumed that schools would not implement curricula or other practices which would go against the laws of the wider society. Thus state-sanctioned education in all nations is primarily a means for maintaining and facilitating the existing social order by reflecting the interests and concerns of the decision makers in power. Such a relationship helps provide continuity in the wider society and build on the past. It is also this reflective or corresponding relationship between schools and the wider society that makes formal education typically conservative rather than an engine of change. In other words, schooling usually serves to mirror and follow, rather than establish, the course for the groups and institutions to which it is aligned (see chapter 7).

An important basis for this conservative posture vis-à-vis schooling can be seen in the personnel who administer and teach. Schools depend on this cadre of individuals (who are usually certified or in some other way sanctioned by the government) to introduce the new generation to the culture and society. Given this role of passing on traditions to others, it should not be surprising that dominant group control over who teaches and administers is strong. This is most visible in private religious schools where there is often insistence that members of their own faith (Christian, Jew, Muslim) serve as teachers to transmit their heritage to a new generation. One reason individuals who become teachers are assumed to represent the values and behaviors of the dominant group is because they were successful students in the schools in which they were trained. Hence their possession of a diploma or teaching credential reflects their ability, if not their willingness, to pass on whatever is agreed to be society's standardized and stereotyped knowledge, skills, values, and attitudes.

To achieve the society's goals of solidarity and loyalty among the populace and to ensure that there is some common ideology to which a diverse polity adheres, the state uses the school simultaneously to subvert local allegiances, including those associated with ethnic groups, and to inculcate a standardized set of symbols. Schools also become the means of maintaining traditions, thus they support the status quo, principally by passing on what must be learned to participate successfully in society. Schools also screen individuals for society by assessing aptitudes for specific roles and statuses. Thus they select and recruit students for the wider society through course grades and related appraisals and hence guide the placement of these individuals into what are deemed appropriate career paths. Again, because not all groups are represented through personnel or the curricula within a given school, such selection and recruitment can be biased in favor or against some students, their families and communities.

Family Interest in Schools

If the nation-state is driven by the need for standardization and conformity, the opposite values typically drive the interests of the family. The family does not operate in stereotyped ways. In the family it is the person—mother, father, brother, uncle—who is most relevant. In contradistinction to the state's interest in what is being taught and learned - irrespective of the personal relationship of the teacher to the student - the family is driven by who does the teaching and how that person can be called on to provide personal support for the student. Confidence in the "teacher" in the family is based on kinship, personal knowledge, and emotional ties with the individual, whereas confidence in the teacher in school is based on diplomas, credentials, and the certification process.

When a child enters school it is usually his or her first major step away from primary involvement with the family. Although gender identification and some level of independence and responsibility may be the most noticeable characteristics carried to school by the individual, many other skills, values, and ways of thinking and communicating have also been established during the early years in the family. The differences in the ways that teaching and learning are carried out in the family and school also require the child to respond to a new basis for judging merit. At home, "ascription," which positions a child acording to his or her family, is generally accepted as the major basis for determining status. In school, however, it is generally assumed that status depends less on who the child is and more on how the child performs teacher-directed tasks.

Even with an emphasis on achievement, however, it is difficult to disentangle background and appearance from what an individual does. Therefore it would be a mistake to assume that ethnic background, physical features, gender, social class, and other background factors do not interact with a teacher's appraisal of a child's performance. In fact, the lack of school success of some students who are poor and/or who are African American, Hispanic American, or Native American can be traced to lower expectations held by teachers for the performance of such youngsters. Such an observation is also relevant in explaining why females are somewhat less likely than males to succeed in schools at certain levels. For example, it has been found that minority and female students receive less attention from teachers than their majority and male counterparts; they are also more likely to be discouraged from pursuing certain subject matter areas, such as math and science; they are discriminated against by standardized tests; and they are held to different classroom standards of behavior. Thus, although merit may be recognized in school, evidence suggests that such judgments are often intimately related to who is judging and who is being judged.

Cultural and Societal Teaching and Learning through Family and School

Families and neighborhoods teach what it takes to survive in a given time and place. Some skills and values a new generation learns are highly particular whereas others are common to all individuals no matter what the society. The more particular process and substance is usually referred to as "enculturation": learning about a particular way of life. The more general process and substance is usually called "socialization": learning to participate as individuals in any society. Most of the content for both outcomes results simply from living in a family and community rather than emerging from systematic, preplanned instruction. The lack of structure associated with such informal education does not impede learning societywide processes, nor does it impede learning particular ways that individuals are named, taught to walk and talk, placed in a kinship system, get married, buried, and so on.

Because of the important influence of a child's environment on growing up, a child is not able to realize all of his or her human potential. In effect, the child's surroundings constrain, often determine, what will be learned. Therefore beyond biological and psychological bases for learning, there are sociocultural processes which involve the interaction of human beings who hold certain things of value which will shape what is to be learned. That is why participation in one society and culture simultaneously makes an individual fit for one lifestyle and potentially unfit for others. This fitness for one culture usually involves learning the rules and norms of acceptable behavior, belief systems, or views of the world, particular ways of functioning cognitively or making sense out of reality, and involves learning expected ways of communicating.

The child's task is to learn about what is socially agreed upon as reality and how to participate in institutions and use available technology. Because of this strong link between the child's environment and what is taught and learned, effective formal education programs depend on understanding the particular social and physical environment in which the teaching and learning occurs; the individuals and institutions responsible for teaching; and the interactions that are typical. This connection between environment and learning is important enough to suggest that it is impossible for administrators, counselors, and teachers to effectively carry out all their educational responsibilities without learning a great deal about learners and their lives outside of the educational institution.

The correspondence between teaching and learning and the wider society can be seen in the ways families and other social institutions carry out daily behavior. The extent to which there is overlap in the ways the family and the school are structured (their purpose, process, and goals) helps explain why children behave as they do. For example, the role and responsibilities of adults and children, the use of time, participation in family chores, discipline and the ability to follow instructions, and other family behaviors have parallels in the school and may or may not be compatible or similar.

As a youngster moves away from those members of his or her immediate family and interacts with others, non-kinship-oriented universal bases of social interaction come into play so that economic, political, and social relations can be productive and predictable. As this process occurs, schools become more important because it is in schools where society institutionalizes teaching and learning and identifies what knowledge and behaviors it expects citizens to acquire. Because the rules that guide behavior may differ between the family and the wider society, the kind of teaching and learning that goes on at home may be similar to, in conflict with, or in competition with that which occurs in schools. Yet stereotypes of what constitutes model family types must be avoided, for families often are able to adapt their particular styles to working productively on school-based agendas.

Alternative Family Styles and their Efficacy

Although the size, organization, and membership of what we refer to as "the family" will vary across ethnic groups and social classes, such units are generally recognized as the source of the most basic and important teaching and learning for children and many youth. Family life sets important foundations for school success. Thus whether the family finds a father at work and a mother at home, both parents in wage-earning positions outside the home, only one parent in the household, or some combination of parents and extended kin in the home, it is through the interaction of a child with parents, siblings, kinsmen, and members of the community that language, basic cognitive and motivational patterns, and problem-solving and other skills are initially acquired, and that values and attitudes are formed.

Some argue that the decline of the two-parent family in the United States has negatively impacted child-rearing practices and readiness for school. Yet because what we mean by "family" has changed, it is difficult to determine what the impact of a single parent raising a child might be. Even though the traditional family model of two parents is the standard of family life, statistics indicate that two-parent families declined by 71 percent between 1970 and 1989; in fact, half of all children—and five out of six African American children— spend most of their early childhood with a single parent, usually the mother. Furthermore, 56 percent of women with children under six years of age were working or looking for work in 1988. The number of teenage mothers was also increasing, especially among Euro-American youth, and often they were living in poverty. Data indicate that 53 percent of all poor families in 1988 were headed by women (Rubin and Borgers 1991).

But we are concerned with child rearing and school readiness, so attending to the issue of how many parents are in the home may be misplaced. It would be better to direct our attention toward the resources available to raise children. Thus poverty rather than number of parents in the home should be the concern. In fact, the number of children living in poverty has been increasing. Of children under eighteen years of age in the United States in the late 1980s, about one in five were living in a home that was below the federally defined poverty line; among blacks, almost half the children were living in poverty.

Those children who are most at risk for school failure come from families that are socioeconomically poor. These risks may be exacerbated if the poverty accompanies cultural backgrounds which are not well represented in school practices and expectations. Poverty is associated with inadequate nutrition and poor or nonexistent health care: it is also associated with child abuse; neglect; violence; the ravages of the drug world; and lack of adult supervision, assistance, and positive role models. The ultimate cost to society for the lack of success of children in school is not only seen in the affected children and families but also in the demands placed on government and private funds for financial support, rehabilitation, institutionalization, or incarceration. Those unable to succeed also cost the larger society potential labor and tax contributions.

In addition to resources available in the family, a growing body of knowledge points to certain characteristics of families that are associated with school success. For example, Yao (1985) reviews selected studies and concludes the more parents and students expect from school, the higher the achievement of students; and the more parents express concern for their children's progress in school, the more the teacher matches that attitude. Yao also asserts that parental awareness of the school program; parental expression of warmth, support, interest, affection, and encouragement; parental establishment of performance goals; and parental guidance with perceived problems are all associated with higher student achievement. Further, limiting the amount of time spent watching television and increasing the amount of time spent on homework is associated with higher school grades. In addition, regularity in daily life and the maintenance of some structure and order for children are conducive to higher school performance.

Rumberger et al. (1990) also review the literature regarding family characteristics and school success. They identify four conclusions from their review: first, parents from high socioeconomic backgrounds are more likely than parents from low socioeconomic backgrounds to participate with teachers and schools and to impact positively their children's academic performance; second, parents can improve their children's school success by spending time in activities which support cognitive development; third, parents impact their children's academic performance by imparting appropriate values, aspirations, and motivation which are needed to persevere and succeed in school; and fourth, particular parenting styles that foster appropriate communication between parents and children and responsible behavior in children also appear to influence students' achievement in school.

Although much of the attention to low school achievement by youngsters from minority backgrounds seeks to identify causes associated with family-rearing practices, it is the child's lack of success with dominant group pedagogy and curricula which establishes the basis for family interventions (e.g., helping parents or older siblings improve a child's study skills and homework; providing discipline; ensuring a child's good health and nutrition). Calabrese (1990) argues that the discriminatory processes of the schools, intended to develop and maintain a disparity in the social class system, explain the lower school achievement of minority youngsters. Such discrimination, he says, is manifested by blaming the poor through suggesting that background factors produce students who are unable to take advantage of school resources and who are thus destined to a life of poverty and failure. Calabrese notes that using this argument excuses schools and the larger society from taking responsibility for low school achievement and results in an alienation of minority families and parents from schools and other social institutions.

The fact that schools can facilitate student achievement also comes from the research literature. Entwistle and Alexander (1990) studied the gap between blacks and whites in mathematic achievement, a gap which increases as students go through school. The researchers found that both groups of children were equivalent in verbal performance and computational skills at the point of school entry, and only a few points apart in reasoning. By the end of the first grade, however, the groups differed significantly in all three areas, and even though socioeconomic status was controlled, there were noticeable differences according to race. The authors' results indicate that school-based factors have a considerable role in explaining student performance throughout schooling.

While we will pursue some of the in-school variables which produce differential achievement by groups (see Chapter 5), the picture from the research evidence regarding the family is useful here in describing parental and related characteristics associated with youngsters who are most likely to succeed in school. However, those who wish to identify family behavior patterns that might help differentiate between family styles which produce successful versus unsuccessful students will be disappointed. Furthermore, ideal characteristics of family styles used to provide a basic foundation for making statements about student achievement are often not applicable or valid when looking at particular families or individuals. This process of taking information in the aggregate and applying it to individual cases is often referred to by social scientists as the "ecological fallacy." This means that ethnic group and social class stereotypes about families which are based on single parenthood, both parents working outside the home, or the child-rearing responsibilities of siblings and extended kin do not indicate an *individual* family's ability to provide primary group relationships which support the learning of values and behaviors associated with success in school. Further, such generalizations do not necessarily indicate a *particular* family's propensity toward changing patterns of behavior in ways recommended by intervention programs aimed at parents to increase their children's success in schools.

Weisner, Gallimore and Jordan (1988) make this argument as it relates to child growth and development. They indicate that it is important not to stereotype family and individual behavior by assuming that everyone within a particular group can be characterized similarly. They point to the importance of studying the individuals who teach and influence children, the motivation of the participants in the process, the cultural guidelines which shape participant behavior, the nature of the tasks in the daily routine, and the goals and beliefs of those present in the activities. Although the authors recognize that families are linked and are interdependent with the world outside their boundaries, they also note that there are certain physical things, individuals, traditions, and activities that characterize what goes on inside families. As such, families become units for analysis by the ways in which the processes, happenings, or activities engage their members.

Three studies are worthy of mention in establishing the notion that individual families do not necessarily represent commonly accepted generalizations associated with a larger cultural group with which they identify or are associated by others. Further, these studies demonstrate that there are multiple ways families can be organized and can function for successful child preparation for school achievement. The first study was carried out in Hawaii among native Hawaiians. The investigators desired to have a better understanding of sibling child caretaking among native Hawaiians, a practice that was often stereotypically associated with such families. In the 1970s investigators Thomas S. Weisner and Ronald Gallimore (1977), among others, began studying and documenting the assumed widespread practice of sibling caretaking among native Hawaiian families. The researchers discovered that although families often used siblings as caretakers, they most often chose to use a variety of childcare practices, one of which was sibcare. Thus statements made about native Hawaiians in general could not always be sustained when individual families were studied.

In another study of families and child rearing, Thomas S. Weisner and Helen Garnier (1990) reported results of a twelve-year follow-up of 205 Euro-American families, 154 of whom lived in what the authors term "nontraditional," or "nonconventional," family arrangements. Such arrangements included families built around voluntary single mothers, social contract couples, countercultural groups, creedal communes, avant-garde families (typically, high-income units strongly committed to countercultural values), and a subgroup of troubled families. The other 51 of the 205 families were living in conventional, two-parent families and were used as a comparison group. In the latest follow-up study reported by the authors, the children were in the sixth and seventh grade. The study focused on several potential risk factors in non-conventional family lifestyles. These included certain parental values, single parenthood, poverty, and frequent change and instability within some families. The study found that there were many alternative family styles and value systems which proved viable as pathways to higher school achievement among children. Especially noted were families in which there was a strong commitment among parents to their particular chosen lifestyle and the values underlying them. Only when a combination of factors involving instability, unconventional family styles, and a low commitment to that lifestyle were present was there an association found with lower school achievement. Again, this study demonstrates that widely held assumptions, often negative in nature, about the effects of non-traditional family organization and practices on school success of children are not validated when subjected to long-term investigation.

A final example of studies which analyze family styles across cultural and socioeconomic boundaries focuses on Latino immigrant families in the United States, a population from which emanate many children who are at risk for low school achievement. C. Goldenberg and R. Gallimore (1990) found that many of the Latino parents shared values typical of mainstream families and that they established efforts at home, especially through homework supervision, to increase the success of their children at school. In fact, many parents were reported to have desired more demanding work from teachers for their children. Goldenberg and Gallimore conclude by pointing to the strong relationship between Latino parents' commitment and ability to assist their children's formal education and their desire to know specifically what they can do to help their children succeed in school.

These studies inform professional educators to be cautious about judging the ability of families to prepare their children for school. In effect, the evidence indicates that there is no "right" or "correct" family style when it comes to ensuring a child's success in school. At the same time, the studies suggest that assisting families in enhancing their children's preparation for school may be not only worthwhile but necessary. We turn, therefore, to the viability of family interventions as a means to enhance family functioning. In general, family intervention efforts designed to raise school performance that have been studied often demonstrate positive gains. Reviewing the literature, Claude Goldenberg, Thomas S. Weisner and Ronald Gallimore (1991) conclude that such interventions have shown immediate cognitive gains, short-term school performance increases, reductions in special education placements and grade retentions, and increases in the positive ratings of parents and teachers regarding the school performance of their children. They also report that parents and teachers hold positive attitudes about such intervention programs. This same kind of positive result is found when teachers make parent involvement part of their regular teaching practice by mobilizing familial support for school achievement (Epstein 1991).

The combined results of the studies of families, and the apparent worthwhileness of family interventions, indicate that poor school achievement may not be due to deep value conflicts between families and schools. In fact, there is reason to believe that socioeconomically poor and minority ethnic families may place as high or higher value on formal education than other segments of society. This high value is likely related to the relatively few means or available paths in society, other than schooling, for vertical, socio-economic mobility for members of such families. The success and receptivity of outside assistance to families are based, however, on an appropriate fit between the changes desired and the patterns of behavior within families. Interventions need to be channeled in ways which build on, rather than radically depart from, common daily family routines which have meaning for parents. As Goldenberg and Gallimore point out, the introduction of entirely new behavior patterns which involve different purposes, motives, and scripts from those with which the family is accustomed are less likely to be self-sustaining once interventions have ended. In effect, families must not simply be treated as passive receivers of new behaviors; instead, they must be involved in deciding which behaviors to change and how to change them.

Although family interventions for improving school performance may often prove successful, it is also true that they are complex. The principal reasons for the complexity are associated with stereotypes regarding what constitutes "normal" family life, especially as it is assumed to relate to the kinds of behaviors needed for success in school; the logistics associated with family intervention programs and the financing of such interventions; and the tradition of family independence. A fourth reason for the complexity concerns the impact of nonfamilial influences associated with the larger economy or lifeways in the community and region on family functioning.

Discussions of "the most ideal family type" or "appropriate family life" have become more common in recent years. Such observations usually assume a norm in which two parents undertake differentiated roles for supporting each other as well as other members of the family. As indicated above, this viewpoint fails to acknowledge the multiple ways that families are structured and organized across socioeconomic and ethnic lines. It also makes false assumptions about how one or more parents are available to provide academic assistance at home or at school, to volunteer to assist with field trips, or to be active in the local parent-teacher association. Perhaps one of the most glaring stereotypes associated with child rearing is that "lesbians and gays are unfit parents." Again contrary to such an assumption, research affirms that there is no appreciable difference between the ability of lesbians and gays to parent and the ability of heterosexuals to parent (Clay 1990). We will look more closely at some of the values underlying such stereotypes (see chapter 6).

Ultimately, intervention programs which are based on stereotypical models and are generalized across society fail to recognize the strengths of particular families. Thus, placing a model family "template" over existing family practice can only generate conflict and failure rather than success as a strategy for family interventions.

Beyond stereotypes leading to self-fulfilling prophecies, the second constraint on school interventions in the family concerns logistics and finance. Both need to be addressed in order to overcome the repetitive reinforcement of family behavior patterns over a multiyear period. Short of paying a salary to someone outside the family to take up long-term residence in the family for purposes of providing advice and counseling, one might ask how the larger society truly increases the probability of changing family-based child rearing? Is it likely, for example, that simply helping parents teach their youngsters successful school skills without altering daily or long-term behavioral patterns within the family or the family's economic resources will have much impact? The studies mentioned earlier indicate no if the new behaviors ask the family to depart too much from their normal daily routines. Again, the studies indicate that at least some of what goes on in families contributes to children's school success and that school interventions in a family designed to increase that success cannot depend on rapid, wholesale change in daily behaviors.

A third reason for the complexity associated with increasing the educational viability of families from outside is the reluctance of schools and the larger society to challenge the sanctity and autonomy of the family. This is complemented by a tradition in the United States wherein parents want to control their children's allegiance and shape their behavior in accordance with particular political, religious, or other value orientations. Hence, rather than intervene directly in the family, there is sometimes a preference to establish educational programs which involve family members but which take place outside the family. Although this is admittedly not as powerful as long-term assistance directly in the family, it is logistically more feasible, may be more cost effective, and preserves the independence of family boundaries. Thus early education programs such as Head Start are designed to remediate and complement what goes on in families and are dependent on the direct involvement of parents as adjuncts to the instructional staff. This combination of early intervention and active parental participation in the child's schooling outside the home has proven to provide the early education gains for youngsters from poverty and multi-cultural backgrounds.

A fourth reason for the complexity of school-based interventions in families is that what goes on inside a family is typically the result of outside social and economic forces over which family members have relatively little control. Thus, rather than remediating families through interventions, some hold it would be more productive to tackle the issues of poverty and access to the opportunity structure in society, variables which affect family life but are not controlled by it. This argument suggests that at best many school-based interventions in communities characterized by poverty will fail because they will be swamped by social and economic realities.

Bringing the Community to the School and Putting the School in the Community

The community often establishes the conditions that influence how the family and school can be linked. Such relationships can be analyzed in accordance with the amount of "social distance" that is maintained among the various community institutions, or structures, and the school. In some instances, this distance is great and few attempts are made to alter it, while in other cases there is value in closing the gap and facilitating interdependence. Basically, the nature and extent of this distance depends on the importance attributed to mutual collaboration for the achievement of the school's, as well as the community's, goals. In the last several decades more and more attention has been given to linking these entities to respond to the problems of drug abuse, crime, poverty, career preparation, and school success.

The urban violence in several United States cities in 1992 is an example of the kinds of social realities which call on schooling to play a more dynamic role in community development and renewal. In spite of such pressures, many educators still view community involvement as extraneous to the principal demands of formal education. At the same time, however, there are others, likely now to be in the majority, who believe that many important educational activities take place in the community and that such processes influence and interact with the methods and goals of the school. John Goodlad (1992), for example, argues that schooling is weak when it comes to the total societal requirements for education, and that thinking of schooling as a means-ends or input-output model of educational effectiveness diminishes the potential linking of schools with other educational resources in the community.

Linking more closely the school and community assumes that the school's resources in subject matter knowledge and facilities can be enhanced through taking advantage of the community's cultural, commercial, political, and industrial resources. Building on the community's actual or potential contribution as catalyst and reinforcer, or inhibitor, of the overall goals held for children is a logical approach to educational, if not socioeconomic, planning. Further, this approach recognizes that siblings, parents, peers, and teachers are all important role models for the personality development and general socialization of the child for adult roles. In effect, making efforts to link the school and the geographic, social, and economic community to which it is tied assumes that transmitting information and designing educational experiences in school should be viewed as only partial inputs into the processes of teaching and learning. In this context, education through schooling is viewed as one crucial, yet partial, contributor to the process of serving the multiple goals of individuals, institutions, and society.

In general it is safe to assume that the teaching in the classroom is more effective, and learning outcomes are enhanced, when there are strong linkages among family, neighborhood, and school. For example, children are more likely to learn the information and skills taught in school when they are surrounded at home, on the streets, and in local businesses and social agencies, by parents, siblings, and others who value learning and reinforce on a daily basis the application of that knowledge and skill to solving daily problems in the home and community. This may be particularly apparent in areas such as health education, where school-based instruction about alcohol and drug abuse or the transmission of such infectious diseases as AIDS, will likely have greater impact in the classroom if older youngsters and parents in the community provide role models for desired behavior. Furthermore, health education campaigns will likely have greater effect if there is a combined effort among community centers, medical doctors, and clinics. Similarly, career education in the schools will not have much impact if there are not apprenticeship and on-the-job training or work-study opportunities that involve the cooperation of business and industry. In each of these examples the intent is to increase the probability that schooling will have an impact by placing the school's efforts in concert with informal and nonformal education efforts in the community.

Although this potential response to the relationship between schools and communities is logical enough, it often breaks down in reality because of the differences in expectation at individual, family, and community levels for what schools are supposed to accomplish. Thus there may be constraints as the day-to-day pressures on family members—finding success in their jobs, earning adequate income, maintaining health status—converge with the requirements for children's success at school. Similarly, youngsters may not further the cause of school-community collaboration, because they may view maintaining distance as their short- or long-term interest. In other words, parents who know little about what goes on in school, and teachers who know little about a student's home life, may facilitate the goals of some independence-seeking youngsters.

At the community level there may also be constraints on building closer relationships with schools. For example, because communities are not typically homogeneous ethnically or economically, there is often tension within communities concerning expectations for schools. In some instances community groups are proactive, desiring almost complete control over what goes on inside and outside classrooms. In other communities a majority of the populace may not have children or may not have the time and resources to further their involvement; thus they may distance themselves from what goes on in schools. There also exist communities where the majority hold a hands-off attitude, leaving schooling to those who they perceive as the professionals.

From the perspective of the schools there are also pressures and oftentimes confusion deciding which priorities deserve the greatest attention and whether and how the community can be of assistance. From childcare to physical and emotional health, from academic competence to career preparation, schools throughout the world typically have been expected to carry a major load in shaping the new generation, often correcting or making up for the shortcomings of the family and the institutions of the community and the wider society. Some administrators and teachers believe that, as professionals (akin to medical doctors and lawyers), they alone possess the knowledge and skills necessary to successfully teach youngsters. More recently, however, other school professionals have taken the position that it is important to reeducate themselves and their institutions so that they can work with others and share in that responsibility.

Even if schools decide to reach out for community assistance, there are signs that many communities are not equipped to provide such assistance. A major question, therefore, is whether most communities are structured and organized enough and whether they have the resources to provide appropriate assistance. Some have argued that the status of the community, like that of the family in the United States, has undergone major changes during the past century, changes which have weakened their respective abilities to provide traditional enculturation and socialization and to reach out and work with schools in achieving mutual goals. According to some, the center of society has shifted from the home to the workplace, thereby decreasing the saliency of the family for child socialization. For example, Coleman (1987) argues that the division of labor in families has lead to parents paying more attention to careers and incomes at the cost of child rearing. He argues that what is missing in North American communities is *social capital*: the norms, social networks, and relationships that support child growth and development. Such support, says Coleman, is found among adults and children in some families and communities —especially those charactericed by strong religious traditions. A gradual increase in children's autonomy and decision-making power combined with growth in individualism in society, both of which exacarbate adult-child relations, makes the task for communities, to identify ways to overcome this erosion in social capital—a problem that is critical in lower socioeconomic neighborhoods. The creation of new public institutions devoted to day-long and year-long childcare is one way Coleman suggests public policy must respond to insure that the kinds of attitudes, effort, and self-conceptions children and youth need to succeed in school (and later in life) are made available.

But increasing the achievement of children in school may be only one of several major goals which brings community attention to the schooling process. Furthermore, concern with community-school relations goes beyond the borders of the United States, for there exist similar concerns and alternative ways to ensure that communities and schools function in an interdependent and mutually beneficial way in many other countries.

In an international review of community-school relations, La Belle and Verhine (1981) were able to identify five models of community schools. These included community schools which 1) increase educational access, 2) enhance learning, 3) foster the transition between study and work, 4) function as community centers, or 5) strengthen nationalism and socioeconomic development. While the first of these models is a community-created response to satisfy the need for schooling among youth (increase the numbers of individuals in schools), the last four stress providing relevant education for the community. Brief characteristics of each type are given in the following paragraphs.

Examples of community schools for educational access predominate in the less developed countries of the world where in rural and in urban areas facilities may be limited and compulsory school attendance may be sporadic. One example is the Harambe school of Kenya. Emerging at the time of Kenya's independence from Britain in 1964, by 1970 Harambe institutions accounted for 62 percent of Kenya's secondary schools. Fueled by a demand for secondary education and initiated independently through self-help efforts within each community, a major problem of these schools has been the quality of their academic curricula and teaching. Although such institutions may provide wider access to education and contribute to local socioeconomic development and community pride in a third-world context, they have also been more likely to reinforce existing community inequalities by emphasizing an academically oriented school ethos and by not adapting to the current needs or projected economic future of the community. Such outcomes are not unusual if academic achievement rather than community problem solving (also a characteristic of some community schools) is addressed.

The other four models of community schooling are devoted to creating mutually beneficial and reinforcing relationships with the community. The first of these is intended to overcome centrally formulated and abstract curricula, to emphasize active learning and replace rote memorization, to encourage greater use of school facilities by community members, and to involve parents in their children's, as well as their own, education. A desire to bring aspects of the community into the schools and apply school learning to community problems can be seen in the Israeli *kibbutzim*. The kibbutzim are collective settlements first established in the early twentieth century by Zionist immigrants. They function as producer and consumer cooperatives, based on mixed agriculture and small industry, in which all members share in the operation of the nearly autonomous village. Formal education in the kibbutz is viewed as a mechanism for preserving the kibbutzim communal way of life, for inculcating a sense of community membership and responsibility, and for preparing young people for productive work.

The third type of community school is one which fosters the transition from study to work. These school-work efforts differ from the kibbutzim in that there is less emphasis on bringing the community into the school but more emphasis on preparing children for employment in the community. The importance of school-work cooperation is seen not only in the kind of curriculum the school offers, which should reflect current and future community employment and development needs, but also in the ways in which the community offers opportunities for youngsters first to experience and then to pursue a chosen career. There are a number of examples of this kind of initiative, and they typically involve school studies and on-the-job apprenticeships or internships. Under Marxist influence Cuba has emphasized this model in the rural areas through its efforts to unite work and study linked to production. For example, Cuba's school to the countryside program places nearly all secondary school students in the rural areas for six to ten weeks each year, during which time they puruse their studies half the day and do farm work the other half.

A fourth community school program employs the school as a community center, or focal point, from which a variety of community services can emanate. Like the learning and work-study schemes, the school community center seeks to dissolve the barriers separating the school from its surrounding environment. In the 1940s and 1950s UNESCO encouraged the development of such programs throughout much of the developing world. In contrast to the other models, however, the community center model has been concerned more with adults than with children and it focuses more on extracurricular activities than on formal instruction. In some instances the implementation of this model emphasizes using the school building for social, cultural, and recreational purposes, and in other instances the school is utilized as a base of operations for technical experts and school personnel attempting to foster social change. We elaborate this particular model of community schooling in our discussion of the relationship between education and social change (see chapter 7).

A fifth and final international model of school community relations is the use of schools for nationalism and socioeconomic development, including raising national identity and consciousness, instilling community change and development, and promoting local and national job preparation. These development and community change oriented programs represent the most broad-based community schooling efforts of the five reviewed here and encompass aspects of the learning, school-work, and community center approach. At various times in history India, Tanzania, and China have employed such schools. Variously, they have attempted to decolonize education, promote indigenous culture, and generate local and national change in ways meaningful to a peasant agrarian society. They are associated with a social philosophy which emphasizes the preservation of traditional values, the importance of "community" to psychological and social well-being, and the need to rely on self-help for local and national progress. The community is intended to be a resource, and the school is intended to encourage students to undertake community projects that contribute to social and economic welfare.

In each of the cases of community schools mentioned above, it is apparent that although schools are often identified as agents of community change and leadership, they are better seen as a reflection of the wider political, cultural, and social concerns of the society in which they exist. In some cases the issues are to stop the migration of youngsters away from the community and to attract their attention to local employment and problem solving. In other instances schools represent the only central facilities in the community and are therefore perceived as important adjuncts to community development. In yet other instances schools represent the arm of the government reaching into the community to socialize and mobilize a nationalism which will sustain the current government.

The United States has experimented with most of the above types of community schools over the past century. For example, Native American schools and community colleges located on federally established reservations often stand behind community development and ethnic identity. Employing work-study and cooperative education programs, using vocational/technical curricula to relate schooling to employment and community problem solving, and bringing the community into the school as part of the curricula describe various educational trends of particular eras. Recently, we have seen variations of these models aimed at increasing the success of at-risk youngsters, often from low socioeconomic minority backgrounds. A program known as Cities in Schools is a national effort to bring health, welfare, police, employment, and other community resources to selected at-risk youngsters so that they will more likely remain in school and be productive citizens in the community and family. The Cities in Schools effort is typically carried out most directly in schools where the coordination of service delivery is maintained through full-time professionals. Together, such individuals constitute an advisory committee which monitors particular student activity and provides appropriate interventions to sustain desired behaviors.

Two additional, more recent community-school efforts in the United States appear to add new dimensions to existing models. One involves parents from the community serving in a governance capacity for the local school. For example, in the late 1980s the Chicago Public Schools began shifting administrative control of each primary and secondary school to elected, parent-led councils which were granted the power to approve budgets, make recommendations on books and curricula, and assign and dismiss principals. Each council is made up of parents, community residents with no children in the school, and teachers, all elected to two-year terms. The decentralization is intended to bring the community into the school and weaken the role of the traditional superintendency and board of education.

Interestingly, in opposition to the above type of parental governance in the school is a model in which parents withdraw their children from schools and provide formal education in the family. Known as home schools, this alternative enables parents to educate their children at home under curricular and testing guidelines prepared by the state. In some respects the home school movement can be seen as a way for parents to pass on their own values to youngsters and thus control the schooling process. As such, it is an example of the influence of values on schooling which we will discuss in more detail (see chapter 6). To others, the home school movement reflects a rejection of the school system and a retreat from efforts to use the school as a center for addressing not only traditional educational issues but also issues of resolution for certain social concerns. Whatever the basis, home schools represent another way to approach the engagement of community-school relationships.

Bridging the Gap among Family, Community, and School from the Perspective of the Student

Although families as well as other private and public institutions outside the school are often the focus of linking parents, community, and school, it is ultimately the student and his or her peers that are intended to be affected by such relationships. Patricia Phelan, Ann Locke Davidson, and Hanh Thanh Cao (1991) assessed such relationships to learn how these interactions affected students in schools. They studied fifty-four students in four desegregated high schools and arrived at four general patterns, ranging from considerable reinforcement derived from life inside and outside schools to almost total estrangement across such institutional boundaries.

The authors argue that most students must navigate the transitions among family, peer group, community, and school with little or no assistance, and that along this path, finding and coping is generally taken for granted. Nevertheless, each student must mediate and integrate experiences across these boundaries, some of which may be viewed as permeable, and others as obstacles and blockages. The authors found that some students moved easily across parallel settings where values, expectations, beliefs, and what was expected for daily behavior were harmonious and uncomplicated. In these situations teachers, friends, and family members had enough in common to avoid establishing competing environments for students. This does not mean that each person a student meets will fit within these reinforcing settings. It does mean, however, that whether one looks to close friends, the engagement of parents in school activities, or the tracking system and extracurricular activities within which certain students participate, one will find the environments generally supportive for those who participate in them.

A second type of student identified by the researchers came from an ethnic or socioeconomic background different from the dominant community background, but had potential for adjustment. Thus, a student's religion or language might set his or her family off from the values and language used in the school. Similarly, the student who was bused to school from the other side of town and whose family and neighborhood were easily separated socioeconomically might represent a considerably different context than that provided by the school and the dominant student population. But such differences for this type of student do not prevent him or her from coping with and crossing over such boundaries and adjusting sufficiently to ensure general success. This does not mean that peer discrimination may not be experienced in school, or that the ethnicity and expectations held by others for school achievement and upward mobility might not differ. Instead, it means that more self-reliant strategies, such as choosing to associate with a high achieving peer group, can be pursued by some.

The third and fourth types of students were found to have much more difficulty negotiating boundaries across the family, peer, community and school contexts. For the third type it is very difficult and hazardous to succeed in school because it means creating distance from peers, family, and community expectations. Thus there is friction and unease, with students achieving in some dimensions but failing in others. These students are at-risk for school failure and can be assisted by special interventions to help them relate to potentially conflicting expectations.

The fourth type of student finds crossing boundaries either extremely difficult or impossible. The student may perceive the home, peer, community, and school to be in opposition and may wish to foster that opposition. Such a student might also be more aggressive in the way he or she views intergroup relationships and issues. Thus such students might hold a general distrust of individuals from one racial and ethnic group, be preoccupied with race or ethnic identity through language and other behaviors, believe that preferential treatment is given to others based on group affiliation and physical features, and/or be suspicious and unconvinced regarding the value of fostering some level of harmony and unity among groups. While not all of these behaviors are necessarily negative, when they are used to distance an individual from what is rewarded behavior in schools, the student might find it acceptable to skip class, ignore homework, get into trouble with legal and school authorities, and become involved in gangs. Such individuals perceive themselves to be outsiders relative to school expectations and thus turn to peers or members of the family or the wider community for respect and support.

Conclusion

Although it may be tempting to identify family, community, or school as the source of problems and solutions in the growth and development of all students, it is not realistic to do so. It is important to recognize these influences for the contribution each can make and to recognize that together they form part of a dynamic and contributory set of circumstances and institutions, all of which are important in the success of students, not only in school but also in the family, in the community, and among peers. How to take advantage of these institutions as resources for enhancing individual and group goals remains the challenge. As resources, they also constitute an important source of potential investment in the nation, an investment which may make for long-term intergroup harmony, competition, or conflict.

The discussion also suggests that school organizations and structures, the nature of school expectations for young people, the ways in which teachers interact with students, and the extent to which extracurricular activities are used to support school and wider social goals all impact the abilities of students not only to negotiate boundaries but also to achieve in accordance with the expectations held for them and by them. In the next section we will explore more in-school characteristics and practices and the ways in which they shape interactions and often mirror what goes on in the wider society.

Part 3

Schools and Multicultural Education

CHAPTER 5

Schools as Centers of Diversity in Teaching and Learning

Throughout the world schools often struggle to reflect the wide variety of social, political, and economic influences which shape their nature and responsibilities. These include the concerns of ethnic and racial groups. In earlier chapters we pointed historically to local, regional, and national pressures on schooling to respond to particular religious, political, and economic pressures; we showed how housing and attendance patterns are shaped demographically along ethnic and racial group lines and how such demographics influence social interaction within and around the institution; we identified the ways in which population segments simultaneously go through a process of integration while using schooling to fulfill their own societal goals; and we looked at ways in which the school relates to other institutions, especially the family and community, in fulfilling its educational mission.

Related but conceptually distinct from these outside influences are the factors associated with what goes on inside schools. These may be inextricably linked to the outside, or they may emanate directly from administrators, teachers, and students who participate daily in the educational process by setting the social climate, interaction patterns, and the institution's traditional ways of operating.

This chapter is devoted to looking at a few patterns of behavior which occur inside institutions, particularly how students from various socioeconomic and cultural backgrounds interact in schools and how teachers adapt or don't adapt their values, ways of communicating, and cognitive patterns in response to those individuals and groups. Thus we focus on structural and organizational issues such as tracking, ability grouping, and extracurricular activities as well as the values, cognitive patterns, and teacher-student language as they interact with school curricula and classroom pedagogy.

Schools as Reflections of the Wider Society

The correspondence between the pressures and constraints from outside the school and the daily activities inside the school can be seen to operate in several ways. As individual and collective lifestyles change, as laws are passed, and as economic pressures are altered in the larger society, there is a rippling effect on schools. Examples include: family structures and community organizations; parental expectations for the achievement of children and youth; population heterogeneity and diversity; social expectations associated with male and female identities; youth and adult role models portrayed by the media; the use of leisure time; trends in personal adornment and clothing; and alternative channels of information and communication. All exert some influence on campus environments as well as the behavior of students, teachers, and administrators. Schools, as surrogates for families, as centers of dispensing means of mental and physical care, and as expected engines of economic and political stability or change, are often bogged down in responding to many of these changing conditions. The courts, for example, are often the source of major civil rights decisions which affect schooling. Such decisions are reflected in dress and speech codes, financial aid and affirmative action, sexual and discriminatory harassment, and access for the disabled. Political and social influences, campus climates and conduct, and institutional administration, continually reflect such external sources of change.

Given such competing pressures, it is no wonder that what goes on in schools reflects the interests of some groups over others. Hence the curricula, organization, and structure of schools are always for some things and against others. Recognizing these differences in schools, Jules Henry (1960) outlined what he considered the dimensions along which educational programs could vary. Among them he included content (e.g., environment, values); teaching methods; eligiblity to become a teacher; behavior in education; selective teaching (e.g., gender, age); limitations to the quality and quantity of information a learner receives from a teacher; forms of discipline used; self-conceptions of learners which are reinforced; and the length of the formal education process.

Although at first glance there is great similarity among schools throughout the world along such dimensions, it is important to recognize that schools do differ, and that to make sense of schooling, it is important to see it function within a particular sociohistorical context. Because our interest is in how schooling interacts with multiculturalism, that context is worthy of a brief overview using the concept of equal educational opportunity.

Because the word "education" does not appear in the constitution of the United States, schooling is a state and local responsibility. At the time of the founding of the United States, each community was typically engaged in providing some form of formal education to its citizens. The curriculum was usually similar for those sectors of the population who had access to schools. With a common curriculum, however, local and state government left the family and student on their own to take advantage of schooling opportunities and to adapt their educational experience to fit their own needs and interests. In effect, government was only responsible for the *provision* of education, ultimately compulsory, while the pursuit thereof was left to the learner.

As economic and political complexities in this country evolved and the control of schooling became less community-based, shaped more by state-level expectations, equality of opportunity meant that the school should respond to the various occupational futures of children by providing different curricula to suit students' particular interests and career aspirations. Thus, and although still segregated by race, schools more commonly tracked students into different curricula, some toward vocational futures and some toward college futures. This was a major change from the common school curriculum.

This pattern remained in place for many decades. Until the 1950s academic and vocational tracking was the dominant way to select, sort, and screen students curricularly. It was during that decade that the federal government, through funding and legislation, and most dramatically through the courts, began playing a more important role in using schools as a means to create social change. The latter influence was especially apparent in the 1954 Supreme Court ruling, *Brown v. Board of Education*, which declared racially separate schools inherently unequal and in violation of basic fundamental freedoms. This decision turned attention away from the idea that communities needed only to provide schools, and that families and students had then to learn how to take advantage of them, toward ensuring that the *effects*, or outcomes, of schooling on students needed to be of equal benefit for all who attended. Thus it was not enough to maintain the school and provide multiple curricula; it was now necessary for all students to be prepared to pursue further education or to secure employment. Importantly, this double emphasis, on equality of opportunity and outcome, created a new mix of students in most schools, primarily because of mandatory busing programs and magnet schools, both of which were intended to further societal integration and reduce segregation. Among the negative effects of this forced school integration policy was the movement of white, middle, and upper socioeconomic populations to the suburbs, where they would be less affected by court-ordered racial mixing in schools.

In 1992 a Supreme Court ruling regarding school desegregation efforts in the Atlanta metropolitan area decreased some of these pressures on schools to maintain a multiracial balance. The ruling found that school districts should not be held accountable for the resegregation of a court-ordered desegregated school system (in this case the DeKalb County (Georgia) school system) when demographic changes in the community were the cause. Some believe that this ruling will encourage more white flight to the suburbs in the 1990s and that society will suffer because of the lack of cross-race interaction inside schools. The concern is that there may be further polarization of racial attitudes and potential conflict between groups.

Looking at the shift during the last half century, from an individual student having to take advantage of whatever the school had to offer to the school being held responsible for satisfying differing student needs and interests, many would say that schools have not been able to satisfy expectations. Nor have other, nonschool efforts been satisfactory to ensure integration and access to the resources of the wider society. Discrimination in housing, the job market, and other areas of society have also been identified as posing continuing barriers to closing income gaps and increasing job opportunities.

Because schools have not been able to deliver equal outcomes, many families and communities during the 1990s have become more involved in attempting to increase the probability of student school success and satisfaction. Implementing this greater balance of responsibility between schools and their respective families and communities, however, has been difficult. The larger society has been accustomed to sending their children off to school, assuming teachers in classrooms would be accountable for a child's learning. Similarly, the professionalization of teaching has established teachers as the authority for doing what is supposed to be in the best interest of the child. Both of these trends—childcare and professionalizing teachers (to be experts like medical doctors)—have tended to separate what goes on inside school from what goes on in a child's life outside school. In effect, expectations on both sides—teachers and parents—have often worked against joint planning and programming on behalf of the teaching and learning process.

Although what schools are expected to accomplish has grown as parents, communities, and other societal institutions have looked to them for building society and resolving social ills, as an organizational entity, the school resembles its nineteenth-century counterpart. The school still represents a curricular and instructional model that attends to the teacher and teaching rather than learning; still has a centralized control of curricula at the level of the community and state; still moves students from classroom to classroom according to a fixed schedule of class times; still follows an annual calendar modeled by traditional agricultural planting and harvesting; and still utilizes a classroom space typically composed of a rectangular layout of rowed desks highlighted by a teacher station at one end.

The continued existence of these traditional patterns does not necessarily mean that no attention has been given to how schools can be organized and administered to effect greater equality of opportunity among all populations. To the contrary, school effectiveness studies have identified characteristics of schools which have demonstrated some success in facilitating academic achievement among low socioeconomic status students from minority backgrounds. These studies show that successful schools place an emphasis on orderliness, often institute systematic monitoring of student progress, and maximize the amount of time students spend on academic activities. Further, they attempt to ensure positive family and community rewards for academic achievement; they place an emphasis on learning basic skills before expanding curricular offerings; and they employ principals who are heavily involved in instructional and curricular issues (Meijnen 1991).

Schools as Centers of Social Interaction

As the activities and climate of schools take shape over time, it is typical for each school to develop a habitual way for students, faculty, and staff to behave as individuals and groups. Like all social institutions, the school contains people, material objects, accepted ways of doing things, and a particular tradition. Said differently, students and teacher come together in a classroom to achieve goals. They use certain materials (e.g., paper, pencils, desks, chalkboards) to achieve those goals. The system revolves around teaching and learning through teacher- or student-designated experiences which are expected to enable learners to achieve desired ends. The tradition evolves or develops as the result of student and teacher coming together regularly in an attempt to fulfill the purposes of the system. Such a tradition includes expected behavior patterns which are based on the values and attitudes of the members and provides a class or set of classes with a predictable set of circumstances which will be in operation each time the group meets and carries on activities. Hence what goes on inside schools is inextricably tied to expectations and mandates from the outside, but the mix of students and faculty inside also constitute another system to which individuals adapt and from which they learn. This aspect of schooling might be close to what Jules Henry called "noise," defined as follows:

A classroom can be compared to a communications system, for certainly there is a flow of messages between teacher (transmitter) and pupils (receivers) and among the pupils, contacts are made and broken, messages can be sent at a certain rate of speed only, and so on. But there is also another interesting characteristic of communications systems that is applicable to classrooms, and that is their inherent tendency to generate *noise*. In a classroom lesson on arithmetic, for example, such *noise* would range all the way from the competitiveness of the students, the quality of the teacher's voice ("I remember exactly how she sounded when she told me to sit down") to the shuffling of the children's feet. The striking thing about the child is that along with his arithmetic—his "messages about arithmetic"—he learns all the *noise* in the system also. It is this that brings it about that an objective observer cannot tell which is being learned in any lesson, the *noise* or the formal subject matter. But—and mark this well—it is *not* primarily the message (let us say, the arithmetic or the spelling) that constitutes the most important subject matter to be learned, but the *noise*! The most significant cultural learnings—primarily the cultural drives—are communicated as 'noise' (Henry 1963).

Henry's observation suggests that what students really learn over the long term in schools is not the recognized curriculum; rather, they learn from the way in which the schooling process is habitually conducted. Such an outcome is not dissimilar to our view of what is learned in the family and community, i.e., children learn skills, information, and values through relatively long-term reinforcement of the ways in which day-to-day behavior is shaped and rewarded by the environment, kin, and friends. Similarly, and perhaps distressing to those who desire the formal curriculum to have greater importance and impact is the fact that in schools it is the habitual ways of carrying out the business of schooling that have greatest impact.

Part of the learning that emanates from the system in process is due to compulsory school attendance laws. Such laws force most students to spend time together in schools, thereby encouraging the establishment of traditions and common ways of carrying out day-to-day activities. The fact that students form a captive audience in this way helps explain why they generate their own "noise" during school hours. Beyond forced interaction, peer groups at all levels of education are among the most important influences on student learning. In effect, the values and interests of youth are brought into school or are generated from the interaction that occurs in school and often challenge both the regular and the extracurriulum for attention. Student-created noise—outside class and outside school clubs—can be seen in the language used by students, in the identity of students with their social class and ethnicity, and in the attitudes and values they hold.

An example from language can be seen in the ways students use vocabulary to set themselves apart from other youth and adults. This certainly is common among social class and ethnic groups, but also reflects overall age group interests. The school simply becomes the convenient venue for transmitting particular vocabulary and language usage. In the early 1990s words such as "dude," "chill," "psych," and "bad" were common, and using 'not' after an untrue statement was widespread. According to an article on slang in *The Los Angeles Times* (Roark 1992), the following slang and its translation demonstrates the extent to which youth can develop vocabulary to increase in-group solidarity. It is akin to the kind of dialect that might be associated with a particular ethnic group. First, the slang:

> It was an on-hit kind of afternoon in L.A. A Mac daddy was scamming on a fly houchy, while one of his homies was clocking some dead Presidents. Meantime, the rest of the $yndicate were trying to kick it, but were being gaffed up by a one time.

The translation read as follows:

It was a good day in Los Angeles. A charming young man was flirting with an attractive young female, while one of his friends was at work earning money. At the same time, the rest of his pals were trying to relax, but were being hasseled by a police officer.

The reporter notes that such slang is so localized and changes so rapidly that it can only be understood by those of particular ages and in particular geographical regions.

A second way the student-generated 'noise' can be seen in schools is through student identity and students' affiliations with one another. Placing emphasis on athletic participation, dating success, good looks, or material resources all reflect the ways in which social origins of students, their future commitments, and the general characteristics of the institution come together to support particular student identities. For instance, athletes and high academic achievers have long held positions of separate social standing in the mix of students within schools. These individuals can be distinguished by dress, language usage, and their tendency to seek one another's association.

More recently, there has been an increase in gangs in urban schools. Again, because of language, dress, intimidation, turf protection, or other characteristics, gang members are also often distinguishable at school. Gangs have become so visible on campuses in Southern California that teacher education programs now include instruction on gang affiliations, graffiti, and values. As athletic, high academic achieving, or gang member identities take form, they shape social perception, including how individuals extract information by watching others and how they interact with others. Some have suggested that membership in gangs occurs partly because the groups represent social activity for individuals who are excluded from formal school rewards, such as high grades and college-oriented classes. The opposite holds for those who value academic achievement and thrive on satisfying the recognized reward structure. In many instances such groups are also natural extensions of relationships built in communities outside schools (Schwartz 1989).

Identities along racial and ethnic group dimensions are reinforced by the social pressure received from the members of a particular reference group to act in accordance with the norms of that group. Thus one's speech, dress, value orientations, and basic daily behaviors are formally and informally monitored by peers to maintain a sense of membership. For African Americans such peer assessment is a method of testing one's "Blackness," or allegiance to in-group solidarity. This kind of identity process can be seen in recent literature which argues that some minority youngsters are pressured to learn to adapt and cope with the dominance of a white majority by "acting white" to succeed in school. This means that if African Americans do not behave according to dominant

ations, they risk not succeeding in school. Simultaneously, their behavior to such dominant group norms, they risk s. Adaptation behavior includes speaking standard English, rs classes, spending time in the library, and getting good ......ypes based on other profiles, however, this argument does not permit a recognition of the ways in which individual behavior, both black and white, vary within groups. Thus labeling of this sort runs the risk of perpetuating self-fulfilling prophecies based on those stereotypes.

While students can be divided along ethnic and social class lines to reflect differences in behaviors, they can also be differentiated by the attitudes and values they hold. We will discuss some of those differences later in this chapter. Despite group differences, students can also be grouped together to learn how they perceive various issues. Such attitudes constitute a third example of the noise they contribute to the schooling process. Philip Altbach (1993) reports that although college and university student attitudes in the United States over the last twenty to thirty years have become more liberal toward some social and political issues, the majority of students remain most concerned with their own career and personal success. Even then, he continues, college students do not evidence liberal attitudes toward all such issues. For example, liberalism can be seen in increasingly positive orientations toward abortion, gender equality, premarital sex, homosexuality, and health care, while conservativism can be seen on issues like the abolition of the death penalty and the use of marijuana. Altbach also reports that students in the United States are less inclined toward political activism than those in most other countries. This is especially the case with many students in third world countries and in Western Europe, where student activism and organizations can often determine policies on major national issues.

The Curriculum and the Extracurriculum in Group Integration and Separation

Apart from student generated noise, there is also the "noise" that is learned from the way in which schools carry out the formal curriculum and the extracurriculum. Our interest is in how intergroup relations are shaped on campuses by these forces. A survey of college and university newspaper editors conducted by the editors of *U.S. News and World Report* (April 19, 1993) found that 64 percent of the editors at large institutions labeled the state of campus race relations as fair or poor, 75 percent noted that self-segregation among blacks was common, and 85 percent reported that there was at least one incident on campus during the year that could be termed racial. Eighty-eight percent of the same editors noted that action taken by campus administrators to deal with racial tensions were not at all or only somewhat effective.

Clearly, schools and colleges in the United States, and often elsewhere, are faced with a dilemma. Teachers and administrators have learned that the best intentions of affirmative action, ethnic-specific curricula, multicultural initiatives, and extracurricular programs, which tend to acknowledge and build group identity, can also produce alienating and segregating effects. Race-based admissions, scholarships, and financial aid programs in post-secondary institutions have sometimes generated a backlash from students who are ineligible for such assistance. Similarly, special race, ethnic, and gender studies programs have sometimes resulted in more segregation among student groups and academic programs. In fact, it can be argued that those who advocate a multicultural approach to education in schools and colleges through race- and ethnic-specific programs promote divisiveness, factionalism, and intolerance. The challenge is finding ways both to build common goals and networks and to enable each individual and group to strengthen their identification with their heritage. To do anything less is to delay the commitment to true societal integration and long-term social betterment.

In the United States the school's role in dividing various ethnic and social classes has long occurred through the formal curriculum. It can be argued that student choices, for example, in pursuing vocational and academic careers, is one major way in which divisions continue to be created. It is often the poor, minority student who is found in the vocational stream and the middle- or upper-class, and dominant group student who is found in the academic stream. This tracking in the formal curriculum can be created and reinforced by the school using standardized test results for ability grouping, often beginning as early as kindergarten. Such tracking is typically based on actual or presumed academic achievement and potential. Because standardized achievement tests tend to be biased against the poor, linguistically different, or culturally different child, minority group students tend to perform less well on them. Once students have been placed in tracks based on such test results, it is often difficult for them to be reclassified. In effect, for many students an academic self-fulfilling prophecy may emerge based on their earliest experiences with school.

Apart from the formal curricula, there is also a tradition in schools and colleges in the United States to support extracurricular activities. Eckert (1989) notes that extracurricular participation is part of a process in which students engage in a competition to control their environment, define their age group, and set guidelines for interaction among themselves and with adults. Many universities in the United States host more than a hundred such organizations, including religious, sports, journalism, political, fraternal, ethnic, and residential bodies. Altbach (1993) reports that such organizations are not as well developed in most other countries because more attention is given to the academic mission.

In colleges and high schools in the United States the establishment of these extracurricular organizations encourages the reinforcement of competencies and interests held by youth. These in turn may reflect particular socioeconomic and cultural backgrounds. As membership builds based on these latter identities, the sanctioned clubs and organizations reinforce separation on campus and may be judged as harmful to creating campus unity. For example, in some schools and colleges in the United States it is not unusual to find academically oriented clubs and certain sports teams, like golf or tennis, dominated by white, middle- and upper-class youngsters and other kinds of clubs and other sports teams, like interscholastic basketball or football, dominated by African Americans from lower socioeconomic backgrounds. Thomas and Moran (1991) studied these relationships in high schools and found that this pattern of differential partici- pation by ethnicity can occur at the expense of academic emphases and is especially common among schools with a high concentration of African Americans. While some of the divisions along racial, ethnic, and class lines in the extracurriculum can be viewed as reflecting student choice, the institution itself also reinforces and initiates such divisions. Oftentimes, separation seems to be valued when institutions sponsor new student orientation programs based on race and ethnicity; endorse divided dormitories, student centers, dances and fraternities; publish special yearbooks; and sponsor graduation receptions.

As can be noted from the above discussion, the result of curricular tracking and participation patterns in extracurricular organizations may be both the integration and the segregation of students along a number of dimensions. These patterns reinforce the idea that schools constitute arenas in which group differences are tested and in which negotiation over the group traditions and visions that will be reproduced through school programs take place (Patthey- Chavez 1993). Just because there is a mix of students attending a given school does not mean that student experiences are truly integrated. Imagine standing across the street from a racially and ethnically mixed secondary school or college in the morning at the time the school day begins. You will see the students from these diverse backgrounds streaming into the school buildings, giving you the impression of a truly integrated institution. Yet the results of resegre- gation by ability grouping and tracking as well as by special interest clubs and organizations limits the substantive interactions among individuals across ethnic, racial, and socioeconomic lines. The interaction that does occur across groups is often limited to brief passing periods between classes, short breaks, and the lunch period. Because these moments are often the only free time youngsters have to exercise choice in their own interpersonal lives on a campus, they tend to seek out individuals who have similar interests and backgrounds to their own, thus limiting the potential for substantive interaction across social and cultural boundaries. This means that it is not sufficient simply to reveal the statistical mix of students within a given school or college to determine whether the school is functionally integrated across social class, racial, and cultural boundaries; it is also important to determine whether students interact on a regular basis within classrooms and special groups and clubs.

There is some evidence that such interaction across group boundaries can be increased by placing a priority on limiting ability grouping and tracking and encouraging extracurricular participation. It has been argued that increasing interaction through the formal curriculum and extracurriculum has the potential for increasing student attachment to the institution, reducing student alienation, providing alternative ways for students to develop self-esteem, and increasing the opportunities for positive intergroup relations (Crain 1981). Although such outcomes may occur naturally under ideal circumstances, at times schools need to pay more attention to these goals through facilitating access to sponsored programs and channeling the behavior of students in them. Some campuses even identify common goals, such as mentoring students in a local elementary or secondary school, and then help extracurricular clubs (crossing racial and ethnic lines) to work jointly in delivering needed services.

Variation in Values, Cognition, and Language as they Affect Classroom Teaching and Learning

In addition to noise, schools offer a place in which backgrounds and characteristics of students can interact with the expectations of the teachers and the curriculum. Variations in how and what is taught and learned outside and inside schools constitute a major challenge for teachers in classrooms with a diversity of students. Lauren Resnick (1987) argues that the educational research community needs to turn its attention to these differences. She outlines four general classes of differences between teaching and learning outside and inside schools.

1. The school's emphasis on individual achievement versus socially shared competence outside of the school.
2. The school's effort to focus on unaided thought while mental work outside school usually involves an array of cognitive tools.
3. The school's emphasis on symbolic thinking in comparison to activity outside which engages individuals in problem solving directly with everyday objects and situations.
4. The school's concern for general skills and knowledge, as opposed to the demands of situation-specific competencies which are necessary outside.

Resnick goes on to argue that these basic differences result in very little transfer of knowledge from schools to everyday life and that there is a need to build apprenticeships and other "bridges" between the world of work and the world of schools.

One of the major obstacles to reducing the discontinuities between what goes on outside and what goes on inside schools is the increased reliance on standardized testing for the placement of youngsters in school classes. This became a major issue in the 1960s as schools became a focal point and a major vehicle for individuals and groups seeking social and economic mobility. Those who could pass the tests gained access to academic tracks and to the education which assured a more financially rewarding career. Mercer (1972) reported that the use of such tests saw two to four times more than expected Hispanic and African American youngsters labeled mentally retarded, the results which prompted placing them in separate special education classes. As such data was being reported, the investigations of educational anthropologists became important in documenting the teaching/learning relationship between and among students and teachers in school classrooms. They developed a special interest in observing and recording the behaviors of students from different socio-economic and cultural backgrounds.

Such documentation enabled educators to argue against a *deficit* explanation of the low achievement of economically poor, ethnic minority students. Akin to blaming poverty on the poor, the deficit explanation for low school performance emphasized so-called inadequacies in the background of minority students which were said to limit their school achievement and require remedial programs for improvement. Typical characterizations included minority African American youngsters came from homes that were "disorganized" (Frazier 1966) and from families that were "deteriorating" (Glazer and Moynihan 1963). People living in poverty were said to evidence a way of life more primitive and violent than that of the middle class (Gladwin 1967). Additionally, some educators believed that the minority child lacked a sense of competition in school, was basically anti-intellectual (Reisman 1962), manifested little intrinsic motivation to learn (Ausubel 1963), and learned less from what he or she heard (Black 1965).

Unfounded claims like these led to the initiation of school-based compensatory education programs designed to make the behavior of the minority child more similar to that of the middle-class child. Programs like Head Start, and family intervention strategies, were initially constructed along these lines. Only in later years did some recognize the negative consequences of attempts to "make over" the culturally different and the poor in the image of the dominant group. Compensatory education resulted in an increase in tracking and ability grouping, and special education classes swelled with minority youngsters. The moral and ethical bases of such programs, the potential long-term homogenizing effect on society, and the questionable role of the school as a locus for changing minority behavior were seldom challenged. Further, the application of the cultural deficit model to educational programs throughout the United States did not produce the intended improvements in school achievement (Averch et al. 1972).

The lack of credibility of the deficit model in explaining low school achievement gave rise to the cultural difference model in which minority behavior was viewed, first, as an adaptation to ethnic discrimination and inequality, and second, as an outgrowth of differences in the minority group's life experiences associated with its historical traditions. The cultural difference model, therefore, did not view ethnic group behavior as deficient or deprived but rather as a logical and expected outgrowth of historical and structural constraints unique to specific populations.

Research which applied the cultural difference model to school achievement assumed that there were certain learned traits or characteristics which differentiated ethnic groups. Such research attempted to identify these traits and the socialization processes by which they were acquired to explain the learning outcomes of members of ethnic groups and to help educators plan educational programs around the traits characterizing the learner.

Value Differences

Underlying many particular characteristics assumed to differentiate cultural groups are the values people hold. One example of such values is pointed to by Stigler and Perry (1988), following their study of mathematics instruction in classrooms in Japan, Taiwan, and the United States. The study yielded data which found that Japanese and Chinese students spent the majority of their time working as a group or entire classroom, whereas American children spent the majority of their time working independently. Specifically, Chinese classrooms put more attention on performance and practice, Japanese classrooms emphasized reflective thinking and verbal discussion, and American classrooms focused on neither; and both Chinese and Japanese teachers relied more on real-life problem situations and word problems than did American teachers. These distinctions in the organization, structure, and general approaches to classroom teaching and learning were extended when the authors learned of the assumptions held by parents regarding individual differences and the nature of learning. For example, American mothers were more likely to believe that mathematics competence was due to innate ability, while Asian mothers believed successful learning was a result of hard work and effort.

A classic study by Gross (1967) concerning value differences among ethnic groups also looked at parental values as they related to student school success. He contrasted Ashkenazic and Sephardic Jewish children in terms of their educational, intellectual, and verbal readiness for preschool. On the basis of knowledge of the cultural background of the two ethnic groups, Gross hypothesized that differences in the learning readiness of the two populations could be explained by analyzing the attitudes and values characterizing each. Thus Gross argued that the Sephardic Jews have historically been found primarily along the North African perimeter and have been surrounded by Moslems, while the Ashkenazic Jews have been rooted in Eastern Europe and have been surrounded by Christians. He went on to suggest that the Ashkenazic communities were affected by the industrial revolution and were victims of anti-Semitism, whereas the Sephardim were isolated from contact with the revolutions of Western Europe and were thus more sheltered from discrimination. Gross concluded that because of their different historical experiences, the Ashkenazim had come to place a strong value on learning through self-study and intellectual productivity, whereas the Sephardim had been more likely to stress economic goals through commercial participation.

To test these theses, Gross took a sample of Sephardic Jews of Syrian descent who had lived in Brooklyn, New York for 50 years and had maintained their own religious congregations, social clubs, and recreational facilities. A nearby Ashkenazic community provided the comparison group. Each community was served by its own all-day Hebrew school; in each group all of the families sent their children to the community private school, all of the children had mothers who were native born, and all spoke English. Gross controlled for social class and administered a battery of cognitive tests to children and a series of questionnaires to mothers. He found that results of intelligence tests administered to the children favored the Ashkenazic youngsters, but that none of the motivational or attitudinal questionnaires administered to the mothers demonstrated any clear relationship with learning readiness in children. Gross explained the results of his study through cultural ideals and stresses characterizing the two ethnic groups. He suggested that although both populations might have shared similar socioeconomic levels and achievement motivation, in all likelihood they acquired their social status through two different portals—the Sephardim through the accumulation of wealth and the Ashkenazim through educational attainment.

Another approach to cultural difference research focuses on the importance of values and assumes that populations can be differentiated by particular traits is the work of Millard Madsen (1971). Madsen developed a series of rather ingenious experimental problem-solving situations to assess competitive and cooperative behavior among populations. One of his techniques involved the use of a marble pull game. The game consists of a small plexiglass marble holder placed in the center of a rectangular table, with a string attached to each of the two sides of the marble holder. By taking hold of one end of the string, each child may pull the marble holder to his or her end of the table and thereby secure the marble; but there is potential for competition if the children pull against each other. In such an instance, because the holder is connected with magnets, the marble holder would break apart and the marble would roll to the side of the table and be lost to both participants.

By using the marble pull, Madsen found considerable difference among several populations in their competitive and cooperative behavior. He reported that Mexican children in a small Mexican town tended to be more cooperative than either Mexican American children or Anglo-American children living in Los Angeles and that differences among children increased with age. In effect, the marble pull game found Mexican children cooperating to *secure* marbles and Anglo-American children competing to *win* marbles; the Mexican-American population fell midway between the two extremes. Even though after the first trial all children were instructed in the way in which marbles could be gained, the Anglo-American sample, aged 7–8, still failed to obtain the marble 44 percent of the time, and the 10–11-year-old Anglo-Americans failed to obtain a marble 62 percent of the time.

These studies of value differences, and the discussion that follows in Chapter 6, demonstrate the importance of ideals, aims, ethical and aesthetic standards which shape school goals and those who work in them. Schools stress verbal attention to uphold values of democracy, individuality, morality, and human perfectibility. They also champion the work-success ethic, independence, thrift, and hard work. But each of these orientations is complemented and challenged in schools by competing values of conformity rather than creativity, relativism rather than absolute standards, and docility rather than challenging authority. Teachers tend to hold in highest esteem those who hold values closest to their own, a bias which is complicated for students coming from other cultural backgrounds.

Related to a concern for values in differentiating groups, some scholars have focused on structural and procedural differences between home and school, indicating that such differences may be more important than academic ability in determining school achievement (Florio and Shultz 1979). Holliday's (1985) study of nine- and ten-year-old African Americans in a desegregated school, for example, found that the students typically changed their behavior between home and school. At home they had high competence in problem-solving skills, whereas in school their greatest attributes were in the areas of interpersonal and social skills. Similarly, in their study of Mexican-American households in the United States, Valez-Ibanez and Greenberg (1992) argue that there is a great difference between what children learn in families and what they are expected to do in classrooms. The authors identify the need to develop more cooperative learning strategies in schools, because social interaction among U.S. Mexican children is a highly developed skill and expectation.

Although such differences exist, there is also an indication that overall, there is an inverse relationship between socioeconomic status and attitudes toward the importance of education. Stevenson, Chen, and Uttal (1990) reported that African American and Hispanic American families were more concerned about education than white families, that children and mothers from the minority groups held high expectations about the children's educational futures, and that minority mothers and teachers working in schools dominated by minority children were more likely than white mothers and teachers to value homework, competency testing, and a longer school day.

Cognition and Conceptual Style Differences

In addition to research on values, and some of their implications for schooling, the literature of the cultural difference model reflects a concern with conceptual style, or the way in which individuals make sense out of reality and the way in which we come to know what we know. The work of Rosalie Cohen, an investigator of conceptual styles, appears to support the cultural difference model as a set of traits, or characteristics, and is illustrative of this line of inquiry. Cohen (1969) analyzed two conceptual styles that emerged from a series of research studies in the United States; one is referred to as "analytic" and the other, "relational." The relational child is said to be unable to deal with linear concepts or the requirements for formal abstraction to produce linear continua. These conceptual styles, which are found to be independent of native ability, are associated with child-rearing practices in the home. The child who demonstrates a relational approach to reality organization is characterized by so-called shared-function environments, found to be common in lower socioeconomic families; whereas the child who demonstrates an analytic approach to reality organization is characterized by more formal, primary-group participation, said to be common in middle-class families. According to Cohen, because of the preponderance of intelligence and achievement tests, schools in the United States require increasingly sophisticated analytic cognitive skills rather than relational skills. Subsequent to Cohen's research, Manuel Ramirez (1982) found that most Mexican American children could be characterized as field sensitive (relational) rather than field independent (analytic) in cognitive style. A liability of cultural difference research is that it supports the stereotyping of an entire ethnic group and establishes labels and self-fulfilling prophecies for the use of teachers. In other words, after reading such studies, teachers may come to believe that all children of Mexican descent are relational in cognitive style.

Although the work of Cohen and Ramirez poses questions regarding the organization of sense data, there is also evidence to suggest that the knowledge applied is culture-specific. The work of Lesser, Fifer, and Clark (1965) is relevant here. They selected four groups of first-grade boys and girls from Chinese, Black, Jewish, and Puerto Rican backgrounds living in New York City. They prepared reasoning, numerical, and spatial tests reflecting experiences common to the various social class and ethnic groups in the area. The children were tested by psychologists of their own ethnic background who used one or more languages appropriate to a given child. It was found that each ethnic group demonstrated a pattern in the ways they used knowledge to solve problems, regardless of social class position. While social class made little difference in the pattern, it did make a difference in the level of scores of each group. The authors concluded "once the pattern specific to the ethnic group emerges, social class variations within the ethnic group do not alter this basic organization" (Lesser et al., 83).

Subsequently, the study was replicated by Stodolsky and Lesser (1967) in Boston with Chinese and Black first-grade children; the results were similar to those observed in New York City. Also as a follow-up, a study of the mental abilities of first-generation, Israeli-born six and seven year-old Jewish children in Israel reconfirmed the Lesser et al. results (Burg and Belmont 1990). In this study, however, different group patterns of verbal, reasoning, numerical and spatial skills coincided with the child's European, Iraqi, North American, and Yemenite historical-cultural background. It should be noted that although the patterns of mental abilities across these studies continued to show strong relationships in cultural background and mental abilities, in each of the Lesser et al. inspired studies it was also noted that there were many individual children whose intellectual pattern did not coincide with the particular norm or dominant behavior of their cultural group. As with the Cohen and Ramirez studies, the risk here is to attribute certain cognitive traits to entire ethnic groups, thereby limiting the potential for youngsters to vary from those patterns and for teachers and others to stereotype youngsters based on such labels.

Language Differences

The third major variable affecting teaching and learning across cultural boundaries in the classroom is language. Because classroom instruction is highly verbalized and because language constitutes a complex inventory of all the ideas, interests, and occupations that take up the attention of the community, it is perhaps the most central of the three variables identified here. Language is said to constitute a sort of logic—a general frame of reference—which some say helps mold the thought of its habitual users. Spoken language further interacts with nonverbal forms of communication through facial expressions, gestures, eye contact, tone of voice, and so on. Nonverbal behaviors also include closeness and touching, the use of space, and personal dress and status.

Because of the way in which forms of communication interact with cognition and values, and because concern is with both separate and distinct languages as well as social dialects, language is perhaps the best researched and most widely discussed characteristic that distinguishes students from differing ethnic backgrounds. While there are no statistics available on the number of students who switch dialects depending on social contexts, limited English proficient students in the United States are expected to increase from 2.8 million in 1990 to 3.4 million in the year 2000. Three quarters of these students speak Spanish, and most of the others speak Vietnamese, Cantonese, Cambodian, Filipino/ Tagalog, or Hmong (Cheng 1990).

✝ As might be expected, some portion of the members of these various ethnic groups desire to preserve their linguistic ability as an important source of cultural identity. There are others, however, mostly outside of these groups, who believe that the preservation of native or mother language abilities by groups threatens the existence of unifying elements in the overall culture of the United States. These latter individuals argue that the society will not sustain its collective consciousness if groups within it are permitted to reinforce a separateness based on language. They also point out that schools should not base their approach to education on the primacy of ethnic or other characteristics to the exclusion of the needs associated with citizenship in the larger society (Imhoff 1990). Nonetheless, because of the importance of language in teaching and learning, schools have become a testing ground for bilingual education and related efforts to increase the likelihood of academic success among populations which speak little or no English.

Perhaps one of the best-known studies identifying the influence of group membership on certain linguistic traits is that of Basil Bernstein (1964). With the assumption that language acquisition influences future learning and cognitive abilities in general, Bernstein differentiated between the language or code used by the middle and lower socioeconomic classes. While he reportedly attempted to avoid being pejorative in his assessment of the languages used by the two populations, Bernstein nevertheless found that members of the middle class spoke what he termed an elaborated or formal language, while members of the lower class spoke a restricted or public language. Because of socialization and environmental factors, the so-called restricted language used by the lower class was said to limit their ability not only with abstract concepts but also with the school in general. Subsequent research refuted Bernstein by finding that higher order cognitive ability is not explained by social class and that the ability to speak more than one language and code is associated with higher levels of cognitive attainment, including concept formation, creativity, and cognitive flexibility (e.g., Diaz 1983).

By the early 1970s proponents of the cultural difference model, especially educational anthropologists, were placing considerable attention on language as a major variable for explaining low school achievement. The work of Dell Hymes (1974), Courtney Cazden (1972), and others pursued studies of communication styles in and out of school settings which provided additional perspectives on how speech and nonverbal communication differences caused problems between teachers and students. As Douglas Foley reports, such studies argued that minority students' "kinesic, proxemic, and communicative competence at turn-taking, question-asking and answering, story-telling, literacy, and general speech style created cultural conflicts or cultural incongruences that led teachers to treat them differently" (Foley 1991, 83). Foley cites the work of Susan Phillips (1983) as an example of this general approach. Philips documented the speech style of Native American adults in the Warm Springs reservation through observation of tribal council and longhouse meetings where there was general egalitarianism and a greater reliance on body language than on verbal ways of communicating. As Philips followed students into Anglo, teacher-centered classrooms, she found that Anglo students were more active verbally when the whole class participated as a group and that Native American students were more active verbally when the teacher used group project-type organizational structures. Philips argued that the Native American students were more active in group projects because such organizational groupings more closely approximated the collective, cooperative, and collateral world to which they were accustomed in their daily life outside the classroom.

The view of language as a major educational variable in the late 1970s was driven primarily by the *Lau* v. *Nichols* United States Supreme Court decision (1974) which found that equal educational opportunity was not satisfied by simply providing limited English proficiency students with the same facilities, textbooks, teachers, and curriculum as were given English-speaking students. This ruling led Congress and the states to fund bilingual education programs intended to increase English language proficiency. It also encouraged competition between two approaches to language maintenance and second language learning. Some of the resulting programs in schools initially approached bilingual education by reinforcing the native language under the assumption that it would provide important cognitive foundations for second language acquisition. This approach is also said to enhance ethnic identity and ease the transition to English. The other major approach to bilingual education has been referred to as "immersion"; it introduces the English curriculum from the student's first contact with schooling. Because of the importance of language in the larger social and cultural context, the effects of these two approaches on English language acquisition remains clouded by complications in research design and methods. But many argue that judging bilingual education through school achievement alone fails to acknowledge the importance of the histories of the respective populations and the use of language in multiple social contexts (Garcia 1990). We will have more to say about bilingual education in the next chapter.

The Importance of Context in Analyzing Cultural Difference

These examples of studies of cultural differences in values, cognition, and language assume that cultural membership, or socialization, which occurs as individuals mature in particular social class and ethnic groups, leads to certain identifiable traits which can be used to differentiate populations. They also share one common and important characteristic: they inevitably view behavior from a comparative perspective, often associated with an idealized set of expectations. These expectations are often measured by how well certain groups, usually the economically and politically dominant, perform on standardized tests. The argument of the cultural difference model, therefore, is derived from comparing the achievement of different populations on the same instrument.

In school classrooms the cultural difference model, although positive in its recognition of variations in backgrounds and resultant behaviors, as we have said, often leads to stereotypes and labeling. While such group-level generalizations may be useful in providing further hypotheses to be tested at the level of the individual, teachers have often used such information to establish self-fulfilling prophecies regarding student behavior. These prophecies often emerge on the basis of a student's surname, skin color, or other alleged symbols of ethnic group membership. The results are teaching methods and curricula which may not sufficiently allow individual variation from the statistical profiles established by group-level generalizations.

A third and alternative approach to the cultural deficit and difference models can be seen in the work of individuals who challenge the assumption that low intellectual achievement is due to culturally distinct traits and that such traits can be isolated from the larger societal context in which they are manifested. Instead, they argue that differences across populations can typically be explained through an analysis of where and how tests for such differences are conducted. Cole et al. (1971), for example, argue that cultural differences in cognition reside more in the situations to which particular cognitive processes are applied than in the existence of a process in one cultural group and its absence in another.

This notion of contextualized, or situation-specific, behavior has primarily been supported by linguists and psychological anthropologists. Foremost among the linguists who supported this position from early on is William Labov (1968). He challenged much of the linguistic deprivation argument frequently central to compensatory education programs. On the basis of his research on nonstandard Black English, Labov emphasized the functional equality of all languages and noted the importance of the manner and means by which language competence is assessed. He supported the contention that an individual learns to cope with the environment within which he or she has been socialized (e.g., neighborhood) and that when the individual is moved from that ecological niche to one that is less familiar or comfortable (e.g., school), failure to cope with the new surroundings may lead to the label of linguistic deprivation. Labov argued that such a diagnosis is situation-specific and that using middle-class linguistic criteria to judge whether or not a Black student can use language effectively is inappropriate both in the selection of criteria and in the situation and tasks used for assessing linguistic competence.

Psychological anthropologists also emerged with data supporting Labov's scholarship. Cole and Bruner put the issue: "The crux of the argument, when applied to the problem of 'cultural deprivation,' is that those groups ordinarily diagnosed as culturally deprived have the same underlying competence as those in the mainstream of dominant culture, *the differences in performance being accounted for by the situations and contexts in which the competence is expressed"* (Cole and Bruner 1971, 870).

This conclusion was the result of several years of cross-cultural studies involving the Kpelle people of Liberia conducted by Gay and Cole (1967) and Cole et al. (1971). The research began by focusing on cross-cultural language-cognition and language-learning relationships and ended with a broader concentration on culture and cognition. The investigators found that by continually manipulating and changing experimental conditions, they were able to more closely approximate the requirements of the task with the learned behavior of the participants. The following example drawn from studies of the Kpelle will assist in clarifying this principle.

In an attempt to assess the relationship between language categories and cognition, the investigators began with a set of twenty objects which, in both Kpelle and English, belonged to the four classes of clothes, tools, foods, and containers. The objects were arranged haphazardly, and the subjects were asked to group those belonging to the same class. At first the Kpelle adults responded either by isolating objects or by putting the objects together on a functional basis. For example, they placed an orange next to a knife. To provide greater clues, the investigators asked the participants to arrange four categories by placing the objects that belonged together on each of four separate chairs. When this technique failed to elicit much sorting by category, the investigators used only two chairs. This manipulation succeeded, and in most cases two categories of objects were placed on each of the two chairs. The results are explained by Glick (1974), who suggests that the Kpelle's first response was contextual and reflected everyday pragmatic reality. When the reduction of chairs increased proximity, the Kpelle shifted from contextual to conceptual thinking and were able to treat the task as a hypothetical rather than a real occurrence. Another similar experiment among the Kpelle people found that they were initially unable to sort beer and soda bottles of various heights and colors because the bottles used were empty and thus were viewed as garbage by the participants. When full bottles were employed, such sorting was carried out.

While context alone does not explain all variabilities in performance, it deserves much more attention in school settings than it has received to date. As Triandis and Brislin (1984) argue, there are similarities and differences due to certain specific group activities. They note universals such as using categorization; using opposites and associations; and grouping evaluative, potency, and activity attributes together. The authors also note that there are deviations from the universals. Literacy, familiarity with certain subject matter, social and cognitive stimulation, nutrition, and prior education can all influence intellectual performance.

Assuming the goal of schooling is to increase the possibility of student learning and the application of that learning, the importance of placing classroom behavior into a more holistic, historical, and comparative perspective in which the context provides a natural rather than contrived explanation for daily behavior cannot be overstated. Foley (1991) argues that Philip's study of speech styles described earlier does not adopt this approach for she fails to provide the individuals themselves an opportunity to explain why they behave as they do and in turn relate those responses back to how white, Anglo domination and reservation life have shaped behavior.

In recent years cognitive development psychologists have embraced the theoretical work of Lev Vygotsky (1978) as a way to further strengthen the importance of sociocultural context and social processes as key to understanding individual cognitive development and hence in the explanation of school achievement. Vygotsky's concepts have lead scholars like Cazden (1988) to develop approaches to teaching which shape the ways adult experts interact with child learners, how they "scaffold" or sensitively interact with children to assist them in acquiring new skills and reconceptualizing skills already known by placing them in various contexts. In effect, it is argued that youngsters can more easily solve new tasks if they recognize from past experience elements of the new situation and the information processing necessary for problem solving.

Others have suggested that research needs to be broadened along several paths to learn more about appropriate ways to minimize discontinuities in learning for culturally different students. Gay (1990) advocates four approaches. First, making modifications in sociolinguistic areas, such as turn-taking rules, duration of utterances, turn-switching pauses, wait time for responses, questioning strategies, and the distribution of opportunities for individuals and groups to participate in verbal interactions with teachers. Second, closing the gap between cognitive frameworks present in the home and cognitive frameworks present in the school by emphaszing common patterns of thought, frames of reference, styles of information processing used to interpret daily reality, to resolve conflicts, and to solve problems. Third, Gay advocates research on modifying the structure of learning activities through examining the amount of physical movement that is required in the classroom; the extent to which sensory stimulation is varied; and how formats like learning centers, individualized programs, and small group activities impact learning. The fourth avenue of research concerns cooperative task structures, where members of particular ethnic groups are encouraged to participate in group settings and communal efforts.

Conclusion

This chapter has shown that dominant-subordinate group relationships are evident in schools through curricular, extracurricular, and pedagogical processes.

To temper the potential impact of an imbalance that may be evident in such intergroup relations, school personnel must be mindful of the need to place teaching and learning into context, must respect the learner's perspective and background, and must be willing to provide him or her with a structured transition from what is already known to what is to be learned. In that regard at least some of what we have identified as differences in values, cognition, and language will likely be reinforced in schools rather than ignored or eliminated. The teaching-learning process, therefore, necessarily involves respecting and recognizing different ways of making sense out of the world, out of values and beliefs that shape an individual's world view, and out of the ways in which reality is described and explained. Both the cultural difference and contextual models also suggest that tracking students on the basis of standardized, norm-referenced tests is likely to result in labeling and stereotyping and thus become self-fulfilling prophecies for teachers. Instead, all tests need to be interpreted in relation to the child's socioeconomic and ethnic background, with special attention paid to the kinds of skills and behavior typically displayed by learners outside schools.

Educators clearly need to know more about how students bridge the gap between the outside world and the school not only in friendship groups, activities, and general interaction but also in the school-based obstacles to learning encountered by ethnic minority children. Securing such data depends on observation methodologies and an opportunity to experiment with school curricula, extracurricular intervention, and assessment devices to uncover ways in which they can be manipulated to match the skills and activity patterns of ethnic minority children. Researchers, therefore, might shift their attention from uncovering cultural traits that will categorize population groups to assessing and promoting classroom procedures that will be advantageous for children from minority ethnic backgrounds. It is conceivable that this kind of research will lead to greater school success for ethnic minority students, to a reduction in the number of youngsters who are inappropriately labeled low achievers or mental retardates, and to an increase in the constructive relationships among and between groups.

CHAPTER 6

The Influence of Values
on Educational Policy and Practice

Introduction

In this chapter we discuss group values and how they shape educational policy and practice. In chapter 5 we saw how variations in values held by different populations can influence classroom teaching and learning. Here, we look at how competing values can influence the nature of other activities in a society's educational institutions. Values guide what group members decide about what counts as knowledge and what their children should learn and do in school. The competition among groups for power and influence often means that the members will pay particular attention to what goes on in schools—institutions whose role it is to socialize and pass on knowledge to the next generation of children. As Jules Henry argued, school is "a place where children are drilled in cultural orientations" (Henry 1963, 320). In a multicultural society, education readily becomes the arena for conflict, as groups battle to determine the cultural orientations into which their own children will be drilled.

As ethnic, racial, economic, and other groups struggle to influence educational systems and institutions, group values influence the curriculum and the content of textbooks, what is or isn't on the library shelves, whether ethnic or other group studies are promoted or ignored, the language teachers speak as they instruct students, who is hired or promoted, and numerous other policies and practices. In addition to influencing academic concerns, group value differences, particularly those of religious groups, engender fierce debate over the schools' role in children's moral development, health, and spiritual guidance. For example, differing values lie at the center of controversies about whether public education should mandate community service, whether school-based AIDS education should encourage students to be sexually abstinent, and whether schools should allow prayer at graduation-related events.

We begin with a definition of values. Next, we review concepts which have been popular in recent decades that are related to group values: that a nation's people can be characterized by a few values or traits (national character); that groups have hierarchies of values which place certain values more centrally than others (core and peripheral, dominant and variant); and that values can be studied across cultures. In doing so, we move from conceptions of societies having a dominant set of values to conceptions of societies having multiple, stratified groups, each containing diverse sets of values.

The differences in these viewpoints are important. Emphasizing a single, dominant set of values overlooks the competition and conflict that value differences engender within education in multicultural societies. More useful for understanding education and intergroup relations are frameworks which recognize that every society has subordinate groups, each with its own set of values, which the group seeks to promote through education. Finally, to show how variation in group values affects education, we discuss examples of educational policies and practices that arise from competing group values in the United States and other countries.

What Are Values?

Values are conceptions about what is desirable. They influence people's behavior and regulate how individuals satisfy their impulses. Values are not dependent on specific situations; rather, they provide the general grounds for accepting or rejecting particular norms, for making judgments, for expressing preferences, and for choosing courses of action. According to a general definition, values are the standards we use for selecting alternatives (Tropman 1989). They have a cognitive element, a selective quality, and some affective component (William 1968). They are more basic—but fewer in number—than beliefs and attitudes.[1] People are usually considered to have thousands of beliefs and hundreds of attitudes, but only dozens of values.

Values have a communal aspect; they are not simply what individuals want or need, but include consideration for other members of society and for the group as a whole. Because they are held in common with others, values can be one attribute by which groups are distinguished. In relation to intergroup relations and education, values shape the preferences group members express for particular educational policies and practices.

Values are strongly held and tend to change slowly. In the United States, most evidence suggests that values endure across generations. A number of studies conducted since the 1970s show that American youth hold many of the same values as youth of several decades ago (Levine and Havighurst 1989). In all the surveys, youth considered economic success, marriage, and parenthood desirable life goals. Likewise, values that the nation's schools currently transmit to students, such as the importance of hard work or learning to speak English, are similar to the values that educational institutions sought to instill in immigrants coming into the United States in the early twentieth century. The strength with which groups hold values, the tendency for values to endure over time, and the recognition that each group must inculcate the next generation ensures that differences in values will generate intense conflict about education.

Values can differ widely between groups whose members live among one another and participate in common economic, civic, and educational activities. For example, the Amish—a religious group concentrated in Pennsylvania and Ohio—live in areas whose population is mostly non-Amish and farm alongside their non-Amish neighbors. Nevertheless, their values guide them toward a simple style of dress and personal behavior; nonparticipation in most formal education beyond elementary school; rejection of modern technology, including electricity and automobiles; and a day-to-day lifestyle that is quite different from their neighbors'.

In the late 1940s and early 1950s, a large-scale research project conducted in the American Southwest demonstrated how groups living close to one another could differ widely in values. "The Comparative Study of Values in Five Cultures" compared values among five ethnic groups, or communities, in the same geographical area (Barnouw 1985). The study's premise was that each person has a ranked order of value orientations which is influenced by his or her culture and is related to the following:

- The innate nature of humans; i.e., Are people basically good or basically evil?
- The relation of humans to nature; i.e., Do people live subjected to nature, in harmony with nature, or attempting to master nature?
- The nature of time orientation; i.e., Do people live for the past, the present, or the future?
- The modality of human activity; i.e., What is most important: what people are or what people accomplish?
- Humans' relationships to one other; i.e., Do people act as individuals or as a collective?

To each of these questions, respondents were offered a threefold set of answers. For example, to the first question they could answer that human nature may be good, may be a mixture of good and evil, or may be evil. The study found significant differences in values among the five groups.

Although not directly linked to education, the project demonstrated the diversity of values held by peoples living in an area no larger than some public school districts. From the study, we can see the potential for great differences in what groups count as knowledge and what they want for their children in educational systems. For example, differences in values about humans' relationship to nature can lead to conflict over whether students should be required to dissect animals, or more broadly, to how issues about conservation and ecology should be presented. Differences in values about human relationships, such as the degree to which children are obligated to support their parents financially versus their obligation to honor them through school success, have been cited as the reason for wide differences in dropout rates between ethnic groups in the same school district.

The diversity of group values within communities sharing the same educational institutions intensifies the struggles that go on among groups as they debate what is desirable to teach and to learn. Thus the rapid increases in immigration in the last decade and the shifting demographic makeup of some urban areas discussed in earlier chapters serves to acerbate the conflicts over values. Likewise, within specific institutions, particularly in higher education, the admission of new groups is likely to intensify conflict as the numbers assert their values about what should be taught and who should teach it. For example, the admission of women to previously all-male universities and the influence of ethnic studies have brought calls for changes in the core literature, social science, and humanities reading lists. At a few institutions, the scornful term DWEM (dead white European male) signifies how some students and faculty have come to reject the "classics' " domination of core courses.

A number of concepts describe how values shape a society and its institutions, including schools. Here we look at several of these concepts, beginning with national character, which emphasizes that a nation has a single set of values or traits guiding what its citizens do.

National Character

Prompted by the need to understand Japan and Germany during World War 2 and other nations in the Cold War that followed, anthropologists carried out national character studies in the 1940s and 1950s to find the major values and related traits that characterized enemy nations' peoples. With the data from these studies, they offered analyses of the Japanese, Germans, Soviets, and Chinese. These studies stressed the common childhood experiences of members of each society and saw national character as the collective expression of a basic personality type largely determined by these early experiences (Pi-Sunyer and Salzmann 1978). Ruth Benedict laid theoretical groundwork for the national character studies in *Patterns of Culture* (1934) and then wrote one of the most famous studies, *Chrysanthemum and the Sword* (1946), based on her wartime study of Japan. Benedict posited that a single cultural denominator could serve as the key to understanding a culture as a whole. Other descriptions focused on single values (e.g., for Americans, the value of independence) that most influenced a nation's people.

National character studies used limited data, were highly subjective, and ignored the complexity of large, industrialized countries (Haviland 1987). They were generally carried out at a distance, using material from novels, films, and émigré interviews rather than from field-based community studies. Moreover, the studies had overt political goals, first to support the fight against fascism and later to combat Communism.

Among those skeptical about national character studies was anthropologist Ralph Linton. Writing in 1951, Linton pointed out that nations are not as culturally homogeneous as the studies assumed and that the studies had methodological problems, particularly when tested across cultures. Despite criticism and a waning interest in national character studies, the use of the societywide profile continued.

Although the national character concept found limited use, some argue that it supports the notion that complex societies have common or core values. Linton, despite his criticisms, granted that many culture patterns are shared by the members of a modern nation, irrespective of their class or regional differences. From these patterns, he argued, one could deduce the existence of common value systems (Linton 1951). He also pointed out how common values make it possible for members of the group holding power to collaborate to control a nation's course.

Others have carried this position further, contending that a complex society can have a single, dominant culture of which common values are an important element. Arensberg and Niehoff (1975) argue that there is an American culture, largely middle-class and Western European in origin, that has modified itself for conditions in the United States. While acknowledging the existence of cultural pluralism, they point out that all people born and raised in the United States will be conditioned to some degree by this culture and that irrespective of group (i.e., gender, race, class, ethnicity), certain points of similarity will occur more frequently among Americans than among groups of people in other countries.

Arensberg and Niehoff emphasize Americans' conformity in language, diet, hygiene, dress, basic skills, land use, recreation and their limited range of moral, political, social, and economic attitudes. Among America's common cultural values are the importance of material well-being; a propensity for making two-fold judgements (success-failure, moral-immoral); a very high value given to effort, achievement, and success; and support for egalitarianism.

Arensberg and Niehoff rather easily dismiss the influence of groups based on gender, race, class, and ethnicity. In contrast to their view, we have seen that different groups, residing in proximity and participating in the same public institutions, may have very different values. Thus the assumption that the United States has one culture and one value system appears too simple. An approach that uses the concepts of core and peripheral values is more useful in understanding the relationship between groups and education.

Core and Peripheral Values

Attempting to distill societies' most important values, anthropologists have developed the concept of core values as the primary values promoted by a particular culture (Haviland 1987). As this concept emerged in the 1940s and 1950s, it was given other labels: key symbols, focal values, dominant values, and themes (Conversi 1990). All, however, refer to the idea that a few specific values are of particular importance. *Peripheral* describes those values which are of relatively less importance in selecting alternatives and judging what is desirable.

One particular definition asserts that core values represent the values of the entire society; they are described as those patterns of behavior that have become well-defined, institutionalized, and accepted by a society's dominant group. They become "the basis for the standards with which the major institutions of the dominant society evaluate their members. These standards, in turn, become the criteria for giving people opportunities for advancement and other rewards" (Pai 1990, 26). In this line of thinking, core values are the primary values that schools transmit (explicitly or implicitly) through a hidden curriculum to generation after generation of students. In the United States, for example, because personal achievement and success are core values, we expect educational institutions, irrespective of location, sponsorship, or age level, to enculturate students toward success and achievement. Likewise, we expect that educational policy will allocate resources and mandate actions which support such enculturation.

Another approach to core values recognizes the existence of multiple sets of values in complex, multicultural societies such as Australia and the United States (Smolicz 1984). Emphasizing that each group within a larger society has its own values, Smolicz rejects the idea of a single set of values for the entire society. Rather, he maintains that every group has a certain core element which acts as an identifying value for its members. The core value is that particular element from its own culture which the group emphasizes most strongly in contrast to the elements of other groups, including the dominant group. For most cultures, the core value is language, but it may also be based on religion, family network, clan, or race. A culture may also have a hierarchy of core values. However, the existence of individual group core values does not mean that multicultural societies have no overarching national values or character. In societies composed of more than one ethnic group where dominant group and subordinate group have a consensual rather than coercive relationship, each group's core values are subsumed under a set of overarching shared values. The shared values and the core values are in dynamic equilibrium. The existence of this dual system of values allows for an ongoing multiculturalism rather than an assimilation of subordinate groups, or a separation thereof.

Dominant and Variant Values

Kluckhohn and Strodtbeck (1961) offer a concept similar to core and peripheral. They divide values into dominant value orientations and variant value orientations. They believe dominant values have been stressed too much and variant values largely ignored. In their formulation, value orientations are complex, patterned principles resulting from the interplay of the cognitive, the affective, and the directive elements which give order to human acts and thoughts as these relate to solving common human problems. They see value orientations as varying from culture to culture only in how they rank a pattern of universal component parts. Cultures' values systems are not single systems of dominant values, but interlocking networks that differ only in how the same value-orientation alternatives are ordered. According to Kluckhohn and Strodtbeck, the number of human problems for which all cultures must find solutions is limited. Likewise, the solutions to these problems are limited; they vary within a range of possible solutions. All solutions are present in all societies but are differently preferred.

The concepts of core and peripheral (and related dominant and variant) clarify the ongoing struggle within societies between a limited set of core values and the values of that society's multiple groups. When these subordinate groups assert themselves and demand their say in the educational process, then policy-makers and practitioners must broker the competing demands.

From this perspective, the day-to-day work of educational policymakers such as school boards or state legislatures is to allocate group values—transforming cultural values into public policy (Marshall, Mitchell, and Wirt 1989). Some of these values are part of the current political culture. Others are values from the past contained in documents like constitutions, statutes, and codes. Many come from direct demands by racial, ethnic, or other groups. Similarly, the day-to-day work of administrators, counselors, and teachers transforms values into specific practices.

Analysis of educational policy, including policy related to multiculturalism, lends itself to values-based frameworks. For example, Kearney (1990) argues that a values framework provides a useful way to focus on ends and goals of policy. To illustrate how this can be done, he describes the Reagan administration's 1981 elimination of the Emergency School Aid Act (which was designed to assist local districts going through desegregation) and its replacement with block grants. The administration's policy was based on its preference for efficiency and choice over equity.

We now turn to specific values, those of the dominant group as well as those of competing subordinate groups, to see how they shape educational policies and practices.

Major Dimensions of Value Differences

In every society the particular set of values which represents the group in power plays a major role in setting the educational agenda. In the United States these dominant group values are generally those of Anglo-Saxon Protestant culture and are similar to the values that schools tried to inculcate into immigrant children in the late nineteenth and early twentieth century. They are the typical American values people in power invoke when they promote their vision of American society. They relate to broad concerns such as work, mobility, achievement, status, equity, independence, religious beliefs, and individualism. Many intergroup conflicts, not just those related to education, derive from differences related to these values (Tropman 1989).

However, as we discussed earlier in the chapter, there is not simply one set of core values in the United States, nor in any other complex, multicultural society. Rather, throughout the last two centuries numerous subordinate groups have been promoting alternative values and the educational policies and practices derived from them. To examine these values-based struggles between dominant and subordinate groups as they relate to education, we provide a number of contemporary examples.

Hard Work, Economic Success, and Education

In the dominant core value system of the United States, economic success should come to those persons who exert individual effort, including effort applied in school. Therefore, for those who hold this value, an important function of schools is to properly prepare people for jobs and the work force. Those who hold this value support educational policies in which schools teach the skills and attitudes needed to achieve career success.

Reflecting this value, the reform reports and related policies of the early 1980s promoted the schools' role in preparing a hard-working, well-trained work force. Warning of the economic challenge facing the United States in dire, nation-threatening terms, the reports recommended heavier student work loads (added courses and graduation requirements) and increased efforts at monitoring students and teachers, usually through state-mandated tests. From the perspective of dominant group leaders, including governors and business executives, asking schools to more rigorously train young people in skills and attitudes was reasonable and necessary. From the leaders' value perspective, the prerequisite hard work and academic accountability would make the United States' economy stronger and would ensure American industrial competitiveness.

However, in the 1980s the relationship between education, hard work, and the job market looked different to subordinate groups whose members had few opportunities for good jobs. Working-class persons, minority racial and ethnic groups, and women expressed a variety of personal and policy priorities, depending on how they viewed their opportunities in the job market and whether they considered "hard work" in education to benefit their own futures. Historically, for women, African Americans, and other ethnic and racial minorities, a level of completed education compared to that of white males has not brought comparable worth in the workplace.

The relative lack of evident payoff for the effort individuals expend in job-retraining programs demonstrates the basis for rejecting the individual effort value. When the economy faltered in the 1980s, various agencies including community colleges, set up retraining programs to prepare workers for new jobs. Underlying these programs was the same dominant group value: hard work and effort applied in education programs and subsequent job search would lead workers to new, relatively well-paying jobs. Unfortunately, what often occurred was that many workers who applied themselves in training did not find appropriate jobs. The programs assumed that if the unemployed strove for success through retraining they would find jobs related to that training at wages sufficient to support a family. The problem was often not in the seekers' lack of job preparation or lack of effort, but in the economy's scarcity of jobs that paid reasonable wages. Moreover, changing urban patterns meant that African Americans, Hispanics, and others would live far from new job locations as factories and other businesses closed.

Student Mobility and Leaving Others Behind

A dominant value in the United States is socioeconomic mobility; i.e., increasing one's status and income relative to others. This is a belief that upward mobility or "getting ahead" is possible for everyone, both individuals and groups. In the quest for upward mobility, Americans are expected to sacrifice personal ties, including at times, friendship. It is not unusual for youth to break off school friendships or group ties as they move on and away to college, or from college to career.

Subordinate groups' values concerning mobility and getting ahead often differ from those held by the dominant group in a way that directly impacts education and intergroup relations within a school. The dominant group's monopoly on mobility and the subordinate group's perception that they are locked into their status are the key factors. Moving from high school to college provides an example. Those with resources have greater opportunity to choose among colleges; the colleges people attend, in turn, often determine not only the quality of education but also the graduates' ability to move into selected careers. A peer group formed in a prestigious university may assure a lifetime of support and all but guarantee occupational success. Among subordinate groups with few resources, peer groups also play an important support function but cannot supply the contacts to insure socioeconomic success.

In an earlier chapter we make reference to information from ethnographic studies in high schools which suggests that some African Americans may fear being accused of "acting white" if they demonstrate academic effort and success. Thus to retain an identity and acceptance with peers, these students consider certain symbols, behavior, activities, and meanings inappropriate for them and adopt their own, building a boundary between themselves and the dominant group, even at the cost of not achieving what from the outside appear to be the skills they need for upward mobility. Those who cross the boundary may be seen as the enemy (Ford and Ogbu 1986). However, for these young people mobility as acted on in school is not as important a value as maintaining group identity. From the inside—from the perspective of these students—we see that adapting to behavior which is based on dominant group values may not be as important as the emotional or social rewards received from continuing group membership.

Achieved Status, Ascribed Status, and Equity

Dominant values that support both achieved status and equity in education are the source of continuing group conflict in the United States. Status refers to a person's sense of self-worth and is based on respect and acceptance in society. An important American value is that people should earn their status through their own achievements, not through inherited wealth or family name. In reality, social class, education, occupation, and power all contribute to status. Nevertheless, Americans tend to support (at least nominally) policies based on the notion that everyone, including students, should earn status through their own efforts. At the same time, the value most people place on achieved status is balanced by the value they give to equity—the idea that every person deserves a fair shake, no matter what they have or have not achieved in life. The equity value leads to policies which guarantee equal opportunity and equal access to public institutions and resources. Over the last few decades the coexistence of the two values has produced an *excellence versus equity* debate that is important to multiculturalism and education.

The push for achievement can be seen in the 1950s, when a concern for excellence improved the teaching of science and mathematics following the Soviet Union's surprising launch of its first space satellite. A similar concern for excellence in the 1980s pushed many states to set higher standards in math, reading, and science to compete with Japan and Germany. The influence of the equity value on the other hand has been provided by Supreme Court decisions in support of desegregation, beginning with *Brown* v. *Board of Education* in 1954, and continuing with federal programs such as Head Start in the 1960s.

In the 1980s school reform efforts emphasizing excellence continued the conflict between excellence and equity. Public demands for educational excellence increased the pressure for improved student outcomes and burdened the professional preparation of teachers with more standardized testing, competency testing, and academic preparation. Critics sympathetic to equity argued that these measures, while designed to improve excellence, reduced equity, particularly when such policies led to lower numbers of minority teachers (Marcoulides and Heck 1990).

Moreover, the reformers were also criticized for their attempts to legislate student excellence with more required tests, added course loads, longer hours, and more homework, without giving schools the resources they need to nurture excellence. Critics claimed the reforms gave lip service to equity and that for dominant political and economic groups, excellence meant only minimally raising the skills of the poor to assure the nation's future economic growth through a low-cost, competitive workforce (Howe 1987).

As a nation, few efforts were made to support the equity value. In mid-1980s there were large inequalities in funding for education. Alaska, Wyoming, and New Jersey each spent more than $3,500 per pupil per year; Arkansas, Kentucky, Mississippi, South Carolina, Tennessee, and Utah each spent less than $2,000 per student (Johnson, Collins, Dupuis, and Johansen 1988, 247). Moreover, the reforms' concern for excellence did little to alter the allocation of resources to subordinate socioeconomic groups. To take Pennsylvania as an example, in 1989 the 53 poorest districts (many of them either rural communities or mill towns) spent an average of $1,752 per student per year on regular instruction; the wealthiest 53 districts, $2,880. Far fewer (50 percent) of the students in the poorer districts than those in the wealthier districts (80 percent) planned to get a post-secondary education (Center for Rural Pennsylvania 1991, 6, 13).

The equity value, in support of cultural pluralism and multicultural education, peaked in the late 1970s and early 1980s. In 1977 the National Council on Accreditation of Teacher Education set multicultural requirements for teacher education program accreditation. *A Nation at Risk* and the numerous reports that followed made little mention of multicultural education.

Values related to status are more complex than simple endorsement of achieved status. There is also value given to ascribed status, which is based on characteristics such as family heritage, gender, race, and social class rather than on accomplishments. Americans have frequently ascribed lesser status to members of minority ethnic groups, women, religious minorities, and persons with physical or mental disabilities, irrespective of their actual capabilities and achievements. Even while claiming to judge people on the basis of performance, employers have paid minorities and women less for doing the same job. In education as in many other institutions in society, some persons, depending on the characteristics assigned to their group, are more likely to be given rewards than are others. A case in point is in women's athletics.

Title IX, the federal Education Amendment Congress passed two decades ago, forbids discrimination based on gender. However, in the twenty years since its passage, although the number of women participating in high school and college sports has risen significantly, the number of women coaches has fallen dramatically. Men have moved into many of the positions coaching women's teams that were formerly held by women. Studies show that male administrators cite the lack of qualified women as the reason for the decline in female coaches and that they perceive women as less qualified. They apparently ascribe to male applicants skills and experience which male coaches have not actually achieved. In fact, research shows that women are at least as qualified as men to coach; they have more professional experience, more experience coaching women, and more formal training. Thus the decline in female coaches under conditions that should have led to improvement for women in high school and college athletics springs in part, from a value held by male decision-makers which assigns capability by group membership and not by performance.

In an arena where many groups and values compete, equity is not always easy. At times, solutions to rectify negative status ascribed to one group may appear to impinge on the claims of others. A case in point involves the academies for African American males in Detroit, Milwaukee, and other cities, as well as the opposition to these academies by those who believe the all-male approach discriminates against females. To their supporters, the all-male academies, which are often associated with an Afrocentric curriculum and which have strong male role models, are the sorely needed solution to saving young, at-risk African American men in the inner city. To others, this approach short changes young women. Each group has rallied its forces in the struggle by those supporting the academies calling on a conservative administration in Washington for endorsement and by both groups using the courts (Walsh 1991).

Another issue related to status and equity values is that of educational tracking. Most schools divide students by ability and offer two or three levels of instruction with varying curricula, based on the belief that students learn best when they have classmates who are not too far advanced for them and who do not move too slowly. However, despite the value placed on individualism, support for the effectiveness of tracking has waned in recent years. As its usefulness is called into question, many proponents have resorted to value-based arguments to support its rejection or its retention. Calls for the elimination of tracking are often based on egalitarian, or equity, values; calls for the retention of tracking are based on values-related individualism. An important factor in the tracking issue is disproportionate representation of some racial and ethnic groups in lower tracks. For example, one large-scale study found in eighth grade

English classes that 40 percent of Asian students and 32 percent of white students were in high ability tracks, but only 15 percent of African American students and 9 percent of Native American students were so grouped (Braddock 1988).

Independence and Conformity

The dominant value of independence demonstrates many Americans' desire for freedom from constraints; the value of conformity harkens back to a long tradition of Puritanism and expectations that people act within strict community morality. In education, Americans have valued independence from control by large bureaucracies, while at the same time they have expected conformity from students and teachers vis-à-vis community norms and behaviors. For over a century Americans have maintained local control over schools, restricting the role of the federal government and giving decision-making power to thousands of school boards.

These values of independence and conformity have sometimes conflicted with educational equality for subordinate groups. In response, the federal government's actions on behalf of equal treatment have restricted the power of local school boards and have forced local communities to implement policies and practices which have not conformed with local custom (Kirst 1984). Court ordered desegregation is a prime example. In numerous cases, federal court-ordered integration and later busing has led to violence in and around public schools, as white parents physically resisted the implementation of judges' orders. The expectation by many parents that schools would conform to local norms about race contributed to the resistance. Indeed, much of the resistance to continued school desegregation has been couched in terms of states' rights, a political manifestation of the independence value.

The value placed at once on independence and on conformity leads to great variation in school policy in nonacademic matters, working to the detriment of subordinate groups. School districts' development and implementation of policies on AIDS is a case in point. In the mid-1980s school districts across the United States, confronted with establishing policies on HIV-positive students, worked independently, unaware of the guidelines developed by the National Center for Disease Control. "It is odd," Kirp and Epstein write, "that each school district has to take up the AIDS question largely on its own. Even in a country that stresses localism in education, it is striking how much each community has been left to sink or swim; there is nothing approaching a national vision or a national consensus" (Kirp and Epstein 1989, 587). They cite a Georgia town whose AIDS policy virtually isolated not only AIDS victims but also their families as a particularly unfortunate case of the independent approach.

The value placed on conformity has generated conflict over school policy related to student behavior. Despite the value many Americans give to independence, students are expected to conform to local mores. Although the Supreme Court declared in 1969 that bans on political expression by students were unconstitutional provided the activity was not disruptive, schools have continued to try to limit student activity and expression, often in the guise of preventing violence. For example, in the early 1990s administrators in one Louisiana district prohibited politically related buttons and clothing as well as clothing with unpatriotic logos. Backpacks whose contents were not visible were also banned. Ironically, the situation came to a head over a piece of clothing related to a contemporary multicultural conflict. In order to obtain the right to wear a T-shirt that read, "Columbus Didn't Discover America, He Conquered It," a student, with the help of the American Civil Liberties Union, had to threaten to sue the district (Chealcalos 1992).

Individualism and Community

A strong value in the United States is individualism, which emphasizes each person's importance and independence. Using this value to choose what is desirable, parents and schools may seek individual therapies for children's learning difficulties, treat behavior problems with counseling, or have high regard for individualized instruction. On the level of policy, the rights of individual persons, families, and groups take on great importance.

The value differences around individualism lead to difficult policy choices. Schools inculcate the common values and related knowledge in a democratic society, which may or may not be those of the individual family, raising the question of whose values should be served if the community at large and individuals (or individual groups) are in conflict. Many argue that given this conflict, it is essential that parents have the right to educate their children as they see fit. Yet at the very time individualism is honored, educators also struggle with how to pass on the common values needed to support and continue the American political system. Benedict (1943) was among the first to do so in an article in which she argued for the importance of transmitting America's democratic heritage to the nation's children.

Throughout almost two centuries of public education in the United States subordinate groups have taken several strategies when faced with public schools they perceived as not properly educating their children. At times, groups have struggled for change, often through the courts or the political process. Parents of special needs' children are one example of a group who won better special education programs through legal challenges and political pressure.

In many cases, groups have established schools where they can pass on their own values to their children. In an earlier chapter we discussed the most massive of these efforts, that of the Roman Catholic church. Some of these schools were not only Catholic, but centered on parishes that were ethnically homogeneous, providing immigrants with control over how their language and ethnic heritage was instilled in their children. A less noble example is the private academies established in the 1950s and 1960s by white parents who did not want their children to attend schools that were integrating across the South.

The impetus to establish private schools is often based on parents' desires for improved academics, for a more moral environment, for firmer discipline, and for the opportunity to teach their children religious or other beliefs that they do not get in public schools. Among the many such schools today are Muslim day schools, established largely in urban areas, enrolling the children of African Americans who converted to Islam and the children of recent immigrants from Muslim countries. Islamic studies and Arabic are part of the curriculum and the school day is built around the noon prayer (Goldman 1992). Japanese, Chinese, and other groups have established similar schools that meet late in the afternoon or on weekends as an adjunct to public education.

The legal support for private schools and the values that back them lie in a 1925 Supreme Court decision which pitted the Catholic Church against an Oregon law requiring public school attendance. *Pierce v. Society of Sisters* established a compromise: public schools could inculcate common values, while dissenters could attend private schools. However, parents would have to pay for these schools and the state would maintain some supervision over the general shape of the curriculum and matters such as safety and health.

The Pierce case arose as America was growing more urban and complex, complicating the original values-inculcation function of the common school in small communities. The Court's decision offered a workable solution, although one which mistakenly assumed that all parents who might wish to educate their children with values different from those guiding public schools had the financial ability to do so.

Because not all groups have equal access to private education, some have suggested that vouchers are one solution to ensure that racial and ethnic minorities and other subordinate groups have the same access to opt out of public education as dominant groups. Massive use of vouchers, however, would potentially draw large numbers of students from the public schools, thereby undermining their ability to transmit majority cultural views, a dilemma for democracy. One possible solution may be to provide tuition vouchers to students who dissent strongly from the values taught in public schools to allow them to attend private schools (Rebell 1989).

Moralism and Religion

Despite the waning influence of many mainline religious groups in the United States, the influence of religion in education continues. Berger argues that religiously based values continue to come into the public life of the nation and that the Constitution, as it has come to be interpreted, while perhaps separating church and state, has not separated religion and politics. Although the Protestant social and cultural establishment has declined, the new secular humanist elite is not dominant either. Instead, the United States continues to be religious, with rising evangelicalism, increasing Catholicism (including a Latin American variety coming with immigration), robust Judaism, and numerous Asian religions (Berger 1986). This implies that conflicts between groups over religiously inspired values and related issues will continue to enter education.

In the United States there has been a connection between the emphasis on moralism and the close association of religion and religious organizations to education. This association has a long history. Religious instruction was a primary reason for founding schools in the American colonies, and state support for organized religion was not unusual in the first decades of the United States (e.g., New York State subsidized church-operated schools from 1795–1825). However, in the first half of the nineteenth century, growing pluralism led to a reduction in state support for religious education. The fight for and against funding for religious (increasingly Catholic) schools became a partisan political issue in the last half of the century, and plans under which some states paid religious school teachers' salaries or funded the construction of parochial school buildings were declared unconstitutional. In the mid-twentieth century the practice of allowing children to attend religious education (often in the public school building) for a portion of the school day spread to almost all the states. By the late 1940s thirteen states required bible reading in the schools. However, required bible reading (and prayer) was struck down in the 1960s by the Supreme Court; then there was a renewed effort to restore them in the early 1980s (Reichley 1985).

Conflicts over religious values and what should be taught have frequently been taken to the Supreme Court. But when fundamentalists have brought suit against the use of what they believe are anti-religious textbooks, the courts have supported school officials. The courts have tended to give school authorities broad control over educational matters (Larsen 1991). Nevertheless, religious groups continue to vie for influence with some efforts focused on getting on school boards through campaigns waged in churches.

In addition to conflicts over the specific teaching or practice of religion in school, many of the most bitter conflicts in schools today represent group conflict—sometimes well organized—between conservative religious organizations and other parent or educational groups. Such group conflict is not new; early in the century similar conflicts raged over the teaching of evolution. Today, the issues often relate to teaching about homosexuality, controlling the morality of books in the library, and providing abortion and contraception information. There are continuing efforts to get books removed from library shelves, sometimes because of the mere mention of practices fundamentalists deem to be outside their religious practice. Children's books which describe the lives of immigrant groups, such as the Chinese, have been particularly susceptible to these attacks if they contain references to non-Christian religious rites.

In New York City appeals to conservative religious values were part of a conflict which developed over a multicultural curriculum that teaches first graders to accept gay people. The local district school board located in a diverse district that has a large immigrant population (49 percent Hispanic, 27 percent white, 18 percent Asian, 6 percent black) rejected the Board of Education curriculum guide, because they felt it gave a positive picture of gay relationships, thereby undercutting parents' moral and religious values (Myers 1992). However, opposition was far from universal, and some immigrant parents lamented the rejection of a curriculum which they felt could help their children adjust to school in a new society. Churches and organized evangelical groups were among those involved in the conflict, supporting the rejection of the new curriculum.

Increasingly, it is clear that attacks on gay rights and other moral crusades from right-wing fundamentalists are not the individual expression of value differences by parents in isolated schools or schools districts. Rather, these conservative values are often promoted by nationally organized, well-funded groups with a clear political agenda. For example, the 1992 Oregon ballot measure that would have required public schools and other government entities to actively discourage homosexuality was promoted locally by groups including the Oregon Association of Evangelicals, but was supported nationally by organizations such as Reverend Pat Robertson's Christian Coalition (Sommerfield 1992). Here as elsewhere, other groups holding very different values organized to oppose the ballot measure, among them mainline religious denominations.

Schools are but one institution that educates and enculturates the young. In many societies youth organizations supplement schools with nonformal education for children and youth (see La Belle 1981). In the United States conservative religious groups exert particular power over organizations such as the Boy Scouts, which receive funds through the United Way charitable giving campaign and establish a public status by using community facilities such as school auditoriums. Influenced by religious groups who sponsor many local troops, the Scouts and other nonformal education groups have limited admission and leadership on the basis of gender, sexual preference, and religious belief.[2] Recent court cases involving the Scouts demonstrate conservative religion's influence in policies and pratices: In 1991 several Illinois families sued the Cub Scouts for not admitting their sons because the boys did not express belief in God. In Miami courts took up the case of an 8-year-old girl who wished to attend a summer Boy Scout camp. In California there was a long-standing suit by a gay man who had been dismissed as a Scout leader. In these and other cases the Mormon and Catholic churches exerted strong influence to uphold the Scouts' right to keep certain people out, particularly homosexuals. Scout officials who wished to change the organization's regulations faced strong opposition from the churches, especially from the Mormons, who refused to make basic changes in the Scout's values (Hinds 1990).

Families, School Policies, and Value Conflicts

Conflict based on group values surfaces in many areas of education, including discipline, classroom management, extracurricular activities, and the relationship of the community to the school. Sometimes the conflict centers around the differences in dominant group values as represented by the policies and practices in a particular school or system and by the expectations and behavior of children who come from families who are members of groups with very different values. The clash in values is often reflected in high dropout rates, school failure, and underachievement by Native Americans, Hispanics, African Americans, and various immigrant groups. Kasten (1992) cautions that there are many groups of Native Americans which have their own cultures, but also suggests that there are broadly held Native American values which conflict with those of Anglo-dominated schools. For example, Anglo teachers often use adult-initiated confrontation, which Native American children find at odds with their value system, where confrontation is inappropriate. Likewise, Anglo educational practice, unlike Native American culture, is based on values that support the urgency of talk and the importance of tight scheduling. If these practices conflict with the values Native American children learn at home, children may be wrongly judged uninterested in learning, or irresponsible, putting them at risk for school failure.

Not all values conflicts relate directly to classroom instruction or management. Some involve the relationship between families, the community, and the school. Groups' values differ, for example, on how much information families should share with educational institutions. Recently, school districts with large immigrant populations have reported losses of federal funds for school lunches, because many parents (including recent Russian arrivals in New York City who have immigrated from societies with a history of control over individuals) refuse to return forms asking for school lunch eligibility information such as family size and household income. In some schools even telephone calls in the parents' language and meetings at the school to explain the purpose of the forms have not resolved the situation (Richardson 1992).

In some cases, particularly for immigrant families, the opportunities to voice values related to education are limited. Many do not speak English and have little experience with the school system their children attend. For them, dealing with the educational institutions can be a new and unfamiliar experience. In Los Angeles the largest immigrant group is from Mexico. Hayes (1992) describes how Mexican immigrant parents, who give high value to a good education for their children, often are not aware of the substandard education their children receive. Thus they do not publicly articulate their strong value for education nor do they voice more specific concerns about school policies and practices.

Value Change and Educational Change: International Examples

We have seen that the values of the dominant group shape the educational agenda, but the changes are made among a constant set of negotiations with other less powerful segments of the society. However, under some conditions radical political changes bring about a rapid shift in prevailing values as one group and its values replace the heretofore dominant group. From the 1950s through the 1970s such transformations occurred fairly frequently in struggles against colonial powers or in revolutions in countries such as Algeria, China, Cuba, Ethiopia, Iran, Mozambique, and Nicaragua (La Belle and Ward 1990). Following these political transformations, the societies' educational systems generally changed in similar ways.

In all these countries except Iran, the radical political changes shifted values toward increased equity. As a result, access to the formal education systems expanded. The expansion brought in more students and altered entry criteria such that previously underrepresented groups would be accepted in larger numbers. For example, China, Cuba, and Nicaragua brought more workers and peasants into their educational institutions. In addition to expanding access by social class, most societies established policies that called for increased participation by women. In Iran, whose new government represented conservative religious values, access to education was limited. New criteria for admission to education included military service, Islamic morality, and gender (Afshar 1985).

Changes in curriculum reflect how these radically transformed societies used the educational system to transmit their own values. In most cases, new governments moved quickly to bring their ideology into the curriculum. For example, immediately after assuming power, China's new government eliminated courses on Confucian ethics and on the old government's philosophy; put Mao's writings and Communist Party documents into the curriculum; and added courses such as dialectical materialism and political economy.

Even as regimes changed curricula to reflect ideological and nationalistic values, they had to deal with their needs for trained work forces. As a result, most of the countries placed a relatively high value on technological and scientific training. Even in Iran, where the humanities were criticized for being too Western and where much of the curriculum was injected with religious material, science textbooks changed very little.

Along with the curricular changes were major changes in educational personnel. Each of these societies needed to build a teaching force whose values coincided with those of the new regime. There were often reductions made in the hiring of foreign teachers, in the training of new teachers, and in some cases, in the ideological retraining of existing teachers.

Conclusion

Several points can be made about intergroup relations, values, and their relation to education. First, the conflicts based on differing group values can be extremely bitter. Parents, and the group to which they belong, compete to pass on a way of life, and the most basic beliefs about what is important, to their children. Thus for some parents whether or not to introduce information about abortions to high school students is not simply one more policy decision. For some it means advising young people on how to commit murder; for others it means giving young women the freedom to control their lives and bodies. For many, there is no middle ground.

Second, proposals for new policies or practices may bring several core values, and the groups holding them, into competition, leaving policymakers with difficult choices: groups which are supportive of one other on most issues may find themselves in conflict; e.g., the case of academies for African American males discussed earlier in this chapter. Some school boards and community organizations have supported such academies in an era when many young African American men are evidently at risk. On the other hand, organizations such as the American Civil Liberties Union and the National Organization of Women's Legal Defense and Education Fund have opposed the academies on an equity basis, arguing that single-sex academies provide opportunities for males which are not offered for females. Ironically, the conservative, Heritage Foundation, has supported the academies because they provided choice by a local community (Miller 1991).

Finally, efforts at increasing diversity, including implementing multicultural curricula, opening systems to participation by more groups, and stressing equity, may bring more conflict, not less, as groups become aware that publicly articulating their values can influence schools and raise the power of their group in the educational arena. On the other hand, as long as dominant group values prevail and guide policy in a district or in an institution, change efforts may be stymied and groups may become silent and inactive. We see in Los Angeles, an example of the increased group assertiveness and resulting conflict that accompanies the opening of a system. Following the retirement of the long-time Anglo superintendent in the early 1990s, an intense debate broke out between supporters of an African American candidate and the supporter of a Hispanic candidate. African Americans, discriminated against in the past, called for the selection of an African American for the position. At the same time Hispanics, growing as a percentage of the city's population called for the selection of a Hispanic (Mydans 1992).

We have discussed how group values influence educational policy and practice. Whatever these policies and practices, individual educational professionals and institutions must develop educational strategies and methods to use when groups and values compete. In the next section we consider various approaches to social change and pedagogy in multicultural settings.

Part 4

Multiculturalism, Education, and Change

CHAPTER 7

Education and Alternative Strategies for Social, Economic, and Political Change

Introduction

Socioeconomic differences among and between racial and ethnic groups remains a major issue facing most countries. These differences are usually associated with differential levels of school achievement, discriminatory barriers barring access to decision-making positions in the political structure, and participation in the job market beyond the entry level among others. As people continue to leave rural areas for city living in most areas of the world, they often end up living in urban poverty, segregated by jobs, housing, and schooling, which, in turn, shapes and reinforces economic and ethnic divisions.

In the United States the 1990 census showed that African Americans were more than twice as likely as whites to be unemployed, were much less likely to work in managerial and professional jobs, and on average were earning 56 percent of whites' incomes. African Americans in 1990 were also three times more likely to live in poverty; they had an average net worth which was only 10 percent that of whites. The 1990 census also showed that the recession of the 1980s had a more negative impact on minority groups. For example, from 1980–1990 Mexican Americans' income fell 13 percent and African Americans' fell 7 percent, while the earnings of whites remained at about the 1980 level.

The growing economic disparity among groups can also be seen in the widening gap between rich and poor and in the decline in the middle class. The 1990 census showed that the lowest 20 percent of United States' households got just under 4.0 percent of total income while the highest 20 percent got 46.5 percent of total income, an increase over 1970 and 1980. During the 1980s the poorest 40 percent of American families saw their incomes drop. In 1979, 12 percent of full-time workers were earning less than the minimum poverty threshold whereas in 1990, 18 percent were earning below that same threshold. Wage rates (in constant dollars) among the less skilled have been falling steadily during past decades, and there has been an overall salary decrease for less skilled workers.

Most agree that income differences reflect other social ills and are intimately related to political power and socioeconomic status. These include prejudice and discrimination among individuals and groups resulting in differential opportunities and social and economic mobility. Some also argue that urban violence is closely associated with economic differences. Others find that those living in poverty lack the knowledge, skills, and work-related attitudes and values to successfully compete in schools and the workplace. All such observations point to the continuing challenge of identifying public and private strategies to combat social, political, and economic disparities through systematic education, capital investment, and various forms of social action—some at the community level and others which transcend community boundaries.

The Atlanta Project

In this regard, the 1990s have found various levels of government, along with numerous private voluntary agencies, giving new attention to poverty, discrimination, and its associated problems. In Georgia, for example, former President Jimmy Carter has launched the Atlanta Project, a community effort to address the despair and hopelessness associated with some 500,000 poor people, primarily African Americans, who live in and around the city. Accompanying the poverty are homelessness, unemployment, teenage pregnancy, lack of health and effective schooling, crime, drugs, and so on. A majority of the families are headed by women, are on welfare, live in substandard housing, suffer from chronic unemployment and are incarcerated at rates far beyond what their ethnic or racial group represent as a percentage of the total population. A special problem apparent in Atlanta, yet common in many other areas as well, is the frequency of low-paying service sector jobs among the poor, (e.g., fast food attendants, housecleaners, retail clerks) which employ many but provide few benefits, little security, and low compensation. The service sector of Atlanta's economy grew by 24 percent between 1985 and 1992.

Atlanta, like most other urban areas in the United States, can document the initiatives it has taken with private and public, state and federal assistance, to address the issues of poverty during the last hundred years. Before 1900 in Atlanta there was a dependence on private charity to respond to poverty. At the turn of the century federal legislation limited labor exploitation and child labor. Subsequently, social security, unemployment insurance, Aid to Families with Dependent Children, Medicare, Medicaid, and Head Start formed the foundations for the city to address the problems of the most needy. In the 1980s, however, the safety net under the poor was cut by a wave of conservatism in the country; the effects of this lack of attention to the poor ultimately reached a crisis point in the early 1990s. The need for career-oriented work opportunities, the proliferation of substandard housing, and the lack of subsidized childcare and universal health insurance became more visible and were identified as priorities for responding to poverty. In the 1990s the affluent and politically powerful became willing to find strategies to ensure long-lasting change in the distribution of power and income.

The basis for the Atlanta Project is instructive, because it represents a recent attempt to employ a long-standing change strategy which will address the problems associated with inner-city urban areas. By clustering neighborhoods around high schools as coordinating centers, and by pairing corporate, educational, and other partners with the various clusters, the Atlanta Project includes and attempts to go beyond soup kitchens, homeless shelters, food stamps, job referral centers, car pools, housing assistance, schools in juvenile detention centers, and emergency health care by proposing more permanent solutions. Such solutions are thought to be found through creating partnerships between civic volunteers and local institutions, and those who are disadvantaged. The Project calls for greater collaboration among federal, state, and local government organizations; the elimination of bureaucratic and legal obstacles to change; the formulation of overarching plans for implementing approaches to community empowerment; the creation of jobs and job training; and a variety of educational programs. Limiting the effort are scarce resources; the program primarily depends on coordinating existing governmental resources and private sources with a massive infusion of volunteers from collaborating organizations. An early achievement of the project was the involvement of some 8,000 volunteers in spring 1993 for the immunization against diseases of nearly 17,000 poor children. Because the Project sought its initial funding from the same public and private sources to which long-standing social assistance programs in the city were accustomed, new relationships with contributors were formed to create additional funding streams.

What is being attempted in Atlanta is not without numerous precedents. Throughout the world there is a long history of efforts to raise educational levels, improve job training and opportunities, build community infrastructure, and generally raise the quality of inner-city living through external assistance and self-help strategies. Much of this history involves the use of formal and nonformal education as a means to cure such ills.

Such education is intended to deliver skills and knowledge to help the poor compete more effectively for jobs; to build attitudes and knowledge among the poor which will help them address the social ills facing their communities; and perhaps most importantly, to motivate and provide information to those from the dominant group whose volunteerism, political support, and financial assistance might make the difference in how a poor community approaches their goals.

Although education is associated with higher earnings for individuals, alone it has proven rather impotent when confronted with economic, social, and political barriers to change. Thus many strategies rely on economically oriented actions, including raising minimum wages, providing incentives for out-of-work individuals to pursue education and other forms of self-development, launching massive public works programs for job creation and community enhancement, providing loans or other incentives for small business development, and offering tax credits to entrepreneurs in "enterprise zones" so that firms can create mostly entry-level jobs. Other strategies depend on achieving political access to decision-making roles or increasing societal pressure to enhance quality of life indicators.

The interest in community and social action activity, and the challenges facing education in addressing the questions of poverty across cultural boundaries, justify the basis for this chapter. We explore the issue of social change, emphasizing working within the existing system and challenging the status quo. Our intention is to provide an analysis of common assumptions, goals, and strategies for involving education in approaches to social change in multicultural environments, with an emphasis on increasing equal opportunity and the likelihood of greater individual and group access to societal resources.

Social Change: Assumptions and Approaches

All societies are constantly undergoing change, much of which is due to unanticipated events, such as natural disasters. Even more of the change may be due to the unanticipated consequences of events, such as satellite communication, electronic mail, the fax machine, and the video camera, to name but a few forms of media which have impacted the way information has been accessed and transmitted throughout the world in recent years. We are concerned with planned change—the design of interventions that are expected to alter individual and social behavior. Thus although the various forms of media mentioned above might be associated with change, we are concerned with how to design and employ them as part of educational strategies.

There is no single theory of planned social, political, or economic change. Further, there is no single way to enhance the quality of life of the poor over a sustained period of time, i.e., to increase their socioeconomic status and their access to societal resources. To guide our discussion, therefore, we suggest two dimensions of concern: the first is an axis of change and the second, an axis of strategy. The axis of change is represented by a bipolar continuum which at one end reflects individuals and groups seeking ways to acclimate (slowly, through small steps) to current economic and political realities, thus ensuring that the social system remains in *equilibrium*. At the other end of the change continuum are individuals and groups seeking to increase access to economic and political resources—seeking to radically realign control over resources—often through confrontation and thus *conflict* with the goals of other individuals or groups.

From the equilibrium perspective, change is accomplished through adaptations to internal and external pressures, including the interests and expressed needs of others. Alternatively, the conflict perspective assumes that if one group achieves the power and control it desires, another group will be limited in achieving the same goals. From the conflict perspective, change corresponds to realignment of the balance of power. In the equilibrium paradigm, education serves the goal of stability and balance by preparing individuals to take positions in the economy and polity. For example, job preparation and basic literacy programs might facilitate the employment of the poor, while voter registration drives might enhance their participation as citizens. From the conflict perspective, education is used as a means to challenge the norms and values of an elite-dominated, maintenance-oriented society either by enhancing awareness and supporting organizations to challenge existing social structures, or (in certain countries of the world) by fomenting violent revolution. In the discussion that follows, we use a *human capital* approach to reflect the equilibrium position on change and a combination of *revitalization* and *new social movement* approaches to reflect the conflict position.

The strategy axis is also a continuum which at one end is highly *prescriptive*, i.e., "top-down," and at the other end, highly *participatory*, i.e., "bottom-up," focusing on the empowerment of the citizen/learner/activist. An emphasis on prescriptive methods places attention on centralized control and planning of curricula and thus on what is taught and who does the teaching. In this method the learner is treated as an object of the instructional program and as such is to be infused with values, skills, and knowledge that are determined by others. On the opposite end of the continuum, the participatory strategy seeks to involve participants in their own teaching and learning either for purposes of adapting to the existing society or for purposes of questioning and changing self and society. In the participatory strategy the learner is regarded as a subject, a protagonist in the learning process who contributes to the vision, adds to the strategies, and helps design the pedagogy and curricula; and the teacher facilitates rather than directs the educational experience. Given these change and strategy orientations—*equilibrium* to *conflict* and *prescription* to *participation*—Figure 1 plots three program types along the change axis.

One end of the change axis is the human capital approach, which is dominant among programs in the United States, and most likely among programs in the world. It is closely associated with a capitalist economy and intended to make relatively minor adaptations in the political and economic system. Often associated with the "trickle-down" perspective on socioeconomic development

FIGURE 1

Social Change Strategies

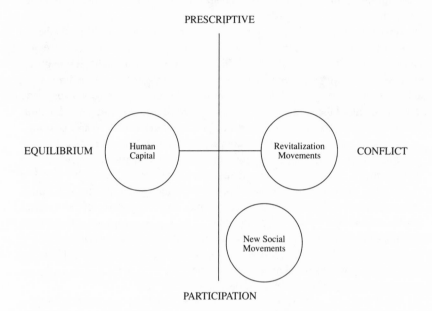

is the intent to create an expanding economy through which individuals secure access to a variety of employment opportunities and higher wages, thereby ensuring an increased standard of living through better quality goods and services. Assuming that the human capital approach represents the equilibrium side of the change axis, the opposite end is represented by revitalization and new social movements geared toward a rebalancing of some economic, but primarily social and political, power. In some countries conflict-oriented revitalization movements result in true revolutions, as has recently occurred in Eastern Europe, where the economic and political system has undergone radical upheavals. In other instances new social movements, oriented toward issues like environmental preservation and enhancement of the overall quality of life, challenge the status quo and are geared to larger, societally based interests.

The human capital approach has a decidedly economic bias while the revitalization and new social movement approaches are more politically and socially motivated. The challenge is to bring these economic, political, and social approaches together in ways that will benefit the poor and disenfranchised. As we discuss these three avenues of change, we will point to some of the educational implications by drawing on both prescriptive and participation-oriented approaches to the strategies employed.

Human Capital

The expansion of job opportunities associated with the human capital approach depends on industrial growth, which involves the processing of raw materials (e.g., steel mills, oil refineries) and investment in manufacturing, agriculture, and the extraction of minerals. The fallout, or effects of such growth, are referred to as "trickle-down", because as the economy grows, opportunities are supposed to expand and the socioeconomically poor are supposed to be provided more productive, better-compensated jobs. Accompanying this increase in economic standing, are expected increases in social status and political participation.

Within this industrial growth model the role of education is to develop workers who fall in line with Adam Smith's statement that a nation's prosperity is determined mainly "by the skill, dexterity, and judgment with which its labour is generally applied." This statement recognizes what economists in the 1950s and 1960s referred to as "human capital"; a concern with the work force and its contribution to economic development. The orthodox economic assumptions underlying the human capital approach state that: product and labor markets are competitive; firms attempt to maximize profits; workers seek to maximize earnings; and the labor force has both knowledge and mobility to take advantage of the best opportunities available.

These assumptions mistakenly treat the labor market as essentially homogenous, determining salaries by the interaction of supply and demand and paying workers in accordance with his or her contribution to a firm's production. This orthodox perspective on the economy assumes that both employers and employees benefit mutually from their investment and work. This is also only partially true. Finally, within this set of assumptions, worker's skills and abilities are held to be at least partially responsible for a worker's productivity and are expected to benefit him or her through employment opportunities, wages, and economic security.

Despite the fact that when the economy grows, job opportunities increase and the poverty rate sometimes falls, the industrial growth model is typically not judged successful based on the distribution of profits but based on national indicators, like the Gross National Product. Thus relatively less attention is placed on who benefits or on the distribution of the profits associated with the growth. When the economy fails to grow or grows slowly, as it did in the 1980s and early 1990s, unemployment increases; competition for jobs among the unskilled and semiskilled and new immigrants is more pronounced; poverty increases; and the restructuring of the labor market pushes many low-wage earners out of work, because cost-saving approaches and the adoption of new technology require higher skills. The result is often inequality and poverty, especially among the culturally different, who are overly represented at the lower skilled levels.

Part of the problem associated with the human capital approach involves the assumptions on which it is based. For example, the labor force is not always as mobile or knowledgeable as it is assumed to be, and its power base may be inadequate when its interests conflict with the interests of owners; and individuals or groups may not be paid in accordance with the contribution made to a company's profits. The economy may expand, therefore, but the benefits may not "trickle down" to most workers. Thus the disparities among rich and poor, as the above statistics from the 1990 census indicate, may expand with the industrial growth.

As the processing of raw materials and the manufacturing of machinery and equipment for the industrial sector and its subsidiaries go forward in an expanding economy, it is necessary that cheap labor be available to fill the need for production. In the United States much of the labor for industrial manufacturing, especially the lesser skilled labor, has come from ethnic minority groups and recent immigrants. Because the success of industrial growth depends on keeping the size and cost of the labor force low, it has been traditionally within the industrialist's interest to promote a reserve set of potential wage earners who are ready to assume the responsibilities of those who currently are employed. For some firms this has meant actively combating labor union movements either by recruiting nonunion labor or by moving to other countries where labor costs are low, thereby challenging domestic workers in the United States to accept lower wages. In the 1980s and 1990s Mexico was one country that served the latter purpose.

Over the long term, workers wish to promote labor scarcity and raise salaries, but industrialists wish to have free access to all potential workers and keep wages as low as possible. Hence, conflict becomes characteristic of relations between workers and owners as the unequal distribution of economic rewards is challenged and protected, respectively. Therefore, in many instances in which unemployment is high, conflict is a result of decisions made regarding the need for labor and the adoption of labor-saving technology on the factory floor. Along with these conscious management decisions, in recent years there has also been a shift in technology away from semiskilled jobs. The result is fewer jobs for the unskilled; and those jobs that do exist often do not pay adequately to support a family.

This interaction between labor, management, and technology can be seen in the efforts to increase investments in business and industry in the poorest areas of cities. Pushed by the Republicans in the early 1990s, the legislation passed by Congress was intended to create so-called enterprise zones through which investors would be exempted from paying capital gains' taxes on some of the profits earned as long as the investment was held for a specified period. Within the zones employers could receive an annual tax break for each worker hired and they could claim an immediate tax deduction for business property bought each year. Additionally, investors could get tax deductions for stock bought in a business within a zone. These incentives for businesses to locate or expand in an area targeted for renewal or growth were intended to increase employment, expand incomes, and improve private property.

Yet, because there are no provisions governing the nature of the employment generated through enterprise zones, it is not unusual for such incentives to find employees locked into low-level, minimal wage positions, with little opportunity to move up a career ladder. Furthermore, many who actually take the jobs often are not residents of the community. These nonresidents are given the jobs because those who live near the industry or business are either unskilled or in other ways unprepared for the jobs. By the early 1990s there were some 600 state enterprise zones in 36 states. A 1989 study of enterprise zones conducted by the General Accounting Office found the zones generally ineffective and recommended a go slow, experimental approach to their use. Nevertheless, Congress passed the legislation, realizing that some action had to be taken to counteract the exodus of middle-class wealth and jobs to the suburbs.

Some argue that because most jobs created through this approach are found at the lower level of the economy, and because many individuals do not have the requisite skills to be employed even at that level, some inner-city residents have found ways to participate in a different economy to earn money. It is referred to as the underground economy and is based on cash or barter; but because the business transactions are not licensed or sanctioned by government, this economy facilitates the avoidance of paying taxes on earnings. The sale of labor, services, contraband, stolen property, and drugs constitute much of the activity. Many of the individuals who participate in this economy have contempt for their mainstream working- and middle-class peers who hold wage-earning positions in regular, socially sanctioned institutions. In the 1980s marketing cocaine for $5 and $10 in neighborhoods created the kind of entrepreneurial climate and profit incentive that pushed many living in poverty into the criminal ranks of illegal business activity. The newfound wealth of these individuals has subsequently created new power brokers in inner-city neighborhoods. These are often the individuals who control the streets through terror, intimidation, and violence and who are typically bound up with the gang warfare that has characterized some urban areas in recent decades.

Part of the critique of the human capital model is that it spawns frustration among the poor because there is little socioeconomic mobility associated with entry-level jobs. So the argument goes: the individuals seeking employment lack basic skills to participate elsewhere in the economy and hence are likely to be frozen at the bottom. For this reason it is inherent in the human capital approach to increase education and job-training programs which are designed to increase worker productivity and thus, economic competitiveness for the industry or firm. Education and job training are also expected to prepare a work force satisfied to work in a hierarchical system which depends on compliance and commitment.

Human capital educational programs usually assist in this process by pursuing a prescriptive curriculum and pedagogy that are in the interests of the state and the dominant group; that are typically more teacher as opposed to student-centered; and that act as sorting and recruiting mechanisms to ensure the reinforcement of existing social relations associated with capitalism. Traditionally, little learner initiation, or participation, in educational decision making has been fostered in this type of program and the learner is usually viewed as a client whose compliance, discipline, and ability to follow instructions are rewarded. In the early 1990s an example of such programs called "workfare" required those on welfare to go to work. One problem with the program was that it failed to provide individuals with real jobs that paid wages above the welfare level. Thus some criticized the program for providing little long-term promise of an opportunity to become self-supporting through wage earning.

Prior to the rise of the high-technology emphasis in the economy worldwide, capitalists were reluctant to go beyond top-down education and invest in participatory processes that delivered more than basic skills. There was said to be an anxiety among managers that a participatory and educated work force would simply lead to challenges to the structure and organization of the workplace. The need for advanced education of the work force grew more acceptable among capitalists in the 1980s as they found that both domestic and worldwide economic competition required such preparation. Thus they became less concerned with the prospect of education leading to unrest and frustration or even challenges to management among a more highly educated work force. The concern instead turned to fostering creativity and participation in decision making. This means that for some workers, education is prized by capitalists because it is an investment in remaining ahead of the competition. The requirements for a more highly educated work force are accompanied by the necessity to incorporate workers into daily management through empowerment. It should be noted that although more schooled employees have been hired and empowered, they have not been incorporated into many of the places of work where the poor predominate; many firms having lower paying manufacturing jobs, and firms associated with the burgeoning service sector, still recruit from the less schooled and implement a top-down management style.

Given the basic assumptions underlying traditional capitalism, it is no wonder that the economic impact of education programs—whether programs are based on schooling, or programs like literacy or technical and vocational education outside schools—may have less to do with pedagogy and more to do with capitalism itself. The idea that the promulgation of education to the poor will enhance their status and power, thereby closing the gap between rich and poor, is most likely to result in the integration of learners into a system operated, and primarily designed to benefit, the political and economic interests at the top. Time will reveal whether capitalists are eager enough to have better-schooled employees throughout the economy and whether they will empower these employees to help shape the decision-making processes in the places they work. In the meantime the human capital approach must be seen, as Paulston (1977) argues, as a means to reinforce basic inequalities, hierarchies, and conflicts in society. He believes that approaches to change based primarily on top-down responses to market demands for defined skills constitute a poor basis on which to design approaches to change.

Human Capital and Education Approaches

The human capital framework treats schooling as important because schooling is supposed to deliver productive skills and because it is a selection device used to filter capable individuals from incapable individuals. Schooling also provides credentials which are used by employers to screen potential employees. Many questions remain regarding the causal linkages among ability, education, trainability, credentials, productivity, income, and occupational status. We are concerned with the way in which those who view education as an important attribute of workers deliver information and skills, reward individuals for their learning, provide credentials, and link education with employment and other opportunities.

The strategies for developing human resources as human capital emphasize individual change and involve potential workers as learners, and collectively, as communities. Much of this kind of education goes on outside schools, yet it is used systematically to reinforce and facilitate change. The methods of instruction range from face-to-face to the use of various forms of print and electronic media. In urban areas such programs are usually of three types: technical/vocational training programs; health instruction and literacy programs; and community social action programs, including community and integrated development and economic cooperatives. We will look briefly at some of what is known about each of these program types.

First, the effects of technical/vocational training programs are increased as they occur on-the-job or under the sponsorship of business and industry. Such programs are sometimes able to guarantee a job to participants after they finish training. Programs found in trade schools separate from the workplace are less viable for increasing an individual's income and status because they are unable to predict job openings and manpower needs in a timely manner, they are unable to afford the high cost of modern equipment or up-to-date instruction, and they suffer from the lower value that is placed on nonschool credentials compared to formal academic training. In effect, business and industry control access to jobs in a capitalist economy, so training must be undertaken in cooperation with employers if it is to facilitate increased income and status for individual learners.

The information regarding systematic programs such as health and family planning, and literacy programs do not permit as easy an analysis, because less research and evaluation has been done on such programs and because they are inherently more complex. Part of the complexity results from the difficulty in isolating health or literacy behavior from other aspects of an individual's daily life, aspects which can act to reinforce traditional behaviors and swamp most attempts at change. For example, the use of birth control devices to limit teenage pregnancies and the use of condoms to limit the spread of AIDS are well known, but campaigns to increase usage have not been as successful as hoped. Most health programs that seek to enter a community have great difficulty overcoming environmental, cultural, and related influences which shape daily, habitual health behavior.

In the area of basic education, economists argue that the highest rates of economic return to a society are associated with reading, writing, and numeracy. Most of this activity is associated with elementary education. However, when conducted for older youth and adults who were ill-served or unserved by schools, outside of schools, it is usually associated with literacy programs. These latter programs typically occur in the workplace, or they depend on efforts to enlist volunteers for each-one-teach-one programs. These out-of-school basic education programs typically have limited impact over the long term and are not very cost effective. Their impact is limited, because like changes in health status behavior, literacy needs to be reinforced through daily use, something which many individuals who want to increase their skills are unable to do given the environment in their workplace or at home. Literacy programs are expensive, because most successful programs require highly individualized instruction, which relies on a one-to-one teacher-student ratio. Of course, much depends on how literacy and illiteracy are defined and what the goals of the program are. Programs that are sponsored by employers and provide incentives for job mobility or increased income are more likely to move individuals into higher levels of literacy. When complemented by family and community values which support literacy, sustaining formal education enrollment among the young is probably the best means to increase literacy in the general population over the long term.

Under the human capital model the results of community social action efforts such as community development are often less than one would hope, as well. The Atlanta Project mentioned earlier is an example of a program in which community development is stressed.

Given the history of other such program, however, it will struggle to achieve its goals. Overall, such efforts have encountered, or have themselves promulgated, a long-term dependency on outside change agents and technical assistance; a faith in self-help community activity without the infusion of necessary resources; a reliance on social-psychological pedagogy to expedite community growth, without sufficient attendance to material changes in the environment; an isolation of programs from ongoing parallel activities associated with government legislation or regional economic planning; and a competition with other similar social action programs in the region which are dependent on the same or similar sources of financial support.

These limitations of traditional community social action can be seen in the evolution of programs during the past thirty years. Community development programs primarily involving social-psychological, bottom-up approaches to lifting a community by its own resources were common in the United States and other countries during the 1950s and 1960s. Realizing that communities were too poor and lacked a history of organized self-help, in the 1970s these programs gave way to something called integrated development. This initiative was built to reflect the multifaceted, complex nature of community life and attempted to take a more coordinated interventionist strategy by simultaneously working on different aspects of the community to reinforce change (LaBelle 1986). However, such programs became too complicated and expensive to implement, and the intervening program agencies did not have a tradition of cooperating with other similar agencies with whom they had goals or methods in common but with whom they had to compete for external funding to remain viable.

In sum, one might ask whether these observations drawn from the research on human capital approaches to education and social change mean, nothing works, or all results are negative? The answer to both questions is no. Clearly, some people do learn new skills, improve their health status, and increase their literacy. Similarly, many communities have experienced the benefits of organization and as a result have been able to improve their schools, solve a social problem, or build and improve the community's physical infrastructure. Thus judgments of success depend on expectations. We are looking at a series of trade-offs in analyzing the success of these human capital efforts. As indicated above, some of the limitations of the approach are inherent in capitalism while others are more related to the complexities of individual and social behavior and what it takes to change that behavior. It is not unusual to find individuals divided on the viability of the human capital approach to change, some seeing the glass half empty and others, half full. Proponents argue that the approach increases all incomes when the economy is growing and that it is discrimination which keeps disparities among groups. Critics argue that the effects of the approach primarily benefit those at the top and such unequal outcomes are exacerbated by intergroup relations. It does seem clear, however, that if one relies on what is known from research and evaluation studies, the results of the approach for socioeconomic development are quite poor relative to the investments made. Partly because of the approach, human capital programs have focused more on adaptation than change and thus generally have not narrowed the gap between rich and poor nor sustained increases in the power and status of the poor.

To some this means that without altering the political and economic interests at all levels of the power structure, such programs will continue to perpetuate a system of inequality in which major economic benefits accrue to the rich while relative economic impoverishment and political impotence remain the plight of the poor. Likewise, critics argue that the search for empirical evidence to support a positive impact of education in capitalist societies is doomed to disappointment because of the inherent contradictions and assumptions made under the human capital model. At the same time, many of these critics also admit that the alternatives to capitalism and industrial growth in most of the world are few and certainly no less problematic.

Revitalization and New Social Movements

When discussing education and change in the United States, it is uncommon to hear of proposals for making more than minor adjustments to the ongoing educational and social system. Thus, like in the human capital approach, it is uncommon to think of schooling and education as part of the larger society within which the control of knowledge is associated with economic and political power, exploitation, privilege, and cultural hegemony. Nonetheless most realize that when the status quo is challenged, new paradigms for the future are created and strategies for change undergo revision. Thus although we are seldom challenged to think within an entirely new framework (one that is not dependent on incremental change of an adaptive sort), it is possible to envision efforts that involve schooling and nonformal education, to assist in establishing new institutions and behaviors.

This larger, more radical approach to change can be seen in other countries where collective actions follow from dissatisfaction with the present system. Usually referred to as revitalization or revolutionary movements, these collective actions are initiated by a minority on behalf of particular political, religious, language, or racial groups to gain access to greater power and status. A second type of action taken by groups is often called a social movement: a collective action which takes place on behalf of an environmental, social, or health issue to enhance the larger societal good. These primarily political and social approaches to change contrast with the basically economic orientation of the human capital model.

Revitalization: Revolution to Civil Rights

Wallace (1961) indicates that revitalization movements are designed to construct a more satisfying culture, one which defines the existing society as inferior and aims toward a utopian image of a better way of life. He indicates that there are commonly six stages which constitute a successful revitalization movement. First, a moral code must be formulated by a prophet, political party, or special interest group to explicate the deficiencies of the existing culture and what needs to happen to achieve the characteristics of a desired culture; second, the formulator of the code must enlist the allegiance and service of others to the goals of the movement; third, a hierarchical organization, with the prophet or formulator at the head, must then be formed to provide direction to those who have become affiliated; fourth, as the challenge to the status quo is pursued, the organization must adapt through modification to the counter-propaganda, or force with which the society's existing leadership responds; fifth, assuming that societal power is transferred to the challengers, a revolution is declared, and direct transformation of the culture begins; sixth, the leadership of the transformed society must now maintain the momentum to further strengthen its position of power.

There are numerous examples of revolutionary societies which have experienced some form of the stages identified above. China, Cuba, and Nicaragua are examples, as are several African nations, such as Ethiopia and Mozambique. Other examples are Middle Eastern states, such as Iran, and more recently, the newly created countries in Eastern Europe. Much of education's contribution to such movements is found outside schools and is intended to communicate the need for change among and between and on behalf of those that desire power. For those in power, the response is to use formal and nonformal education to defend the status quo. For the challengers in some countries, private religious schools might be an important source of strength. (This occurred with the Catholic schools in Nicaragua and the Islamic schools in Iran). More frequently, however, enlisting the support of the masses through education depends on out-of-school efforts through clandestine publications, wall posters, and geographically-based-but-networked communication groups.

While not all revitalization movements are intended to result in a major political and economic revolution, some clearly are. One example of such an orientation was Cuba in the late 1950s and early 1960s. Castro's revolutionary vanguard, or leadership group, originally established itself in an area of Cuban rural discontent—Oriente Province—principally populated by sugar producers, many of whom were landless peasants, squatters, or sharecroppers. Che Guevara (1967) was a member of the vanguard group in this area prior to the revolution of 1959, and he reports there was much to learn and teach among this unskilled and unstable peasant population. In the military training area there was instruction on the use and care of firearms, packing equipment, keeping accurate records of casualties and events, guerrilla tactics, and so on. While both knowledge and practice were important for military preparation, as the guerrillas came into closer contact with the daily problems of the peasants, there were more specific ideological lessons to learn as well. For example, Guevara describes himself and others providing instruction in the importance of agrarian reform collectivization, literacy, and principles of social change.

Guevara describes the movement from the rural guerrilla point of view, but others argue that Castro's victory did not reside exclusively in the strength of the rural militia, nor with the proletariat, but rather was due to the support of the urban middle classes, structural circumstances, and the errors and incompetence of the enemy (Pope 1980). Part of the strategy was to highlight the structural dominance associated with a Cuban economy shaped by U.S. investment in infrastructure, to highlight the hotel industry, and to highlight sugar processing. These investments were backstopped by direct U.S. political and military intervention throughout the twentieth century. Economically, during the late 1950s, for example, North Americans reportedly owned 40 percent of the sugar mills, 90 percent of the cattle ranches, 23 percent of industry, 50 percent of public railways, 90 percent of telephones, light and power services, and 99.9 percent of the oil refineries (Bhola 1982).

As a revitalization movement, the revolution in Cuba ultimately took on a self-perpetuating momentum of its own, often aided by nonformal education through mass communication channels. Castro's 1957–1958 publications, "The Manifesto to the People of Cuba" and the "Twenty-Sixth of July Manifesto" provided him with vehicles to offer criticism and solutions to sociopolitical issues relevant to all social classes. As an ideological expression of the not-yet-Marxist revolution, the former publication mentions the need for industrial incentives, agricultural diversification, and enforcement of tax collection without imposing an overall net increase. The latter publication identified the need for social harmony and increased productivity for the mutual benefit of owners of capital and owners of labor. These manifestos followed Castro's earlier published statements in newspapers calling for drastic changes in the political structures; the elimination of government corruption; reflections on class, race, and regional inequalities; land reform; the abolishment of torture and repression; and the dismantling of U.S.- and foreign-owned monopolies on Cuban soil (Dominguez 1978). It is assumed that these publications played a critical role in informing the urban populace of the goals and values of the revolutionary cause and in solidifying support among disparate groups (La Belle 1986).

Although it can be argued that the revolution in Cuba failed to satisfy many inside and outside the country, Cuba represents a rather far-reaching and relatively contemporary revitalization movement from which to draw lessons about education and revolutionary change. As one contemplates this case, it is important to note the socioeconomic and political conditions on the island at the time as well as the clandestine use of nonformal education to orient the population toward radically transforming those conditions. It is also important to note how the example follows Wallace's outline of revitalization movements. Specifically, in the Cuban case Castro served as the prophet who developed with Guevara the moral code for the movement. They initially sought the allegiance and support of peasants, and then others, through the establishment of a hierarchical organization. The movement adapted to counterforces as the struggle ensued, and ultimately, a transformation of the existing society occurred. Because of the repressive nature of the government established by Castro, the effects of the revolution involved the exodus of large numbers of Cubans to the United States and elsewhere. Yet as a less developed country, Cuba has remained at or near the top of the list of similar nations for the provision of education, for health status, and for overall quality-of-life indicators for its population.

While the Cuban case is at the revolutionary end of our change continuum, balancing the human capital approach at the other, there are examples that fall in between. These other revitalization movements seek to challenge the status quo from the perspective of gaining greater group power and status, but they do not necessarily anticipate overthrowing the current economic and political structure. For example, in recent decades several civil rights activists in the United States have pressed demands for greater access to political and economic power. They also laid the foundation for other social action movements related to, but not limited to, women's rights and the environment.

Although segments of all ethnic and racial groups in the United States have protested and engaged in confrontations to redress grievances at some time during their history, the most pervasive civil rights movement traces its history to 1955 in Montgomery, Alabama. It was here where Rosa Parks, an African American department store seamstress, was arrested for not moving to the back of a municipal bus when ordered to do so by the white bus driver. Parks attended the Highlander Folk School, where she and other civil rights activists were exposed to the ideas of Miles Horton, an advocate of personal and community participation in the social change process (Horton 1973). Parks' arrest lead to a boycott of the buses in Montgomery and subsequently throughout the South, initially orchestrated through the coordination and leadership of predominantly black Baptist Church ministers. The Reverend Martin Luther King, Jr. was one of these ministers, and it was his church in Montgomery where much of the early organization of the boycott occurred. By adopting variants of the nonviolent doctrines of Ghandi, church meetings were turned into nonformal education efforts to prepare parishioners in nonviolent resistance and in taking direct action to put pressure on the status quo. Through King's oratory ability and with the collective strength of the Southern Christian Leadership Conference, the movement relied on both hierarchical decision making and broad-based empowerment of the masses. It lead to parallel movements by other African-American organizations, and in turn facilitated sit-ins at restaurants to guarantee access, the desegregation of bus terminals, and the elimination of the separation of the races within public schools.

As the nonviolent-oriented civil rights movement impacted long-held discriminatory behavior, local and state law enforcement, and federal laws, several more radical civil rights initiatives like the Black Power movement, argued against the goals of integration and nonviolence as a long-term vision and a strategy for change. One of these latter efforts can be seen in the work of Elijah Muhammad and his disciple Malcolm X, whose work was initially conducted through the Muslim religion. The movement advocated racially separate social, economic, and educational goals, and thus criticized the integrationist efforts of King and others. Employing principles of black nationalism combined with religious ideology, Malcolm X remains, even after his assassination in 1965, a representative of the civil rights goals of some African Americans. He came from a family who followed the teaching of Marcus Garvey, an African American who believed the United States would never be a country that would provide the opportunity for real equality for blacks. Garvey encouraged African Americans to return to Africa to make their home. As a youngster, the home of Malcolm X was burned by the Ku Klux Klan. He grew up on welfare, became a street hustler in Harlem, and was sent to prison at the age of twenty-one. It was during his time in prison that Malcolm X became self-schooled and embraced the teachings of the prophet Elijah Muhammad.

The Black Muslims believe that the black man is the original man, that he is part of Allah, that he is divine and supreme. They advocate the separation of white from black and the practice of a strict moral code which includes abstaining from alcohol, gambling, profanity, and drugs. Malcolm X believed that integration was invented by white liberals as a smokescreen to confuse the true desires of African Americans. He believed that human rights had to precede civil rights and that armed self-defense and revenge against the Ku Klux Klan and other white terrorists is necessary. The Muslims' most essential goal is economic independence, an objective they feel will foster both freedom and power (Haley and X 1964). They also advocate schools which separate the sexes and which are taught and administered by people who adhere to Black Muslim values of righteousness, decency, and self-respect. Students are taught Muslim duties, dietary laws, character development, the history of the black man and the Muslim Movement, English, and Arabic. The objective of a Muslim education is to re-educate the African American so that each can be proud to identify as a black person and take a place in an interdependent, segregated but economically viable black community.

When Malcolm X was assassinated, he was just beginning to articulate a broader vision of African-American unity within a world body politic. To him the movement was neither a social nor a moral phenomenon; it was a struggle for power between whites, the oppressors, and blacks, the oppressed. After a trip to Africa and a journey to Mecca, Malcolm X attempted to link the African-American movement with Blacks in other countries, specifically Africa, through the Organization of Afro-American Unity. The charter for this organization calls for voter registration and other efforts to form strong political clubs and related organizations to foster political actions. Through such action he felt a unity would emerge that would permit blacks to confront the questions of working relationships with whites and facilitate the interests of other movements, specifically those of labor (Clarke 1990).

Apart from African-American revitalization movements, other ethnic groups have strong traditions of confrontation for greater access to economic and political rights. In the early 1960s Caesar Chavez led primarily Mexican American and Chicano farmworkers in California to unionize for better working conditions and compensation by boycotting nationwide the sales of table grapes and lettuce. American Indian groups during the last few decades also coalesced into the American Indian Movement to challenge authorities over the use and ownership of land which in the middle and late 1800s was granted to them. The Ogala Indians of South Dakota, for example, were granted exclusive use of the Black Hills in 1868 only to see them taken from them in 1877. During the last thirty to forty years such names as Leonard Peltier and Dennis Banks have been associated with these American Indian efforts to restore these lands to their former owners. These groups have used strategies which included conflict and violent confrontation, at least one march on Washington, and several court cases. Such strategies have been employed to better the economic, political, and social status of the Indians who, both on and off reservations, continue to suffer extremely high unemployment and welfare rates, alcoholism, and overall poverty.

These brief introductions to revitalization movements demonstrate that achieving goals depends on the willingness of people to be lead; on the existence of vision, organization, and leadership; and on an educational program that can rally the support of a broad-based constituency. Even in the absence of prophets such movements can remain strong. Both Martin Luther King, Jr. and Malcolm X, long after their deaths, were well-known on high school and college campuses in the early 1990s. In each case, these individuals continued to represent alternative approaches to civil rights issues. Although Malcolm X was perhaps more prominent during this period, the actual work of the Black Muslim sect in recent years has primarily focused on work among ex-prisoners, drug users, and prostitutes rather than civil rights. While not detracting from the success of sit-downs, sit-ins, boycotts, and teach-ins associated with individuals like Martin Luther King, Jr. their popularity reflects a growing impatience with such nonviolent tactics, arguing instead for more confrontation in the future rather than evolutionary change.

New Social Movements: Women's Rights and the Environment

Apart from revitalization movements that seek to make revolutionary change or to redress grievances on behalf of a specific ethnic or racial group are more issue-oriented efforts referred to as new social movements. Dalton, Kuechler, and Burklin (1990) trace some of this type of movement to the student activism of the 1960s in which critical protests generally challenged the goals and functioning of Western society. These earlier movements coalesced around free speech, peace, and individual rights. The evolution of such movements has grown to where they now represent a range of social, cultural, and quality-of-life issues. The women's movement, consumer and self-help groups, pro-life and pro-choice groups, environmental activists, the communitarians, a revitalized peace movement, and so on, are among the examples.

The resulting organizations transcend geographical boundaries and translate changing values and interests into potential political action. Dalton, Kuechler, and Burklin suggest that there is something qualitatively new with such organizations in that they stress highly participatory decision making, a decentralized organizational structure, and opposition to bureaucratic methods of operation. Thus in contradistinction to revitalization movements, new social movements are not dependent on a prophet and are collaterally organized rather than hierarchical in nature. In the authors' analysis of such movements, they indicate that new social movement members often have especially intense feelings about their cause, that they are drawn from across social classes with leadership often coming from the middle or higher socioeconomic status groups, and that they are typically characterized by collective social gain, or altruism. Challenging material self-interests and well-being predominates among these groups. Such can be seen with attitudes toward environmental issues and overall quality-of-life concerns which challenge typical growth-oriented paradigms.

The women's rights movement is probably best understood linked to the civil rights activities of the 1950s and 1960s and the free speech and peace movements of the 1960s. Burns (1990) argues that the initiation of the movement came from many women who participated in the civil rights marches, sit-ins, and boycotts and who realized that they were being exploited by the male leaders of these various organizations. Volunteering to go to the South and participate in the movements, these women brought a history of political engagement for change from their own Northern and Western communities. Given the egalitarian and democratic goals of the civil rights efforts on behalf of the African American oppressed, many of these socially active women felt they were not being recognized for their leadership and instead were being assigned exclusively to secondary roles making posters or serving food. As some began to speak out against such subordination and as they saw what could be done through collective action, they turned to organizing themselves for their own liberation.

In the early years author Betty Friedan (1963) became a national spokesperson for exposing the narrow ways in which women were constrained to contribute to self and others. Friedan encouraged women to fulfill themselves as human beings and to seek careers outside of the home. By 1966 the National Organization for Women (NOW) was formed to provide leadership for the women's movement, and as Friedan left the presidency of the organization in 1970, she called for a national strike in favor of abortion-on-demand, twenty-four-hour childcare services, and equal opportunity in jobs and schooling.

Although the women's movement had Friedan to spark the interest of others, it was not dependent on a prophet to propel its activities. It also differed from most revitalization movements in the nature of the issues addressed and in the way in which the movement was organized and structured. For example, the strength of the women's movement was not found at the national level but rather at the community level, in local women's groups and activities. It was process rather than prescriptive in orientation. Some of these grass roots organizations called for more political involvement and some aimed at taking action on specific causes like abortion. Overall, however, the various local units shared a concern for women's oppression and for raising consciousness about their actual and potential roles and contributions to themselves and the wider society. As a result, the activists left no area of North American life untouched, from public office to the family, from the mass media to education, and from the Equal Rights Amendment to gaining greater access to the world of the professions (Cassell 1977). In 1973 many of the diverse array of women's organizations took credit for the Supreme Court's decision to strike down all state abortion laws and provide women with a right to abortion during the first trimester of pregnancy. The 1980s and 1990s saw the women's movement deepen its commitment to its cause as it pursued greater equality in status and compensation in the workplace, political representation through elected representation, women's studies in higher education, and abortion rights.

A second example of a new social movement, this one most directly linked to the anti-Vietnam war movement of the late 1960s, is Greenpeace, an organization devoted to protecting the environment. Greenpeace was started in the early 1970s as a nonviolent yet action-oriented effort to stop nuclear testing. By 1975 it had launched campaigns against whaling and against the annual slaughter of harp seal pups. In the 1980s it took credit for being the catalyst for saving the entire continent of Antarctica from mining and oil drilling. The organization's rather unorthodox tactics have set it apart from others. For example, to gain attention to its concerns, it has plugged toxic waste pipes, entered directly into nuclear test sites, and intervened directly to stop the dumping of wastes in waterways. Still a relatively small organization in the early 1990s—probably less than five million individuals worldwide—the numbers belie its impact on the policies and practices of multinational corporations and independent nations. Because of Greenpeace efforts, the annual harvest of whales dropped from 25,000 in 1975 to 1,000 in 1988, and the European community banned the import of white seal fur products. Sometimes drawing the enmity of countries on one issue while receiving praise on another, the organization remains one of the few which can crosscut national boundaries in a nonviolent and nonpartisan way (Harwood 1988).

A final example of a new social movement are the communitarians. According to Etzioni (1993), this movement was initiated during a 1990 meeting of a small group of public figures and scholars who believed the United States needed a social movement to enhance social responsibility, private and public morality, and the collective interest of the society at large. Communitarians are committed to weaving what they view as a reasonable path between individual rights and individual responsibilities. While such a goal makes common sense to many, others confront the movement with wanting to protect the rights of the individual against the interests of the public, even in instances of safety and health. As with other social movements, the success of the communitarians will depend in part on empowering local citizens to organize and elaborate the principles that Etzioni and others espouse.

In contradistinction to some human capital and revitalization movements which tend to employ top-down, prescriptive pedagogical strategies, new social movements such as women's rights and Greenpeace are more inclined to empower individuals and to extend that empowerment horizontally. While a central organization exists for overall coordination and leadership, the participatory structure through which it operates relies on educational methods which generally contributes to such goals. One pedagogical strategy used in this regard has been called consciousness-raising; currently it is called popular education. It originated in Brazil in the late 1940s and 1950s as a means for people to come together in opposition to a repressive military government. The method involves members of a group or community who through a facilitator discuss their social reality and concrete historical experiences. The intent is for each individual in the group to become more aware of their individual political, economic, and social situation through an analysis of themselves, their family, educational, occupational, and social problems. Burns (1990) reports that a variant of this method was used early on in the civil rights movement at the Highlander Folk School and elsewhere, and that the method was widely employed in the women's rights movements as organizations sprouted in communities across the country.

Unlike educational programs associated with human capital approaches, consciousness-raising does not represent a fixed curriculum intended to integrate an individual into the present society. Instead it represents a normative process which juxtaposes a utopian future against the contradictions of the present. Consciousness-raising assumes that the poor and oppressed have their own ideology, born out of their experiences for their struggle to survive. Sometimes added to consciousness-raising is empowering the community to analyze its collective reality with the intent of promoting some social transformation. Referred to as popular education, this approach involves the community identifying its needs and expectations, analyzing obstacles to attend to them, and designing tactics and methods to overcome them. Some of these activities resemble community development or integrated development efforts.

Conscious-raising is integral to certain revitalization movements and nearly all new social movements that are intent on increasing access to greater economic and political power for the poor and oppressed. But like its prescriptive, human capital counterpart, consciousness-raising typically is not sufficient to overcome the constraints for achieving such goals. In the absence of adequate jobs, educational efforts of various types can provide knowledge, skills, and differing perspectives on reality, but can lead as much to frustration as to change. In effect, education plays its most important role in transmitting information, enlightenment, and motivation to accompany an agenda already set. It is strongest in a supportive rather than catalytic role and is seen thus in the civil rights, women's liberation, and environmental movements.

Conclusion

In appraising the human capital, revitalization, and new social movement approaches to change, one must note that there are strengths and weaknesses associated with each. The human capital approach represents a slow, methodical effort to retain the status quo while challenging individuals and groups to work their way up and through the social ladder. It deals most directly with the economy but fails to shift power or resources from one social class to another and thus appears inadequate as a way to narrow the gap between rich and poor. Its pedagogy most often depends on filling people with information and skills rather than releasing what is already pent up inside them. Revitalization movements depend on the vision and articulateness of a dynamic prophet and appear most useful for gaining political power. Educationally, revitalization movements combine prescriptive and process pedagogy often resulting in skills and empowerment. And whether through legislation or confrontation, revitalization movements threaten to turn the ways in which the larger society operates on their end. They have not done so well, however, in building the economic status of their constituencies and thus they have often left newly found political power in a burned-out neighborhood (as was the case in Los Angeles in 1992), without any economic backing. Finally, new social movements tend to be most effective at changing traditions, long explained through habit. The pedagogy here is process-oriented, challenging day-to-day behaviors and proposing new relationships as models for emulation. The new social movement appeal appears to rest with the empowerment that accompanies the combination of moral certitude and grass roots activity. Yet in this case, both political power and economic power may be left in the wake of accomplishing what the membership has determined is right or correct.

In attempting to untangle these distinct paths to change, Burns (1990) notes that it is difficult to determine cause and effect since change can occur in sporadic ways, often involving considerable time lag and often moving in a domino like manner. The 1964 Civil Rights Act, and the 1965 Voting Rights Act, which abolished literacy tests, followed the previous decade of sit-ins and marches. In the field of women's rights, the effects were far reaching but took time. In both instances, incremental change continues to be seen even after several decades have lapsed. Similarly, getting every nation in the world to agree to provide full protection from mining and drilling in Antarctica for at least fifty years followed a decade of behind-the-scenes work by Greenpeace.

Revitalization and new social movements suggest that those who step out front and challenge the status quo not only receive attention but can actually create change. In an analysis of several such movements, Burns (1990) notes that even though the 1960s and 1970s represented periods supportive of liberal reforms, there were problems nonetheless. He points to internal divisiveness, disillusionment, and lack of funding within various movements. The dependence on volunteers often meant that at some point individuals had to return to their regular jobs, schools, or other activity. Leaving the various movements also occurred as short-term goals were achieved or as leadership waned. The result often meant that there was little follow-through on some intended actions. Other issues confronting the movements included a lack of widespread understanding both theoretically and practically of nonviolence, of democracy, and of the importance of differentiating between intermediate and ultimate goals. Combined with moral absolutism and an impatience for results, movement means and ends often became intermixed and confused. Independent and parallel groups often fought for turf and media attention rather than for strengthening each other in coalitions.

Although there are differences among the internal characteristics of such organizations, there is a common thread used by all to achieve their outcomes: education. Revitalization and new social movements use education to feed their primarily political and social agenda, and human capital programs appear more likely to use education for skills and knowledge which can make a difference economically. This should not be surprising, for human capital proponents are protecting the economic status quo and desire to create strategies, often in political and social arenas, to work within those conditions. The revitalization and social movement advocates however, realizing that they are challenging those in power and that they have little access to economic clout, focus their efforts on opening the political and social doors with the hope that economic change will follow. It is the combination of economic gains and political and social change which is needed, but which has become so allusive, to all of these efforts. When the bricks are thrown from the ghetto, sociopolitical change seems to follow; but the question is whether economic betterment can develop as well. The challenge of the 1990s and beyond is to attempt a coming together of these strategies for change. The delivery of skills through education, career paths through economic and political action, and access without discrimination or prejudice in the society in general, must be evident in any successful action. The other challenge is to achieve such outcomes peacefully, without the need for violence and conflict.

CHAPTER 8

Approaches to Multiculturalism and Educational Pedagogy

Education professionals who live and work in multicultural societies ultimately must choose what and how to teach in classrooms filled with students who vary by race, ethnicity, language background, and social class; what to include in a curriculum when community groups holding different values support opposing goals; and how to administer a school or university to honor both diversity and excellence. The purpose of this last chapter is to provide an overview of some of the approaches to multiculturalism and education that teachers, administrators, and other staff choose where multiple groups compete inside educational institutions.

We begin by surveying approaches to multicultural education in elementary and secondary schools. Then we look in some detail at one type of multicultural education, bilingual education, before discussing multiculturalism in higher education and campus climate. We conclude with suggestions for how individual education professionals can use the insights and techniques of ethnography and educational anthropology to prepare themselves for work in a multicultural society.

Approaches to Multicultural Education

As multicultural education programs expanded in elementary and secondary schools in the United States in the 1960s and 1970s, a variety of approaches emerged, differing in assumptions about the nature of the relationship between dominant groups and subordinate groups; about what groups should be included and which groups should be emphasized under the increasingly broad umbrella "multicultural" (i.e., racial, ethnic, social class, gender, disability, age, language); about the relative importance that psychological, cultural, and structural factors play in changing society; and about how best to ensure success in school for subordinate group children.

During the last two decades the first of two significant developments has been the emergence of the view that multicultural education is education for subordinate group empowerment and social change, and second, the broadening of the multicultural definition to include characteristics such as language, gender, disability, sexual preference, and age. Thus the focus now for education professionals at the elementary and secondary level is how to provide their students with the knowledge and tools they need to promote change in an increasingly diverse, democratic society. These developments have come in addition to the long-standing debate about whether multicultural education should seek primarily to assimilate groups into society or to provide them with means to acculturate while maintaining their own traditions. In the midst of these developments and debates many practitioners have continued to be most concerned about improving the academic success of subordinate group children.

Multicultural Education for Empowerment and Social Change

Most approaches to multicultural education in the last thirty years have assumed that cultural diversity contributes positively to society, that formal education programs should help to preserve this diversity, and that multicultural education efforts ultimately increase intergroup understanding and cooperation. Educators have assumed that teaching all students about society's various groups, about the concept of culture, and about the worth of cultural differences would raise students' knowledge, increase subordinate groups' cultural pride, reduce prejudice, and eventually increase social justice. Not surprisingly (and given these assumptions), multicultural education generally has not analyzed dominant group power and its role in the oppression of minorities.

However, in recent years some practitioners have grown concerned not only with teaching about, or to, subordinate groups, but also with analyzing intergroup relationships and giving students the skills required to help change society. Reviews of the multicultural literature in the mid-1980s (Grant, Sleeter, and Anderson 1986; Sleeter and Grant 1987) revealed that some multicultural educators had begun preparing students for cultural diversity and teaching them to challenge structural inequality in an approach Sleeter and Grant label "Education that is Multicultural and Social Reconstructionist." By this phrase they mean an approach to education that deals directly with society's structural inequality based on race, social class, gender, and disability; that prepares students to change society to better serve all people, particularly members of groups which have been oppressed; and that works with young people to help them understand the nature of oppression and develop the skills needed to work for constructive social change (Sleeter and Grant 1988).

Even though some educators have adopted an approach to multicultural education that emphasizes empowerment and change, national reports and major documents on multicultural education typically represent a more traditional position. A recent example is *The American Tapestry: Educating a Nation* published by the National Association of State Boards of Education. The report does not discuss how multicultural education efforts might serve to teach group empowerment, but rather emphasizes the maintenance of subordinate group cultures while assuming their overall acculturation to the dominate culture. It recommends reexamining policies and practices so they are multicultural, assuring diverse group representation on all committees and commissions, adding more multiculturalism in teacher education and staff development training, encouraging more subordinate group members to enter teaching, infusing multiculturalism into the curriculum and texts, and administering student assessments that are culturally diverse.

The United States is not alone in this tendency to downplay the empowerment aspects of multicultural education in formal or official documents and policies. In some countries multicultural education has taken an acculturation approach, especially through language and cultural adjustment programs for immigrants and resident foreign workers. In Australia, for example, multicultural education has focused primarily on assimilating large numbers of new ethnic groups into society. Since the 1970s, the government has provided multicultural services for immigrants to help them integrate and adjust, including English as a Second Language courses, expanded multicultural educational materials, and increased ethnic broadcasting opportunities.

Broadening Definition of Multicultural

The first expansion of multicultural education to include groups other than those based on ethnicity and race occurred in the late 1960s, when the women's movement raised issues of justice and equality related to gender. Many of these issues were closely associated with education, ranging from inequality in opportunities for women in educational institutions to the culture of the school and the expectations and images school culture transmitted to and about women.

The revival of interest in ethnic movements broadened the scope of multicultural education. Many Americans with origins in Eastern and Southern Europe were introduced to positive images of their group history and culture. However, the ethnic revival process also revealed that the values of Northern European Protestants still dominated much of American education, just as they had for over a century. During this period multicultural education programs expanded to include new ethnic groups such as those from Southeast Asia who immigrated following the United States' withdrawal from Vietnam. Throughout the 1970s and into the 1980s groups other than those based on ethnicity and gender emerged and grew in power and visibility. Among these groups, gays and lesbians, persons with physical disabilities, and organizations based on age were the most prominent. Their concerns were incorporated into multicultural education as it became apparent that these groups, like others before them, were bringing particular values and interests into their contentions for power inside educational institutions.

The recognition of new groups and their concerns over the last two decades has generally contributed to more discussion of intergroup relationship issues and group power issues in multicultural education. Nevertheless, a broad definition of multiculturalism does not necessarily lead to support for the empowerment approach For example, some educators include class, ethnicity, race, gender, exceptionality, religion, language, and age within their definition of multiculturalism but limit their multicultural education strategies to building on students' cultural backgrounds in developing classroom instruction and school environments (Gollnick and Chinn 1990).

Subordinate groups continue to question the practice of multicultural education, expressing skepticism about whether goals of diversity and pluralism may not be coming at the expense of their groups' traditional values. For example, Dupris (1979) argues that given the history of dominant group control of Native American education (particularly federal government control), multicultural education and bilingual education efforts must include the rejuvenation of Native American languages and culture.

Multicultural education advocates differ over which group characteristics should receive the most emphasis, race being but one such characteristic. For some, racism is not the primary form of social inequality to be addressed in multicultural education, asserting that race, class, and gender are of equal importance (Grant and Sleeter 1988). For others, race is the most important group characteristic. In fact, criticism has been leveled at educators who adopt an inclusive, comprehensive framework of multicultural education, because such adoption is considered not facing up strongly enough to racism (Nieto 1992). Another aspect over which there is disagreement is how much to emphasize improving individual performance and how much to raise consciousness. Even for some proponents of group empowerment approaches, alleviating subordinate group educational failure is as important as giving students opportunities to become critical participants in a democratic society (Nieto 1992).

The emerging empowerment approach recognizes that many groups share a concern for increased democracy and justice as well as desire a voice in what values should shape education. As a result, multicultural education is increasingly teaching about diversity and is analyzing the relationship of subordinate groups and dominant groups within a broader critique of society and education. Various theories of conflict, cognitive development, and culture have influenced this critique and the practice that follows from it.

Conflict, Cognitive Development, and Culture

A multicultural education program that emphasizes social change raises questions about the relative importance of conflict, cognitive development, and culture in changing society. Each has implications for multicultural education pedagogy.

Conflict theories see society organized in groups which struggle with each other for resources and in which dominant groups structure social institutions in ways that maintain or increase their advantage. People, consciously or not, resist oppression. It is assumed that teaching children of different groups about each other, or engaging them in activities about the value of diversity is not sufficient to prevent future discrimination. Instead, conflict theories argue that the structures dominant groups use to perpetuate their advantages must be changed and that people need to be taught how to do this.

Cognitive development theory views learning as a process of structuring knowledge through the interaction of the mind and experience. In practice, this means that people in a democracy learn about critical thought and social action by practicing them, not by reading about them in school. This concept is the educators' basis for using the experiential or active learning strategies to teach students empowerment and social change. For example, cognitive development theory contends that if teachers wish to change gender relations, it is not enough for the girls in a class to read about women taking leadership. Instead, they need opportunities to experience leadership in class activities.

Finally, the empowerment approach sees cultures not as passed on from one generation to another, but as continually constructed and re-constructed in response to social and political conditions. This concept shifts multicultural education from a concentration on ethnic group traditions and practices to understanding how groups of all kinds and their members construct knowledge. This view of culture promotes the inclusion of many groups, including those based on attributes such as age or disability.

These three concepts lead those who promote an empowerment approach to specific pedagogical practices (Sleeter and Grant 1988):

- Practicing democracy—Students not only study about democracy but also participate in activities which help them learn how to seek representation, ensure justice, and acquire power while exercising democracy, beginning with relationships in the classroom.
- Analyzing life circumstances—Students learn to analyze their own lives as they already understand them from practical common experience using more formal explanations of how society works. Here multicultural education draws on consciousness-raising theory and the experience of selected movements, such as women's groups in the United States and new social movements throughout the world, to develop specific techniques to link the individual to the nation.
- Developing social action skills—The school becomes the training ground to prepare a socially active citizenry. Students might not only learn about

how a local school board works, but also practice lobbying the board for a desired change.

• Building coalitions—Students learn to form coalitions across race, class, and gender to address common problems, seek access, or ensure justice.

Curriculum materials for an empowerment and social change approach may resemble standard materials but may also have revised objectives which include these principles. For example, a lesson might engage students in some of the following: discussing the idea that English should be the only official language of the United States; role-playing in groups using a new language such as signing; role-playing members of dominant and subordinate language groups with different access to supplies, information, and leadership positions; planning a mock election campaign through building coalitions and voter registration campaigns; or analyzing the criminal justice systems from the perspective of race and ethnicity.

Proponents of empowerment and social change approaches suggest other principles and practices for bringing this approach to multicultural education into the classroom:

• The commitment by educators to a strongly stated antiracist position.
• The development by teachers of positive concepts about their own ethnic identities and the use of their own ethnic experience as a bridge to their students.
• The commitment to multicultural education as a long-term, slow-change process involving parents and the community.
• The infusion of multicultural education across the curriculum with both affective and cognitive activities.
• The democratization of teaching practices to include techniques that give student voices a chance to be heard in the curriculum.
• Attention to increasing student achievement including enhancement of basic skills.
• Exposing students to an understanding of oppression and inequality and identifying ways to eliminate these problems (Nieto 1992; Suzuki 1984).

As identified above, the move toward empowerment in multicultural education does not mean that previous approaches have been abandoned. Empowerment is a concern of only some proponents of multicultural education; much more common are traditional approaches which emphasize diversity and pluralism but limit or ignore attention to social class, empowerment, and social change.

Improving Academic Success of Subordinate Group Children

Amidst the emergence and expansion of the empowerment approach, concern for the success of subordinate group students has continued. In the

1960s some progressive educators and social scientists, attempting to counter programs developed in the 1950s which "compensated" poor and minority children for supposed deficits in their cultures, concluded that differences between mainstream and ethnic minority cultures, which were manifested in the schools, produced discord for minority children who then had learning difficulties and lower achievement levels. In response, educators assisted subordinate group children to make their school lives and home lives more culturally compatible. They reasoned that if multicultural education programs could change schools' cultures to be more like students' home cultures, then subordinate group children could have more access to, and higher achievement in, formal education. Although an improvement over the compensatory approaches, this "cultural difference" approach did not seek to empower students or to bring about change in intergroup relations.

A more recent approach to improving subordinate group academic success reflects the emergence of the empowerment and social change approach and seeks to provide curricula based on the concept of equity as comparability (Gay 1988). This concept means that subordinate group students have the right to learning opportunities that are as likely to be as successful for them as current practices are for dominant group students. In addition, the allocations of materials and resources is representative of a school's culture and ethnic groups. While all students are to be held responsible for achieving the same level of academic mastery, the ways to accomplish this vary with the students. A unit on critical thinking might have students read and view films about oppressive practices against ethnic and social groups, then dramatize what they conclude are the effects these practices have on individuals. Questions such as the following help to shape this approach:

- Does the curricular rationale reflect sensitivity to student diversity?
- Does diversity permeate the core content and activities?
- Are the culturally diverse content, examples, and experiences comparable to those selected from the majority culture?
- Are the suggested methods for teaching content and skills, and the proposed student learning activities, responsive to the learning styles and preferences of different students?
- How do the content and learning activities affirm the culture of diverse students?
- Do the evaluation techniques allow different ways for students to demonstrate their achievement? Are these sensitive to ethnic and cultural diversity? (Gay 1988).

Bilingual Education: Assimilation to Empowerment

We now turn to bilingual education, a major component of multicultural education, which demonstrates the shift over the past several decades from approaches that are primarily assimilationist and status quo to those that promote empowerment and social change. Because those associated with bilingual education have often advocated empowering speakers of minority languages, bilingual education has been extremely controversial in the United States.

Research Findings

Bilingual education uses two languages—that of the majority and that of a minority—to teach both academic content and language skills. The question is when is each used, for how long, and for what purposes. Research on bilingual education has generally shown it to be pedagogically effective. Recent findings show that sustained use of students' native language, combined with English instruction, is a positive approach. It grounds students in the language of their home while also helping them to acquire the language of America's economic opportunity structure and its dominant political and social discourse. Moreover, students' knowledge of their first language and culture can assist them in learning a second. Thus the time non-English speaking children spend receiving instruction in their first language is not wasted; on the contrary, the self-esteem and intellectual tools children gain in this instruction help them later in other formal schooling.

In brief, research on bilingual education over the last twenty years has concluded:

• Early childhood may not be the best time to learn a second language, so pushing children into English instruction too early may not be appropriate.
• Language is more than simple, social conversation. Children need time to learn the more complex academic language skills.
• Skills learned in one language transfer to another.
• Reading should be taught in the native language; the reading skills will transfer into English reading later.
• Bilingualism does not handicap children cognitively. (Crawford 1992, 89)

Although they may appeal to persons who believe children should be immediately introduced to the majority language, programs that completely immerse children in a second language don't work as well as bilingual education. Research has offered an explanation: Language learners must understand the messages coming in. Good bilingual education programs—with an English as a Second Language component, or with specially designed subject matter teaching in English—actually provide more comprehensible input in English (Krashen 1992). Having subject matter classes in the native language helps make the English language context more comprehensible.

History of Bilingual Education in the United States

The United States has a long history of educational instruction in languages other than English. In the eighteenth and nineteenth centuries, German was widely taught in many states. In the Southwest, Spanish was used to instruct children in New Mexico and California. Native American groups such as the Cherokee educated youth in their own languages. By the 1820s the Choctaws in Mississippi had formalized bilingual education using textbooks printed in Choctaw. As their social structure changed, and as their leadership confronted the need to survive as a nation, the tribal leadership accepted schools operated by Protestant missionaries where bilingual education was practiced (Noley 1979). Finally, religious groups, particularly the Catholic Church, sponsored educational efforts using languages other than English. However, as we saw in a previous chapter, in the early twentieth century intense pressure for Americanization, heightened by United States involvement in World War 1, led schools to drop languages other than English.

In the 1930s the Bureau of Indian Affairs' Division of Education, influenced by progressive education and the work of anthropologists, attempted reforms which included bilingual education efforts. Long-standing negative attitudes toward Indian languages, opposition toward bilingual education within the Division of Education, a lack of qualified instructors (at that time BIA teachers had only to pass a Civil Service exam; they needed no knowledge of Native American culture or language), and a lack of bilingual books. Some books were created and teachers trained, but the approach remained one based on the values of English speakers. By the early 1940s the effort waned (Szasz 1974).

Bilingual education reemerged in the early 1960s in direct response to the needs of the Spanish-speaking Cuban immigrants who had fled to Florida after Fidel Castro assumed power. A number of factors encouraged these bilingual programs: having fled Communism, the Cuban population was politically favored, was perceived as only temporarily residing in the United States before returning to Cuba, and included many middle-class professionals and teachers with an understanding of the educational and political institutions their children encountered. More generally, the emerging civil rights movement, the concerns in the 1960s that the United States become a more diverse society, and the increased activism by various Hispanic groups supported the expansion of bilingual education. Congress enacted the Bilingual Education Act of 1968 and Massachusetts mandated bilingual education in 1971. By 1980 federal funds were supporting 950 bilingual education projects in seventy languages. The debates over bilingual education, particularly over federally funded programs, grew more intense in the 1980s during the Reagan administration. Although the research and evaluation agenda for federally funded bilingual education programs became an important aspect of the debate, the conflict they engendered was not about whether specific programs or methods work, but about language diversity and how those who value and promote it have asserted group power within a prevailing national ideology (Ovando 1990).

As much as any educational program related to multiculturalism, bilingual education exemplifies the competition that occurs between dominant and subordinate groups in educational policy and institutions. It also demonstrates the potential that multicultural educational efforts have for student, parent, and community empowerment. Moreover, like supporters of other multicultural education efforts, bilingual education proponents, even as they have critiqued the educational system and sought ways to use education to bring about social change, have been extremely concerned with raising the educational achievement of individual non-English speaking children.

Although bilingual education shows multicultural education's movement toward empowerment and social change, it differs from other multicultural education programs in several ways. First, multicultural education programs generally include all students, even the children of parents who differ strongly on specific aspects of a program (i.e., whether to include information about gays and lesbians). In contrast, dominant group members rarely voluntarily participate in bilingual education programs: the learning of a second language is almost always the burden of subordinate group children. Second, the level of internal debate among parents and others in minority language communities about bilingual programs has been intense and has been sustained because language competence is closely connected to future job opportunities, and as we discussed in an earlier chapter, because groups include members with a wide range of individual differences and values. It should not be surprising that within a minority language community some parents may wish for their children to learn English immediately while others wish theirs to continue with their mother tongue.

Despite the controversies arising from its alignment with empowerment and change rather than assimilation, bilingual education seems effective in teaching both academic content and English. We now look at pedagogical issues, including types of bilingual education, suggestions for practitioners, and issues in the field.

Approaches to Bilingual Education

A number of categories of instruction are associated with bilingual education and with the different degrees of empowerment and change for minority language groups. They include: Transitional Bilingual Education, Maintenance Bilingual Education, Immersion Bilingual Education, and English as a Second Language.

Transitional Bilingual Education (TBE) programs begin with content courses in students' native language and are accompanied by English as a

Second Language (ESL) instruction. In many TBE programs, students are moved to English-only instruction as soon as possible, usually after no more than two or three years. TBE tends to be associated with those who see dominant/subordinate group relationships as best served by subordinate group assimilation. In fact, the goal of federally funded TBE programs in the United States has never been the production of fully bilingual, bicultural adults capable of functioning competently in two languages and cultures (Spener 1988). Because programs terminate students in their native language after just three years, children often face limited bilingualism, i.e., are not fully proficient in their native language, but also are not able to use the language for academic purposes. Likewise, TBE programs may not offer enough English instruction to get students ready to do academic work in English.

Maintenance Bilingual Education (MBE) programs also begin with content taught in students' native languages and ESL instruction. However, these programs do not seek to move students as quickly as possible to English only. Associated with those who see society as more pluralistic, with group languages and cultures equally valued, MBE programs' goal is to develop students' linguistic and cultural skills both in English and in another language. These programs may last six or more years and appear to help maintain family relationships, to aid students emotionally and scholastically, and to encourage parent involvement in schools and their children's education (Nieto 1992).

Immersion (or enrichment) Bilingual Education programs (IBE) place students in the new language *before* they get academic content in their native language. This approach is usually used for the few dominant group students—often middle class—who participate in bilingual education. English speakers learning French in Quebec are one example. An immersion program first begun in Quebec in the mid-1960s gave English speakers competence in French, while also retaining English identity and normal levels of English language development (Genesee and Tucker 1985). However, the immersion approach, when used for subordinate students whose language lacks the social prestige of the dominant group, can turn into a bilingual education program that will not benefit children (Nieto 1992).

English as a Second Language (ESL) instruction is often an important component of bilingual education programs. In addition, ESL is offered in many schools with immigrant student populations but in which no single group is large enough to need a bilingual program.

Placing children in a new language environment with little or no support is not a bilingual education program. However, such "submersion" describes the experience of the many children who are put into an English-only classroom environment with the expectation that they will learn to function, sink or swim, without special help. It is associated with those who take a strong assimilationist position which promotes minority language group members rapidly dropping their old culture and adopting dominant group culture.

Districts with students who speak different languages face a more difficult situation than districts with students of one or two minority languages. Increasing immigration to the United States, with persons settling in communities beyond the large coastal cities, means that education professionals in many areas must now develop approaches to working with language minority students where there is no bilingual education program. Trueba (1988) offers some suggestions for these situations. Cognitive skills, he says, are best acquired through a child's native language. Therefore in situations where there are many different languages represented in a school or classroom, the use of tutoring or peer teaching in each student's language should be encouraged. Teachers need to have knowledge of the students' cultures, and they need authorization to be flexible as to when they introduce specific curriculum units, so they can present material at the time they judge most appropriate for students. Trueba recommends teachers adopt specific strategies that include placing students in learning environments which guarantee success; identifying learning strengths, skill levels, and preferences in order to make activities culturally congruent; and experimenting with diverse instructional settings, experiences, and strategies. Finally, he emphasizes the need for personal relationships to develop between teacher and students.

In developing approaches to bilingual education, education professionals should consider several additional issues. First, the answer to whether transitional programs or maintenance programs are more effective lies in group values, not in the results of language acquisition research. Second, despite the progress made in empowering groups whose first language is not English, students and staff who work or study bilingual education may be marginalized. Bilingual education programs may create a kind of tracking when children are pulled out of regular classes. Instead of empowering children, such efforts can stigmatize them as the subjects of remediation unless efforts are taken to counteract this marginalization. Finally, school success through bilingual education does not guarantee individuals success in the job market or change in their subordinate group position. In the United States many subordinate groups are native speakers of English.

Higher Education—Curricular and Administrative Issues

Although multiculturalism presents somewhat different issues in higher education institutions than it does in elementary and secondary schools, the approaches to multiculturalism in each setting have developed in similar ways. Proponents of multiculturalism in higher education have moved from teaching about differences to promoting change based on difference and from simply acknowledging growing campus diversity to actively empowering students and others to build on this diversity.

Whereas elementary and secondary education institutions have been primarily concerned with programs for multicultural and bilingual education, colleges and universities have faced a broader set of issues related to multiculturalism. These issues include the role of ethnic studies, women's studies, gay and lesbian studies, and other group studies; ways of adjudicating competing claims for what should be included or excluded from the curriculum; and administrative concerns relating to such matters as affirmative action, admissions, interracial campus climates, and intergroup relations across race and ethnic boundaries.

From Group Studies to Basic Curriculum Change

Multiculturalism's impact on the academic side of higher education has primarily come from curriculum expansion and change in response to successful subordinate group efforts over the last two decades to redefine what counts as knowledge. These efforts have been aided by beliefs that diversity can contribute to student learning and that the curriculum should reflect the diverse groups who are part of an educational institution. These pressures for change led first to the creation of individual group programs, departments, and disciplines (e.g., Afro-American studies, women's studies, Native American studies, Chicano studies, gay and lesbian studies). More recently, under the rubric of multiculturalism have come increasingly forceful calls for more fundamental change in general education core requirements and in the content of basic courses. Subordinate group student organizations have played an important role in calling for such change.

The roots of ethnic studies, women's studies, and other group studies lie in the civil rights movement and protests of the 1960s, which were frequently led by university students and faculty members. During the same period affirmative action programs were bringing African American, Hispanic, Native American, and other minority group students into colleges and universities in significant numbers for the first time. When these students encountered racism and isolation, they often demanded the creation of ethnic studies departments, programs, and cultural centers.

Higher education institutions, growing rapidly with an influx of baby boomers and relatively high levels of funding, found it relatively easy to meet these demands by creating centers and institutes but not by creating academic departments. Such programs were comparatively inexpensive and did not require major changes in the college or university structure. The same process held true for women's studies. Increasing female enrollment, general support within the community, and the need for relatively small amounts of funding eased the establishment of marginalized programs. Funding and support continued for groups and their programs in the 1970s.

Accompanying the growth of these group studies programs was the parallel growth in other measures of academic output related to gender, ethnicity, and race: increased publication of books and journal articles; establishment of new journals; specialized conferences; and collaboration within fields and within individual universities. The growth of the knowledge base related to these areas has been very rapid in some fields. For example, at the 1970 annual meeting of the American Philosophical Society, no papers on race or gender were presented; in 1990, 21 of 224 papers were on these topics. Over the same twenty-year span the growth at the Modern Language Association was from 21 papers on race and gender issues to 212 papers. From these programs and increased pace of scholarship, independent disciplines were born (Butler and Schmitz 1992).

Despite the eventual creation of full-fledged departments, the success and isolation from much of traditional higher education disciplines has meant that group studies have often been controversial. Their presence in a university represents a group claim about what knowledge should be transmitted to future generations of students. That an institution has ethnic, women's, or other studies programs, or that journals for these disciplines exist, is testimony to an intellectual diversity that some have found unsettling.

Other issues have been raised related to these programs. Often founded by activists or in a spirit of activism, group studies programs have faced charges that they lack proper scholarship and intellectual rigor. In addition, competition for funds intensified in the 1980s as higher education budgets shrank. Likewise, group studies programs, born in a time of student idealism, began to feel greater competition for students in an era when many young people were more concerned with education for a lucrative career than with ethnic identity. While group studies may be well established in academia, they often do not link directly to specific job opportunities after graduation. Finally, group studies programs have themselves felt the intergroup competition that is continually a part of a multicultural society. A case in point is conflict over the focus of ethnic studies programs; in some black studies programs faculty desire programs to concentrate on the African-American experience while others feel a department should focus on African culture and African peoples.

Fundamentally, however, the creation, growth, and productivity of ethnic, women's, gay and lesbian, and other group studies represents a pluralistic approach to multiculturalism in higher education. Diversity is encouraged, but the wider structure and culture of the university is not challenged. For example, even though a university may have a major Latino studies program, in the great majority of the institutions students have virtually no contact with, or knowledge of, Latino culture, history, or politics. Group studies have not fundamentally changed university curricula nor empowered subordinate group faculty and students beyond their program or department.

In recent years another approach to multiculturalism has presented a more compelling challenge to higher education. This approach has questioned what should be included in the campus-wide curricula, in core courses required of all students, and in various disciplines such as history and literature. In this more global approach, ethnic groups, women, gays and lesbians, and members of other groups have criticized higher education for its bias toward white, European, male scholarship. A typical critique might be that the syllabus for a freshmen humanities course contains almost exclusively male-authored works from the Greeks, the Bible, European history, and dominant groups represented in the United States. The multiculturalists would argue that the syllabus is too narrow, provides material from traditions that are not reflective of many students, and that it is not possible to separate the supposedly universal themes the course proposes to examine from basic characteristics of the writers and their experience. In response, the arguments for retention of the syllabus (as is) would be that it represents a core of Western learning necessary to be an educated person in the United States and that the traditional works included in fact deal with themes which transcend ethnicity, race, gender, or sexual preference. Moreover, the argument would run, while encouragement of diverse scholarship may now be producing work by people from many groups, the fact remains that white males produced much of our historical, literary, and social science canons.

Through such critiques and challenges to the basic curricula, how, and by whom it is presented, multiculturalists are attempting to empower groups by changing what higher education recognizes as core knowledge to include subordinate group perspectives. Unlike the earlier creation of compartmentalized group studies programs, the current multicultural approach attempts to empower and change by claiming for subordinate groups a share of limited academic goods such as the content of the syllabus in a required first-year course or in a distribution or general education requirement. An equally radical challenge has come to specific departments and disciplines when groups such as Afrocentrists have called into question the fundamental assumptions and basic knowledge of a particular field. At the same time some are suggesting that ethnic studies be included as part of broader themes such as American Studies (Takaki 1993).

Finally, for some groups—most recently Native Americans—influence in the curriculum has come through the creation of their own institutions of higher education (Stein, 1992). Since 1968, Native Americans have founded twenty-four tribal colleges. These colleges provide services for local communities, teach vocational education courses, offer instruction that reinforces tribal culture, and prepare students to transfer to four-year institutions. The tribal colleges represent Native American control; most of them were founded by local groups with no outside support (Tierney 1992). At the same time they promote tribal empowerment and affirmation of tribal culture, the colleges have struggled to meet the accreditation rules and have faced the pressures for good vocational outcomes that other higher institutions face. Tierney suggests that what the colleges offer Native American students is an entire experience framed in tribal norms and values, rather than in decontextualized techniques. Similarly, for faculty, particularly dominant group (white) faculty, professional growth includes intense learning and participation in the culture and community of the particular college and tribe (Tierney 1992).

Other Issues for Higher Education

Educational practitioners, whatever their positions on specific debates about the content of the canon or the legitimacy of a challenge to traditional scholarship, must determine how they will teach students (many from diverse groups, but more often from the dominant culture) with little understanding of the basic issues related to multiculturalism. One answer used in many institutions is to establish courses that directly address multiculturalism. Issues developers of these programs must deal with include:

- Establishing a clear definition of what they mean by multiculturalism. Does it have largely to do with ethnicity and race, does it include the broad variety of groups discussed throughout this chapter, or does it focus on issues and themes studied comparatively and internationally?
- Setting the pedagogical goals for a multiculturalism course or curriculum early in the process to help focus the work and balance the competing claims that various groups will make on the process. For some, the goal may be to concentrate on learning about ethnic groups. For others, the goal may be for students to gain a better understanding of the interplay of groups and political and economic power. For advocates of an empowerment approach, the goal may be to teach students both critical analysis and the skills needed to further change the university and the larger society.
- Presenting a multicultural approach, when students lack understanding and insight into their own culture(s) and the dominant culture in the United States.
- Solving the problems common to any curricular change within a traditional university setting—e.g., should a course be required or not required, offered separately or as a sequence, modified from an existing model, or built anew.
- Selecting and developing faculty for courses in multiculturalism requires particular care since the topics may be emotionally charged and because various groups may have strong beliefs about who can teach—or more likely who should not teach—particular topics. Institutions will have to decide, for example, if courses primarily focusing on women's studies can be taught by males (Gaff 1992).

Although the current approach to multiculturalism has centered largely around the curriculum, there are many other issues associated with multiculturalism and higher education. Among these are controversies about affirmative action, housing, financial aid, and admissions. With subordinate groups underrepresented in higher education and college degree attainment rates highly skewed toward higher-income families (Pitsch 1992), administrators must decide within the confines of various legal constraints or directives about whom to admit and whom to hire. These questions have become particularly important with recent research showing that over the long term, minority recruitment programs can overcome social disadvantage (Zweigenhaft 1991). In efforts to maintain diversity some institutions have monitored admissions by ethnic group. For example, during the 1980s the law school at the University of California at Berkeley maintained separate waiting lists for Asian Americans, African Americans, Hispanics, and Native Americans. An investigation by the U.S. Department of Education as to whether such a policy violated civil rights laws resulted in some modification to the practice (DeWitt 1992). Continued group pressure for empowerment and change will undoubtedly continue as long as higher education is perceived as a pathway to upward mobility, leaving no easy solutions for those who make admissions and financial decisions. Similar dilemmas exist for faculty hiring, promotion, and tenure.

School and Campus Climate

As various groups contest who controls what is taught in schools and universities, they have also contended with the more general social atmosphere in secondary schools and on higher education campuses. For many students the reality of school or university life is constructed around the people they socialize with, the sorority or fraternity they pledge, the people they live around, and the people they encounter in day-to-day activities. Students are often less concerned about courses and more concerned about the overall learning experience, including their life outside the classroom. Racial, gender, and sexual preference issues take on very personal meaning for students who are living, often for the first time, in a diverse and conflictual world (Moffatt 1989).

In recent years campus climate has become an issue increasingly associated with multiculturalism. As subordinate groups assert their claim to full participation in higher education they have pointed out that racial taunts and violence, sexual harassment and date rape, and intimidation of gay and lesbian students are not isolated events, but are evidence that they are still subordinate groups on campus, subject to oppression from dominant group students. Moreover, higher education students are becoming increasingly diverse, not only ethnically and racially, but in terms of age and previous life experience.

Thus the inflexibility and rigidity of universities, once seen as a general problem for students, is now seen as marginalizing nontraditional students who are usually older and often female.

Campus climate presents some difficult issues that present administrators with conflicting value choices. For example, at some institutions there has been conflict over what is and what is not protected free speech when the message in question—whether "jokes" on campus computer mail networks, statements made by professors about intergroup relations, or public sanction of a date rapist made by women's groups—may contribute to intergroup tension on campus.

In the late 1980s and early 1990s in response to incidents on their campuses, a number of colleges and universities instituted hate-speech codes that ban speech that offends or demeans another individual's race, gender, age, religion, sexual orientation, or handicap. Such codes focus on speech that is addressed directly to individuals and that speakers know (or should reasonably know) are "fighting words," likely to provoke violence or imminent harm. Criticized by civil liberties organizations, the codes have resulted in few students being expelled. More often, infractions have been punished with community service or required attendance at sensitivity or multicultural workshops (Dodge 1993). The codes may also be part of a broader discriminatory harassment policy which covers oral, written, graphic, and physical conduct (for a sample of such a code see Illinois State Bar Association 1991).

Another issue associated with multiculturalism relates to the extent to which administrators should support the formation and maintenance of separate group organizations, centers, and activities. Many argue that such activities and institutions provide safe emotional and intellectual havens for subordinate groups amidst a hostile campus climate; others argue that the very separateness isolates and ultimately marginalizes subordinate group students (Frohnen 1991). Finally, for some colleges and universities the degree to which sexual relationships between students and faculty should be regulated has been an issue for debate. The basis for considering such regulation is that the relationships often involve persons from two groups with very different levels of power within the university, in particular between faculty and students.

Suggestions for practice

Efforts to improve campus climate have ranged from quick, decisive responses to specific incidents of racism or sexual harassment to one-time human awareness days or multicultural weeks. Orientation programs often include general sessions on multiculturalism as well as on specific topics such as date rape. The American Jewish Committee's Institute on Human Relations has described the growth of incidents based on intergroup conflict on campuses and has formulated suggested responses, both short- and long-term. They recommend immediately following an incident that an institution's president respond firmly and quickly by stating prejudice will not be tolerated. Other first steps include activating an organized response team, immediate suspension and quick implementation of the disciplinary process, hotlines to prevent rumors, help for victimized students, and institution-sponsored rallies. They point out that a long-term prejudice reduction plan should accompany preparations for crises (Stern 1990).

More comprehensive approaches include those which attempt to empower students, faculty, and staff to change campus climate. For example, the National Coalition Building Institute (Brown and Mazza) utilizes principles which can be applied more generally to improving campus climate. Like the trend in approaches to multiculturalism, the Institute emphasizes empowerment and change.

• Training peer leadership teams empowers people to take action when, as individuals, they may feel powerless to face the increasing intergroup conflict on campus.
• Ongoing, campuswide efforts led by groups which include faculty and administrators as well as students are required, since experience shows that student-only groups are not nearly as effective.
• Building ongoing programs is more effective than responding to specific incidents of racism.
• Programs that address intergroup relations on campus need to include a wide range of individuals from a variety of interest groups.
• Programs work when they are not based on guilt, but are upbeat and hopeful.

To this point, we have discussed approaches to multicultural education, bilingual education, and multiculturalism as they have developed in schools and institutions of higher education over the last several decades. We have argued that these approaches have moved from supporting group assimilation to emphasizing empowerment and social change. In each area we have suggested issues facing practitioners and have suggested a limited number of practical ideas and techniques that go with each approach. We now turn to one approach that individual educational professionals can take to prepare themselves to work in an increasingly multicultural society.

Developing Personal Understanding

As we have seen, multiculturalism is not only a complicated concept but also a reality in most societies. It is not surprising, therefore, that many individuals find it difficult to comfortably relate to the competing values, interests, and goals of the various social class, ethnic, racial, and other groups which comprise the population. Such complications are especially visible to classroon teachers and school administrators who are called on to sort through these interests and lifestyles to find ways to build on differences while preserving common ground for teaching, learning, and productive social relations.

As advocates of multiculturalism attempt to bring to the curriculum and to their respective campuses the heritage and interests of the groups which comprise the wider society, they must be convinced themselves of the coexistence of unity and diversity. An important step in this process is for each individual to assess his or her own position on the issues of multiculturalism. If a teacher or administrator has little respect for students who have grown up in poverty; who have had to cope with family instability; who speak a different language; or who challenge dominant group conventions in music, scholarship, or belief, it is difficult to provide the kind of leadership and mentoring needed to foster these same young people's intellectual and social-emotional growth. Similarly, if control rather than respect for difference and diversity is valued by the teacher or administrator, it will be difficult for such individuals to establish the kind of social climate which will provide space for each individual and group to demonstrate an agenda which responds to their special needs and concerns.

The uniqueness of each community, family, school, and classroom makes it difficult to provide standard recipes for the promotion of multiculturalism. Instead, what is called for is a recognition of the influence of such natural settings on the behavior of individuals in them. These settings provide regularities which go beyond individual behavior; they constitute a framework within which individuals interpret their thoughts, feelings, and actions. Thus to adequately function in communities and institutions, the outsider must go beyond sensitivity and empathy and attempt to observe and learn from sharing the daily life of the individuals who regularly participate in a given setting.

The anthropologist refers to the systematic use of observation as ethnography, or the coming to know individuals, their language, and lifeways through daily interaction over time. This is an effort to control oversimplification, bias, and emotion in order to understand why people behave the way they do from their own perspective. The anthropologist does this by both participating and observing simultaneously. As a study goes forward, the participant-observer attempts to understand each event or fact and place it into a larger picture of relationships between and among individuals and groups. Thus it is a systematic attempt to discover the knowledge a group of people have learned and are using to organize their behavior.

The teacher or administrator in a multicultural school or university whose interest is in understanding more about the population that makes up the institution and its surroundings can adapt ethnography to such goals. The assumption underlying such study is that all people have aims and that they also have some knowledge about the means to achieve them. The interests and valuations of people become the central pivot around which the conduct and interpretation of the participant-observer is guided. In such study it is not just what the observer sees people doing, but what the people who are doing it see themselves doing. By raising what is observed to a conscious level and by seeking ways to explain those observations from the individuals themselves, the intent is to come closer to appreciating and learning how to build on diversity.

The methods for carrying out this type of study are many, ranging from one-on-one interviews, to observations of classrooms and other delimited areas of social interaction, to long-term participant-observation by taking a new role in an unfamiliar cultural setting. The information gathered can include demographic variables, social structures, values and attitudes, nonverbal and verbal behavior, artifacts and documents, patterns of action and nonaction, folklore, formal organizations, and logs of how people spend their time or effort. The resulting information can be set in a variety of frameworks, from cognitive maps which seek to discover and make explicit all the cultural rules a person needs to know to carry out a particular function in a society; to microeth-nography, a precise analysis of the interactions between individuals in a very limited setting; to frameworks that attempt to link what occurs in limited social settings to wider political-social movements. Extensive educational anthropology literature and ethnography of education literature found in journals such as *Anthropology and Education Quarterly* offer further details on these methods and frameworks, as well as a wealth of cases studies.

Once we begin to observe with a desire to understand and comprehend multicultural contexts, we come to appreciate the interrelationships which influence everyone's life. The difficulties in analysis often lie in the failure to see the whole and thus the significance of the parts. In school settings, this whole is the variety of students, staff, teachers, and counselors and their daily activity in numerous settings. These individuals and activities in turn are linked interactively to life outside the school. Thus to explain what goes on inside schools, it is necessary to be systematically engaged in the community where individuals prepare for or follow-up on the school's agenda. These outside influences also include the actions of citizens groups, parents, school boards, the economic opportunity structure, and the political climate. Thus, each school is a living entity, changing and adapting to inside and outside influences and emerging from a historical tradition.

Within this interactive framework, educators need to learn how schooling fits into the life of different groups of students and how teachers and students relate to the institution and perceive its utility. Educators also need to assess the expectations they hold for students, the relationship of student background and aspirations to the school curriculum, and the ways these various influences impact on school and classroom events and behaviors. In this effort to comprehend the interactions of individuals and groups in and around schools, the educator must therefore be willing to move out of the school and into the community. Only in this way can the linkages between and among behaviors in multiple settings be studied and analyzed with the intent of contributing to the success of educators and students alike and creating a more just and satisfying climate within communities and schools.

Conclusion

In the preceding chapters we discussed issues related to multiculturalism and education in an era when the global information flow makes national boundaries increasingly less important but when conflict between ethnic and other groups shows no sign of abating. Our purpose is to show how multiculturalism—broadly defined to include ethnicity, race, and social class as well as gender, sexual preference, age, and other characteristics—interacts with education. We emphasize that educational institutions are often the arena in which groups struggle for power, control, and access to opportunities.

We briefly reviewed the long relationship between multiculturalism and education in the United States, one that has taken on a new urgency in the last decade. We maintain that the historical issues and the contemporary struggles in this relationship can be understood within frameworks which explain how groups contend to influence policy and gain opportunities in the push and pull for societal integration or group independence. Amidst these struggles, political and social entities—the nation, the family, the community—have interests in education and therefore collaborate with schools in various ways. On a more individual level, persons from different economic and cultural groups interact differently with schools in terms of values, cognitive patterns, and language, and this affects their school achievement, and in many societies, their later life success. We also explored how group values—which may come from competing value systems—shape educational policy and practice. In the final chapters we reviewed how education plays various roles in different strategies for social change, and we touched on approaches to multicultural education, bilingual education, campus climate, and how individuals can prepare for work in the complex arena of intergroup relations and education.

We close by stating our belief that for the educational practitioner, the issue of multiculturalism is not primarily about learning the culture of a particular group or debating which groups should be included in a multicultural curriculum. Rather, it is most important to understand that multiculturism and education is a continuing drama of intergroup relations played out in schools and other educational settings. We hope that the history, frameworks, values, and other topics discussed throughout the book have offered some insights into how groups interact and how this interaction plays out in education.

Notes

Chapter 1

1. The report was published in two volumes of the College Study in Intergroup Relations, the first describing the projects at the twenty-four colleges and the second analyzing the findings. They are L. A. Cook, *College programs in intergroup relations.* (1950). Washington, D.C.: American Council on Education; L. A. Cook, *Intergroup relations in teacher education.* (1950).

Chapter 6

1. Values, as a component of culture, are independent of individuals, whereas attitudes are located in the individual. Unlike values, attitudes are connected to specific activities or environments. Attitudes determine for each individual what she or he will see, hear, think, and do. In contrast to the rather abstract nature of values, attitudes are more specific.

2. The largest single Scout sponsor is the Church of Latter Day Saints; the second largest, the United Methodist Church; and the fourth largest, the Roman Catholic Church; Presbyterian, Lutheran, and Baptist churches are fifth, sixth, and seventh respectively.

References

Afshar, H., ed. (1985). *Iran: A revolution in turmoil*. Houndsmills, England: Macmillan.

Altbach, P. G. (1993). Students: Interests, culture, and activism. In *Higher learning in America: 1980–2000*, ed. A. Levine, Baltimore: Johns Hopkins Univ. Press. 203–221.

Ambert, A., and S. Melendez. (1985). *Bilingual education: A sourcebook*. New York: Garland.

American Association for Colleges of Teacher Education. (No date). *No One Model American*.

Arensberg, C., and A. Niehoff. (1975). American culture values. In *The nacirema*, ed. J. Spradley and M. Rynkiewich, 363–378. Boston: Little, Brown, and Company.

Asante, M. K. (1991). Multiculturalism: An exchange. *The American Scholar*, 267–272.

Ausubel, D. P. (1963). A teaching strategy for culturally deprived pupils: Cognitive and motivational considerations. *School review* 71: 454–463.

Averch, H. A., S. J. Carroll, T. S. Donaldson, H. J. Kiesling, and J. Pincus, (1972). *How effective is schooling? A critical review and synthesis of research findings*. Santa Monica: Rand.

Bach, C. (1946). *The Pittsburgh council on intercultural education: A descriptive study*. Master's thesis, University of Pittsburgh.

Banks, J. (1979). Shaping the future of multicultural education. *The Journal of Negro education* 48(3): 237–252.

Barnouw, V. (1985). *Culture and personality*. Homewood, Ill.: The Dorsey Press.

Barth, F., ed. (1969). *Ethnic groups and boundaries*. Bergen: Universitets.

Barth, F., and D. Noel. (1972). Conceptual frameworks for the analysis of race relations: An evaluation. *Social forces* 50: 333–348.

191

Benedict, R. (1934). *Patterns of culture*. Boston: Houghton Mifflin.

_____. (1943). Transmitting our democratic heritage in the schools. *American journal of sociology*, 722–727.

_____. (1946). *Chrysanthemum and the sword*. Boston: Houghton Mifflin.

Berger, P. (1986, May). Religion in post-Protestant America. *Commentary*, 41–45.

Bernal, M. (1987). *Black Athena: The Afroasiatic roots of classical civilization*. New Brunswick, N.J.: Rutgers Univ. Press.

Bernstein, B. (1964). Aspects of language and learning in the genesis of the social process. In *Language in culture and society: A reader in linguistics and anthropology*, ed. D. Hymes. Evanston: Harper and Row.

Berry, F. B., and J. W. Blassingame. (1982). *Long memory: The Black experience in America*. New York: Oxford University Press.

Bhola, H. S. (1982). *Campaigning for literacy: A critical analysis of some selected literacy campaigns of the twentieth century, with a memorandum to decision makers*. Paris: UNESCO/ICAE.

Black, M. H. (1965). Characteristics of the culturally disadvantaged child. *The reading teacher* 18, 465–470.

Burg, B., and I. Belmont. (1990). Mental abilities of children from different cultural backgrounds in Israel. *Journal of cross-cultural psychology* 21(1): 90–108.

Burns, S. (1990). *Social movements of the 1960s*. Boston: Twayne Publishers.

Butler, J., and B. Schmitz. (1992, January/February). Ethnic studies, women's studies, and multiculturalism. *Change*, 37–41.

Calabrese, R. L. (1990). The public school: A source of alienation for minority parents. *Journal of Negro education* 59(2): 148–154.

Cassell, J. (1977). *A group called women: Sisterhood and symbolism in the feminist movement*. New York: McKay.

Cazden, C. (1988). *Classroom discourse: The language of teaching and learning*. Portsmouth, N.H.: Heinemann.

Cazden, C., V. John, and D. Hymes, eds. (1972). *Functions of language in the classroom*. New York: Teachers College Press.

Center for Rural Pennsylvania. (1991). *Rich schools—poor schools: Challenges for rural Pennsylvania*. Harrisburg, Pa.: Author.

Chealcalos, C. (1992, October 6). Youth battles Louisiana dress code: High schools ban political clothing. *The Atlanta journal/The Atlanta constitution*, no page number.

Cheng Li-Rong, L. (1990). Recognizing diversity. *American behavioral scientist* 34(2): 263–278.

Children's Defense Fund. (1990). *A vision for America's future.* Washington, D.C.

Churchill, S. (1987). Policy development for education in multicultural societies: Trends and processes in OECD countries. In Centre for Educational Research and Innovation, *Multicultural education,* 64–93. Paris: Author.

Citron, A., C. Reynolds and S. Taylor. (1945). Ten years of intercultural education in educational magazines. *Harvard educational review.* 15(2): 129–135.

Clark, J. H., ed. (1990). *Malcolm X.* Trenton: African World Press.

Clay, J. W. (1990, March). Working with lesbian and gay parents and their children. *Young children,* 31–35.

Cohen, R. A. (1969). Conceptual styles, culture conflict, and nonverbal tests of intelligence. *American anthropologist,* 71(2): 828–856.

Cole, M., and J. S. Bruner. (1971). Cultural differences and inferences about psychological processes. *American psychologist,* 26(10): 867–876.

Cole, M., J. Gay, J. A. Glick, and D. W. Sharp. (1971). *The cultural context of learning and thinking.* New York: Basic Books.

Coleman, J. (1987). *Public and private high schools: the impact of communities.* New York: Basic Books.

Conversi, D. (1990). Language or race: The choice of core values in the development of Catalan and Basque nationalisms. *Ethnic and racial studies* 13(1): 50–70.

Cook, L. A. (1947). Intergroup education *Review of educational research,* 17(4): 266–278.

———. (1950). *College programs in intergroup relations.* Washington, D.C.: American Council on Education.

———. (1950). *Intergroup relations in teacher education.* Washington, D.C.: American Council on Education.

Coughlin, E. (1992, January 29). Scholars confront fundamental question: Which vision of American should prevail? *The chronicle of higher education,* A8–A11.

Crain, R. L. (1981). Making desegregation work: Extracurricular activities. *The urban review* 13(2): 121–127.

Crawford, J. (1988). *Bilingual education: history, politics, theory, and practice.* Trenton, N.J.: Crane Publishing.

Cremin, L. (1962). *The transformation of the school: Progressivism in American education, 1876–1957.* New York: Alfred A. Knopf.

Cubberly, E. (1929). *Changing conceptions of education*. Boston: Houghton and Mifflin.

Dalton, R. J., M. Kuechler, and W. Burklin. (1990). The challenge of new movements. In *Challenging the political order*, ed. R. J. Dalton and M. Kuechler, 1–20. New York: Oxford University Press.

Daniels, R. (1986). Changes in immigration law and nativism since 1924. *American Jewish history* 76: 159–180.

DeWitt, K. (1992, September 29). Berkeley law school to change admissions policy. *The New York times*, 1.

Diaz, R. M. (1983). Thought and two languages: The impact of bilingualism on cognitive development. *Review of research in education* 10: 23–54.

Diop, C. A. (1991). *Civilization or barbarism*, trans. Y. L. M. Ngemi; ed. H. Salemson and M. de Jager. Brooklyn: Lawrence Hill Books/Chicago Review Press.

Dodge, S. (1992, February 12). Campus codes that ban hate speech are rarely used to penalize students. *The chronicle of higher education*, A35.

Dominguez, J. (1978). *Cuba, order and revolution*. Cambridge: Belknap Press.

Du Bois, R. D. (1945). Introduction to *Democracy's children*, by E. M. Duncan. New York: Hinds, Hayden, and Eldredge.

Dupris, J. (1979). The national impact of multicultural education: A renaissance of Native American culture through tribal selfdetermination and Indian control of education. In *Multicultural education and the American Indian*, 43–54. Los Angeles: American Indian Studies Center, University of California.

Eckert, P. (1989). *Jocks and burnouts*. New York: Teachers College Press.

Entwistle, D. R., and K. La Alexander. (1990). Beginning school math competence: Minority and majority comparisons. *Child development* 61, 454–471.

Epstein, J. L., and S. L. Dauber. (1991). School programs and teacher practices of parent involvement in inner-city elementary and middle schools. *The elementary school journal* 91(3): 289–305.

Etzioni, A. (1993). *The spirit of community*. New York: Crown Publishers.

Fishman, J. (1972). *Language and nationalism*. Boston: Newbury House.

Florio, S., and J. Shultz. (1979). Social competence at home and at school. *Theory into practice* 18: 234–243.

Foley, D. E. (1991). Reconsidering anthropological explantions of ethnic school failure. *Anthropology and education quarterly*, 22: 60–86.

Ford, S., and J. Ogbu. (1986). Black students' school success: Coping with the "Burden of 'acting white.' " *The Urban Review* 18(3): 176–206.

Foster, L., and D. Stockley. (1984). *Multiculturalism: the changing Australian paradigm*. Clevedon, Great Britain: Multilingual Matters.

Frazier, E. F. (1966). *The negro family in the United States* Rev. ed. Chicago: Univ. of Chicago Press.

Friedan, B. (1963). *The feminine mystique*. New York: W. W. Norton.

Frohnen, B. (1991, Fall). Liberal apartheid thrives at American colleges. *Campus*, 2, 4, 16.

Gaff, J. (1992, January/February). Beyond politics: The educational issues inherent in multicultural education. *Change*, 31–35.

Garcia, E. (1988). Attributes of effective schools for language minority students. *Education and urban society* 20(4): 387–398.

———. (1990). Educating teachers for language minority students. *Handbook of research on teacher education*, 717–729.

Gay, G. (1983, April). Multiethnic education: Historical developments and future prospects. *Phi Delta Kappan*, 560–563.

———. (1988). Designing relevant curricula for diverse learners. *Education and urban society* 20(4): 327–340.

———. (1991). Culturally diverse students and social studies. In *Handbook of research on social studies teaching and learning*, ed. J. P. Shaver. New York: MacMillan.

Gay, J., and M. Cole. (1967). *The new mathematics in an old culture: A study of learning among the Kpelle of Liberia*. New York: Holt, Rinehart, and Winston.

Gillmoor, D., and S. Doig. (1992, January). Segregation forever? American demographics, 48–51.

Gladwin, T. (1967). *Poverty U.S.A.* Boston: Little, Brown.

Glazer, N. (1977). Public education and American pluralism. In *Parents, teachers, and children: Prospects for choice in American education*, 85–109. San Francisco: Institute for Contemporary Studies.

Glazer, N., and D. P. Moynihan. (1963). *Beyond the melting pot: The Negroes, Puerto Ricans, Jews, Italians, and Irish of New York city*. Cambridge: MIT Press and Harvard University Press.

Glazer, N., and D. Moynihan. (1970). *Beyond the melting pot*. Cambridge: MIT Press.

Glick, J. (1974). Culture and cognition: Some theoretical and methodological concerns. In *Education and cultural process: Toward an anthropology of education*, ed. G. D. Spindler, 373–383. New York: Holt, Rinehart, and Winston.

Goldenberg, C., and R. Gallimore. (1990). *Local knowledge, research knowledge, and educational achievement: A case study of first-grade Spanish reading improvement*. Paper presented at the annual meeting of the American Educational Research Association, Boston.

Goldenberg, C., T. S. Weisner, and R. Gallimore. (1991, June). *Families and adaptive change: Re-thinking training and intervention.* Paper presented at the conference on New Directions in Child and Family Research: Shaping Head Start in the Nineties, Washington, D.C.

Goldman, A. (1992, October). Reading, writing, arithmetic, Arabic and Islam. *The New York Times*, A12.

Gollnick, D., and P. Chinn. (1990). *Multicultural education in a pluralistic society.* 3rd ed. New York: Macmillan.

Goodlad, John I. (1992). *Toward educative communities and tomorrow's teachers.* Work in Progress Series, No. 1. Seattle: Institute for Educational Inquiry.

Granrud, J. (1945). Preface to *The history of the Springfield plan*, by C. Chatto and A. Halligan. New York: Barnes and Noble.

Grant, C., and C. Sleeter. (1985). The literature on multicultural education: Review and analysis. *Educational review* 37, 97–118.

_____. (1989). *Turning on learning: Five approaches for multicultural teaching plans for race, class, gender and disability.* New York: Merrill.

Grant, C., C. Sleeter, and J. Anderson. (1986). The literature on multicultural education: Review and analysis, Part II. *Educational studies*, 47–71.

Greeley, A. (1974). *Ethnicity in the United States.* New York: John Wiley.

Greene, V. (1982). Ethnic confrontations with state universities. In *American education and the European immigrant*, ed. B. Weiss, 189–207. Urbana: Univ. of Illinois Press.

Gross, M. (1967). *Learning readiness in two Jewish groups: A study in cultural deprivation.* New York: Center for Urban Education.

Guevara, C. (1967). *Episodes of the revolutionary war.* Havana: Gauiras Book Institute.

Haley, A., and Malcolm X. (1964). *The autobiography of Malcolm X.* New York: Ballantine Books.

Harwood, M. (1988, October). Daredevils for the environment. *The New York times magazine.*

Haviland, W. A. (1987). *Cultural anthropology.* 5th ed. New York: Holt, Rinehart, and Winston.

Hawkins, J., and T. J. LaBelle, eds. (1985). *Education and intergroup relations.* New York: Praeger.

Hayes, K. (1992). Attitudes toward education: Voluntary and involuntary immigrants from the same families. *Anthropology and education quarterly* 23(3): 250–267.

Henry, J. (1960). A cross cultural outline of education. *Current anthropology* 1(4): 267–305.

_____. (1963). *Culture against man*. New York: Vintage Books.

Hinds, M. (1991, June 23). In test of who can join, Scouts confront identity. *The New York times*, 1, 12.

Holliday, B. G. (1985). Towards a model of teacher-child transactional processes affecting Black children's academic achievement. In *Beginnings: The social and affective development of Black children*, ed. M. B. Spencer, G. K. Brookins and W. R. Allen, 117–130. Hillsdale, N.J.: Lawrence Erlbaum.

Holm, T. (1979). Racial stereotypes and government policies regarding the education of Native Americans, 1879–1920. In *Multicultural education and the American Indian*, 15–24. Los Angeles: American Indian Studies Center, Univ. of California.

Horton, M. (1973). Decision-making process. In *Educational reconstruction: Promise and challenge*. ed. N. Shimahara, 23–42. Columbus, OH: Merrill.

Howe, H., II. (1987). Remarks on equity and excellence in education. *Harvard educational review* 57(2): 199–202.

Hymes, D. (1974). *Foundations in sociolinguistics: An ethnographic approach*. Philadelphia: Univ. of Pennsylvania Press.

Illinois State Bar Association (1991). *If words could kill*. Springfield, Ill. Author.

Imhoff, G. (1990). The Position of U.S. English on bilingual education. *ANNALS* 58: 49–61.

Jackson, E. (1948). *The Pittsburgh council on intercultural education: A study in community organization*. Master's thesis, University of Pittsburgh.

James, G. (1954). *Stolen legacy*. San Francisco: Julian Richardson Associates.

Jasso, G., and M. Rosenzweig. (1990). *The new chosen people: Immigrants in the United States*. New York: Russell Sage Foundation.

Johnson, J., H. Collins, V. Dupuis, and J. Johansen. (1988). *Introduction to the foundations of education*. 7th ed. Boston: Allyn and Bacon, Inc.

Kasten, W. (1992). Bridging the horizon: American Indian beliefs and whole language learning. *Anthropology and education quarterly* 23(2): 108–119.

Kearney, C. P. (1990). Shifting national values: The education block grant and school desegregation. *Education and urban society* 23(1): 80–92.

Kirp, D., S. Epstein. (1989, April). AIDS in America's schoolhouses: Learning the hard lessons. *Phi Delta Kappan*, 585–593.

Kirst, M. (1984). *Who controls our schools? American values in conflict.* New York: W. H. Freeman and Company.

Kluckhohn, F. R., and F. L. Strodtbeck, (1961). *Variations in value orientations.* Evanston, Ill.: Row, Peterson and Company.

Krashen, S. (1992). Sink-or swim "success stories" and bilingual education. In *Language loyalties: A source book on the official English controversy,* ed. J. Crawford, 354–357. Chicago: Univ. of Chicago Press.

La Belle, T. J. (1981). An introduction to the nonformal education of children and youth. *Comparative education review* 25(3): 313–329.

————. (1986). *Nonformal education in Latin America and the Caribbean.* New York: Praeger.

La Belle, T. J., and R. E. Verhine. (1981). School-Community interaction: A comparative and international perspective. In *Communities and their schools,* ed. D. Davies, 211–268. New York: McGraw Hill.

La Belle, T. J. and C. Ward. (1990). Education reform when nations undergo radical political and social transformation. *Comparative education* 26(1): 95–106.

La Belle, T. J., and P. S. White. (1980). Education and multiethnic integration: An intergroup-relations typology. *Comparative education review* 24(2): 155–173.

Labov, W. (1968). The logic of non-standard english. In *Linquistic-cultural differences in American education: Vol. 7,* ed. A. C. Aarons, B. Y. Gordon, and W. A. Stewart, 60–74. [Florida]: Florida Reporter.

Lambert, W., and D. Taylor. (1990). *Coping with cultural and racial diversity in urban America.* New York: Praeger.

Larson, E. (1991). Constitutional challenges to textbooks. In *Textbooks in American society: Politics, policy, and pedagogy,* ed. P. Altbach, G. Kelly, H. Petrie, and L. Weis. Albany: State Univ. of New York Press.

Lazerson, M. (1977). Consensus and conflict in American education: Historical perspectives. In *Parents, teachers, and children: Prospects for choice in American education,* 15–36. San Francisco: Institute for Contemporary Studies.

Lefkowitz, M. (1992, February 10). Not out of Africa. *The new republic,* 29–36.

Lesser, G. S., G. Fifer, and D. H. Clark. (1965). Mental abilities of children from different social-class and cultural groups. *Monograph of the society for research in child development* 30(4, Serial No. 102).

Levine, D., and R. Havighurst. (1989). *Society and education.* 7th ed. Boston: Allyn and Bacon.

Linton, R. (1951). The concept of national character. In *Personality and political crisis,* A. Stanton and S. Perry ed. Glenco Ill.: The Free Press.

MacCracken, H. N. (1945). "Intergroup relations" and American education. *Harvard educational review* 15(2): 76–78.

Madson, M. C. (1971). Developmental and cross-cultural differences in the cooperative and competitive behavior of young children. *Journal of cross-cultural psychology* 2(4): 365–371.

Mansnerous, L. (1992, November 1). Should tracking be derailed? *The New York times educational life*, 14–16.

Marcoulides, G., and R. Heck. (1990). Educational policy issues for the 1990s: Balancing equity and excellence in implementing the reform agenda. *Urban education* 25(1), 55–67.

Marger, M. (1991). *Race and ethnic relations: American and global perspectives.* 2nd ed. Belmont, Calif.: Wadsworth.

Marriott, M. (1992, February 26). Indians turning to tribal colleges for opportunity and cultural values. *The New York times*, A13.

Marshall, C., D. Mitchell, and F. Wirt. (1989). *Culture and education policy in the American states.* New York: The Falmer Group.

Martin, P. (1991). Labor migration in Asia. *International migration review* 25(1): 176–179.

Mazza, G. and C. Brown. (No date). Peer training strategies for welcoming diversity. National Coalition Building Institute.

McClymer, J. 1982. The Americanization movement and the education of the foreign-born adult, 1915–1925. In *American education and the European immigrant: 1840–1940*, ed. B. Weiss, 96–116. Urbana, Ill.: Univ. of Illinois Press.

Meijnen, G. W. (1991). Cultural capital and learning progress. *International journal of educational research* 15: 7–19.

Mercer, J. R. (1972, February). *Sociocultural factors in the education evaluation of Black and Chicano children.* Paper presented at the Tenth Annual Conference on Civil and Human Rights of Educators and Students, Washington, D.C.

Miller, C. (1945). The meaning. Introduction to *The history of the Springfield plan*, by C. Chatto and A. Halligan. New York: Barnes and Noble.

Miller, J. (1991 September 18). Bush endorses civil-rights revisions to permit academies for black males. *Education week*, 24.

Moffatt, M. (1989). *Coming of age in New Jersey: College and American culture.* New Brunswick, N.J.: Rutgers Univ. Press.

Mydans, S. (1992, January 25). Seeking shelter in the U.S. after the Soviet storm. *The New York times*, 1, 7.

_____. (1992, October 5). Black and Hispanic groups battle over schools post in Los Angeles. *The New York times*, A12.

Myers, L. S. (1992, October 6). Schools find that diversity can place values in conflict. *The New York times*, A18.

National Association of State Boards of Education. (No date). The American tapestry: Educating a nation. Alexandria,Va.: Author.

National Commission on Children. (1991). *Speaking of kids: A national survey of children and parents*. Washington, D.C.: Author.

Nieto, S. (1992). *Affirming diversity: the sociopolitical context of multicultural education*. New York: Longman.

Noley, G. (1979). Choctaw bilingual and bicultural education in the nineteenth century. In *Multicultural education and the American Indian*, 25–39. Los Angeles: American Indian Studies Center, University of California.

Novak, M. (1972). *The rise of the unmeltable ethnics*. New York: MacMillan.

Ogbu, J. (1978). *Minority education and caste: The American system in cross-cultural perspective*, 410–411. New York: Academic Press.

Orfield, G., and C. Ashkinaze. (1991). *The closing door: Conservative policy and Black opportunity*. Chicago: Univ. of Chicago Press.

Otheguy, R. (1982). Thinking about bilingual education: a critical appraisal. *Harvard educational review* 52(3): 301–314.

Ovando, C. (1990). Politics and pedagogy: the case of bilinqual education. *Harvard educational review* 60(3): 341–356.

Pai, Y. (1990). *Cultural foundations of education*. Columbus, Ohio: Merrill.

Patthey-Chavez, G. G. (1993). High school as an arena for cultural conflict and acculturation for Latin Angelinos. *Anthropology and education quarterly* 24(1): 33–60.

Paulston, R. (1976). *Conflicting theories of social and educational change: A typological review*. Pittsburgh: Univ. of Pittsburgh Press.

_____. (1977). Social and educational change: Conceptual frameworks. *Comparative education review* 21(2–3): 370–395.

Phelan, P., A. L. Davidson, and H. T. Cao. (1991). Student's multiple worlds: Negotiating the boundaries of family, peer, and school cultures. *Anthropology and education quarterly* 22: 224–250.

Philips, S. (1983). *The invisible culture: Communication in classroom and community on the Warm Springs Indian reservation*. New York: Longman.

Pi-Sunyer, O., and Z. Salzmann. (1978). *Humanity and culture: An introduction to anthropology*. Boston: Houghton Mifflin.

Pitsch, M. (1991, September 18). Study charts students' diversity, school progress state by state. *Education week*, 1.

_____. (1992, September 9). Income gap in college participation persists, democratic study conclude. *Education week*, 17.

Pope, A. G. (1980). *American Latina en el sistema politico internacional*. Mexico City: Ediciones Gernika.

Postiglione, G. (1983). *Ethnicity and American social theory: Toward critical pluralism*. Lanham, Md.: Univer. Press of America.

The rainbow comes to Prince George's County. (1991). *American demographics* 10–11.

Ramirez, M., III. (1982, March). *Cognitive styles and cultural diversity*. Paper presented at the Annual Meeting of the American Education Research Association, New York.

Ravitch, D. (1990). Multiculturalism: E pluribus plures. *The American scholar* 59(3): 337–354.

Rebell, M. (1989). Values inculcation and the schools: The need for a new Pierce compromise. In *Public values, private schools*, ed. N. Devins, 33–62. London: Falmer Press.

Reichley, J. (1985). *Religion in American public life*. The Brookings Institute: Washington, D.C.

Reinhold, R. (1991, September 29). Class struggle. *The New York times magazine*. 26–29, 46–47, 52.

Reisman, F. (1962). *The culturally deprived child*. New York: Harper and Row.

Resnick, L. B. (1987). Learning in School and Out. *Educational researcher*, 13–20.

Richardson, (1992, November 7). Immigrant's fear of forms imperils aid to New York schools. *The New York times*, 10.

Riche, M. F. (1991, October). We're all minorities now. *American demographics*, 26–34.

Rippa, S. A. (1988). *Education in a free society*. New York: Longman.

Roark, A. C. (1992, August 18). It's dope, so chill. *Los Angeles times*, E7.

Rubin, L. J., and S. B. Borgers. (1991, September). The changing family: Implications for education. *Principal*, 11–13.

Rumberger, R. W., R. Ghatak, G. Poulos, P. L. Ritter, and S. M. Dornbush, (1990). Family influences on dropout behavior in one california high school. *Sociology of education* 63: 283–299.

San Miguel, G. (1987). *"Let All of them take heed": Mexican Americans and the campaign for educational equality in Texas, 1910–1981*. Austin: Univer. of Texas Press.

Schermerhorn, R. A. (1970). *Comparative ethnic relations*. New York: Random House.

Schlesinger, A., Jr. (1991). A dissent on multicultural education. *Partisan review* 58(4): 630–634.

Schmidt, P. (1992, January 15). Study shows rise in the segregation of Hispanic students. *Education week*, 1, 19.

Schwartz, A. J. (1989). Middle-class educational values among Latino gang members in east Los Angeles county high schools. *Urban education* 24(3): 323–342.

Sleeter, C., and C. Grant, (1987). An analysis of multicultural education in the United States. *Harvard education review* 57(4): 421–444.

———. (1988). *Making choices for multicultural education: Five approaches to race, class, and gender*. Columbus, Ohio: Merrill.

Smolicz, J. (1984). Multiculturalism and an overarching framework of values: Some education responses for ethnically plural societies. *European journal of education* 19(1): 11–23.

Sommerfield, M. (1992, October 21). Ore. schools in eye of storm over anti-gay measure. *Education week*, 15.

Spener, D. (1988). Transitional bilingual education and the socialization of immigrants. *Harvard educational review* 58(2): 133–153.

Spring, J. (1990). *The American school 1642–1990*. New York: Longman.

Stein, W. (1992). *Tribally controlled colleges: Making good medicine*. New York: Peter Lang.

Stern, K. (1991). *Bigotry on campus: A planned response*. New York: The American Jewish Committee, Institute of Human Relations.

Stevenson, H. W., C. Chen, and D. H. Uttal. (1990). Beliefs and achievement: A study of Black, White, and Hispanic children. *Child development* 61(2): 508–523.

Stigler, J. W., and M. Perry. (1988). Mathematics learning in Japanese, Chinese, and American Classrooms. In *Children's mathematics*, ed. G. B. Saxe, and M. Gearhart, 27–54. San Francisco: Josey-Bass.

Stodolsky, S. S., and G. S. Lesser. (1967). Learning patterns in the disadvantaged. *Harvard educational review*, 37 546–593.

Suarez-Orozco, M. (1991). Migration, minority status, and education: European dilemmas and responses in the 1990s. *Anthropology and education quarterly* 22(2): 100.

Suzuki, B. (1984). Curriculum transformation for multicultural education. *Education and urban society* 16(3): 294–322.

Szasz, M. (1974). *Education and the American Indian.* Albuquerque: Univ. of New Mexico Press.

Takaki, R. (1993). A different mirror: A history of multicultural America. Boston: Little, Brown & Company.

Thomas, W. B., and K. J. Moran. (1991). The stratification of school knowledge through extracurricular activities in an urban high school. *Urban education* 26(3): 285–300.

Tierney, W. (1992). *Official encouragement, institutional discouragement: Minorities in academe—The Native American experience.* Norwood, N.Y.: Ablex Publishing.

Triandis, H. C., and R. W. Brislin. (1984). Cross-cultural psychology. *American psychologist* 39(9): 1006–1016.

Tropman, J. (1989). *American values and social welfare.* Englewood-Cliffs, N.J.: Prentice-Hall.

Trueba, H. (1988). Instructional effectiveness: English-only for speakers of other languages? *Education and urban society* 20(4): 341–362.

Tyack, D. (1974). *The one best system: A history of American urban education.* Cambridge: Harvard University Press.

U.S. Bureau of the Census. (1991). Statistical abstract of the United States: 1991. 111th ed. Washington, D.C.

U.S. Department of Education. (1991). *The condition of education, 1991,* Vol. 1, *Elementary and secondary education.* Washington, D.C.: Author.

U.S. news and world report. (1993, April 19.)

Velez-Ibanez, C. G., and J. B. Greenberg. (1992). Formation and transformation of funds of knowledge among U.S.-Mexican Households. *Anthropology and education quarterly* 23(4): 313–336.

Vygotsky, L. (1978). *Mind in society: The development of higher psychological processes.* Cambridge: MIT Press.

Waldvop, J., and T. Exter. (1991, March). The legacy of the 1980s. American demographics, 32–38.

Wallace, A. (1961). Schools in revolutionary and conservative societies. In *Anthropology and education,* ed. Frederick C. Gruber, 40–54. Philadelphia: Univ. of Pennsylvania Press.

Walsh, M. (1991, September 4). Under court order, girls admitted to schools for black boys in Detroit. *Education week,* 1, 24.

Weisner, T. S., and R. Gallimore. (1977). My brother's keeper: Child and sibling caretaking. *Current anthropology* 18: 169–190.

Weisner, T. S., and H. Garnier. (1990, April). *Stability of family structure and student learning in elementary school*. Paper presented at the American Educational Research Association, Boston.

Weisner, T. S., R. Gallimore, and C. Jordan. (1988). Unpackaging cultural effects on classroom learning: Native Hawaiian peer assistance and child-generated activity. *Anthropology and education quarterly* 19: 327–351.

West, P. (1992, February 19). Scientists debate claims of Afrocentric teachings. *Education week*, 10.

Williams, R. (1968). The concept of values. In *International encyclopedia of the social sciences*, ed. D. Sills. Vol. 16, 283–287. New York: Macmillan; Glencoe, Ill.: The Free Press.

Woodson, C. (1933). *The miseducation of the Negro*. Washington, D.C.: Associated Publishers.

Yao, E. L. (1985). A comparison of family characteristics of Asian American and Anglo American high achievers. *International journal of comparative sociology* 26(3–4): 198–208.

Zweigenhaft, R. (1991). Blacks in the white establishment: A study of race and class in America. New Haven: Yale Univ. Press.

Index